Bodies of Knowledge

Bodies of Knowledge:
Sexuality, Reproduction, and Women's Health
in the Second Wave

Wendy Kline

The University of Chicago Press :: Chicago and London

Wendy Kline is associate professor of history at the University of
Cincinnati. She is the author of *Building a Better Race: Gender, Sexuality,
and Eugenics from the Turn of the Century to the Baby Boom.*

The University of Chicago Press, Chicago 60637
The University of Chicago Press, Ltd., London
© 2010 by The University of Chicago
All rights reserved. Published 2010
Printed in the United States of America

19 18 17 16 15 14 13 12 11 10   1 2 3 4 5

ISBN-13: 978-0-226-44305-8   (cloth)
ISBN-13: 978-0-226-44308-9   (paper)
ISBN-10: 0-226-44305-1   (cloth)
ISBN-10: 0-226-44308-6   (paper)

Library of Congress Cataloging-in-Publication Data

Kline, Wendy 1968–
    Bodies of knowledge : sexuality, reproduction, and women's health in
the second wave / Wendy Kline.
        p. cm.
    Includes bibliographical references and index.
    ISBN-13: 978-0-226-44305-8 (hardcover : alk. paper)
    ISBN-10: 0-226-44305-1 (hardcover : alk. paper)
    ISBN-13: 978-0-226-44308-9 (pbk. : alk. paper)
    ISBN-10: 0-226-44308-6 (pbk. : alk. paper)
    1. Women—Sexual behavior.   2. Women's health services.
3. Reproductive health.   I. Title.
    HQ29.K58 2010
    306.7082'09045—dc22

                                                    2009050077

♾ The paper used in this publication meets the minimum requirements of
the American National Standard for Information Sciences—Permanence
of Paper for Printed Library Materials, ANSI Z39.48-1992.

For my daughter, Emily

Contents

Preface

When I was five years old, my stepmother was diagnosed with ovarian cancer. She was given six weeks to live and was instructed to undergo radiation and chemotherapy. She refused both treatments, choosing instead to change her diet and adopt a positive mindset. My father would not allow anyone to visit her who did not believe that she would get well. Thirty-five years later, she is a vibrant, youthful, cancer-free feminist who travels the world to teach about self-empowerment and creating a learning environment.

This is not a book about cancer, or sickness of any kind. But I begin with this image because it helps to explain my early fascination with the relationship between body and mind. It was not a connection I understood well at age five, when faced with the probability that my young stepmother would die. That she didn't die, and that it was presented to me as a choice—she had chosen to live by her positive thinking—suggested to me a dynamic interplay between the body and the mind.

Growing up in the 1970s, most of my assumptions about the female body were negative. It was messy, it was hairy, it was smelly, and it was almost always too large. It was meant to be controlled and then dismissed for intellectual pursuits. I identified with the feminist poet Adrienne Rich's remark, "I know no woman—virgin, mother, lesbian, married, celibate—whether she earns her keep as a housewife, a cock-tail waitress, or a scanner of brain waves—for whom her body is not a fundamental problem: its clouded meaning, its fertility, its desire, its so-called frigidity, its bloody speech, its silences, its changes and muti-lations, its rapes and ripenings." But Rich then proposed something rad-ical: "There is for the first time today a possibility of converting our physicality into both knowledge and power."[1] She was controversial, but she was right. In the 1970s, many women—some with activist back-grounds, but some with none at all—turned to the body along with the mind as inspiration for feminist thought. They used their own bodies and individual experiences to interpret reproductive functions. They used their stories to weave a composite portrait of what the female body means and does.

There were, and still are, many such women: artists, poets, scholars, writers, activists, scientists. This is just one part of the story.

Acknowledgments

I have been fortunate to have had the luxury of researching and writing this book. As with all such projects, it has been a journey and a process full of discovery. Writing about the recent past yields opportunities sometimes intimidating to the archival researcher suddenly confronted with the living (this was not the case with my first book, the chronology of which ends in the 1950s). I am grateful to the subjects of this book, women who felt strongly about preserving the recent past by donating their records and agreeing to share their memories, through both interviews and the Internet.

A special thanks goes to the 275 readers who answered my online questionnaire about their memories of reading *Our Bodies, Ourselves*, and to George Mason University's Center for History and New Media for financial and technical support with the questionnaire. Jim Sparrow was particularly helpful in setting up the site, which Judy Norsigian generously agreed to have linked to the *Our Bodies, Ourselves* official Web site. Fran Ventre, Carola Eisenberg, Judy Norsigian, Judith Weisz, Jess Stribling, Terri Kapsalis, Tanya McHale, and Joan Goldberg all generously consented to personal interviews, which helped me enormously in structuring the project.

Many institutions provided me with the funding that enabled the completion of this project. The University of

Cincinnati has been extremely generous, granting me sabbatical leave and summer research funding through the College of Arts and Sciences, the University Research Council, and the Charles Phelps Taft Research Center. In addition, the Taft Center awarded me a yearlong fellowship in 2005–6, which proved invaluable in terms of time, funding, and interaction with the five other Center Fellows. In 2004–5 I held a fellowship at the Francis A. Countway Library at Harvard University, and was also a Margaret Storrs Grierson Scholar-in-Residence at the Sophia Smith Collection at Smith College. I received library research support grants from the Schlesinger Library at Harvard University in both 2001 and 2003.

Individual archivists, librarians, assistants, and scholars helped me track down valuable sources and provided me with special access to materials. Becky Kluchin arranged for me to work with Pat Rush's personal papers, currently housed in Estelle Carol's attic in Chicago. Estelle was extremely generous with her time and her living room while Becky and I read through files. Suzanne Junod and Cindy Lachin helped me obtain access to the U.S. Food and Drug Administration manufacturer files at Fisher's Lane in Rockville, Maryland, despite massive security measures and a bomb threat while I was there. Lyle Jaffe aided me with the FDA Depo-Provera material on microform in the FDA Division of Dockets Management despite an aging microform reader that threatened to stop printing every few pages. Mary Hyde allowed me complete access to the Depo-Provera material in the Resource Center History Library Archives at the American College of Obstetricians and Gynecologists. John Rees, curator at the National Library of Medicine, combed through the massive records of the American College of Nurse Midwives for relevant information. Sherrill Redmon, director of the Sophia Smith Collection, provided me with unprocessed material on women's health. Just as important, several people at the Schlesinger Library provided me with materials and ideas on my many visits. Diana Carey searched through the Ventre papers for the perfect photograph, while Sarah Hutcheon and Ellen Shea patiently supplied suggestions and documents. Shortly after 8:45 a.m. on September 11, 2001, I was the sole researcher in the reading room when I noticed Sarah, on duty at the research desk, leaning toward her radio with marked intensity. Perhaps because of what happened on that day, I feel a special bond with all of those working at the Schlesinger Library, especially Sarah and Ellen.

The hospitality of friends and family made my research trips not only rewarding but also comfortable and affordable. In Cambridge and Boston, Dan and Helen Horowitz, Jeff Kline and Julie Anderson, Jonathan Roosevelt, and Kelsey Wirth all provided me with places to stay and willingly listened to me rant about my latest research discovery. In Washington, D.C., Stephanie and Doug Desjardins and Barbara and Dick Gardner shared their homes and kitchens with me. In Evanston, Judith Allen and Robert Kluchin offered up their condo to me and Becky Kluchin, making for an adventurous and fun-filled research trip. Other family members and friends have also offered support and interest, especially Chandrika and Karthik Kasturi, Maureen Kline, Nancy Kline, Amy Klein, Jen Lloyd, Amanda Mangialardo, Susan Shorr, Shelly Webb, and Jodi Wyett.

This project has benefited greatly from scholarly feedback. At the University of Chicago Press, I am particularly grateful to the three readers of my manuscript, Susan Reverby, Regina Morantz-Sanchez, and one anonymous reviewer. Their comments challenged me to make this a better book. Robert Devens has been a fantastic editor and a pleasure to work with, as has his assistant, Anne Summers Goldberg, and Senior Manuscript Editor Sandy Hazel. I also benefited from feedback at invited talks, including the History of Science Program at the University of Pennsylvania, the Clinical Scholars Program at the University of Michigan's medical school, the Department of Anthropology, History and Social Medicine at the University of California, San Francisco, the Department of History at the University of Iowa, the Department of History at the University of Prince Edward Island, the Women's Center at California State University at Sacramento, the Department of Women's Studies at the University of Cincinnati, and the Social Studies of Medicine Department at McGill-Queen's University.

Portions of this work have appeared in national conferences, including multiple meetings of the American Association of the History of Medicine (2002, 2003, 2005, 2006, 2007, and 2009), the History of Science Society (2007), the Berkshire Conference on the History of Women (2005, 2008), and the European Association for the History of Medicine (2005). Thanks to the AAHM regulars who asked insightful questions and provided me with a sense of scholarly support: Rima Apple, Charlotte Borst, Jacalyn Duffin, Janet Golden, Judy Houck, Joel Howell, Becky Kluchin, Judy Leavitt, Debbie Levine, Beth Linker, Ellen More, Marty Pernick, Heather Prescott, Leslie Reagan, Naomi Rogers, Dominique Tobbell, Andrea Tone, Keith Wailoo, and Liz Watkins. You all make me never want to miss an AAHM conference. A special thank-you to Becky Kluchin for our weekly "check-ins," and for all of her ideas, feedback, and support.

These past nine years at the University of Cincinnati have been productive and rewarding. I am grateful to my sociable colleagues who have been very supportive of my work, particularly David Stradling, who read through every chapter and helped me brainstorm over numerous lunches and coffees. Willard Sunderland, a great departmental chair, has made every day in the main office entertaining and fun. Our interdisciplinary reading group read through my very first version of the *Our Bodies, Ourselves* chapter and helped me realize that I had a bigger and more promising project ahead of me—thanks to Todd and Hillary Herzog, Maura O'Connor, Willard Sunderland, and Katharina Gerstenberger. The third floor of McMicken is blessed with not only history colleagues, but also some of the English Department fiction writers who have become good friends: Michael Griffith, Nicola Mason, Brock Clarke, and Leah Stewart. Thanks for keeping me smiling and for reminding me that there are many ways to tell a good story.

As I write this, my five-year-old daughter, Emily, is trying to show me a cut on her finger and desperately wanting me to get off the computer. She reminds me of how my work has resulted in hundreds of hours away from my family. They are very thankful that I am finally done with this project. But they have been supportive from the beginning, especially my husband, Stefan Paula. He has done more entertaining, cooking, and bathing of little people in the past nine years than many fathers do in a lifetime, I'm sure. He has patiently stood by through countless conferences, symphony rehearsals, and wedding gigs. Thank you, Stefan, for waiting.

Introduction: Body Knowledge

"What are our bodies?" asked the Boston Women's Health Book Collective in the first edition of *Our Bodies, Ourselves*. "First, they *are* us. We do not inhabit them—we *are* them."[1] In 1970, this was a controversial claim, particularly among feminist theorists. "Difference" feminists, such as the authors of *Our Bodies, Ourselves*, placed the female body at the center of their identity, whereas "equality" feminists sought to transcend that biological barrier by deemphasizing the body.[2] This ideological divide had profound implications for women's health and feminism in the late twentieth century. Historically, claims of difference between men and women had been used to reinforce a gender hierarchy, thereby marginalizing women.[3] Why, then, would some second-wave feminists turn to an essentialist argument of female biological difference—the same position previously used to subjugate women—to combat oppression?

The key to understanding this feminist paradox lies in the historical relationship between scientific knowledge, women's bodies, and medical practice. In the late nineteenth century, a new paradigm of experimental science altered this relationship by privileging laboratory research over clinical observation. Supporters of the new laboratory science touted it as more rational, detached, and objective. Critics viewed it as flawed, challenging its claim of objectivity as impossible to achieve and its desire to seek knowledge free of specific context as problematic. Many of these critics, which included female physicians such as Elizabeth Blackwell, feared that this new modern, scientific approach to medicine would lose sight of its subject: the patient. They believed that empathic expertise based on a connection with and compassion for the patient trumped a mechanistic scientific model.[4] But they were outnumbered and overpowered by their adversaries.

This historical moment provides an intellectual antecedent to the 1970s debates between feminists by establishing binary, oppositional approaches to science that were distinctly gendered. The new experimental science of the late nineteenth century dismissed empathy and nurturing as feminine and as bad science, replacing these approaches with objectivity and clinical detachment—which they saw as masculine. Nearly a century later, feminist philosophers returned to this historical moment to trace the trajectory of medicine and its disconnect from all things feminine. They sought to challenge the division between subject and object in medicine and to introduce a different form of knowing based on subjective experience.[5] In the process, they resuscitated and restructured essentialist claims of female difference. Evelyn Fox Keller, for example, proposed replacing "static objectivity" with what she termed "dynamic objectivity"—which, as she explains, "is not unlike empathy, a form of knowledge of other persons that draws explicitly on the commonality of *feelings* and *experience* in order to enrich one's understanding of another in his or her own right."[6] Such proposals suggested the possibility of destabilizing subjectivity and objectivity as oppositional theoretical models.

Others, however, saw no need for restructuring earlier claims of difference, instead proposing that feminists embrace it wholeheartedly. "We need to imagine a world in which every woman is the presiding genius of her own body," the feminist poet Adrienne Rich declared in 1976. "In such a world women will truly create new life, bringing forth not only children (if and as we choose) but the visions, and the thinking, necessary to sustain, console, and alter human existence—a new relationship to the universe."[7] Rich, along with a growing number of "difference" feminists in the 1970s, struggled to position the female body at the center of women's liberation. Women would never attain equal status, they argued, without the authority and knowledge that came from their own bodies. Thinking *through* the body, rather than around it, remained a neglected yet central component of female empowerment. "I have come to believe," Rich explained, "that female biology . . . has far more radical implications than we have yet come to appreciate." Though patriarchal ideology and practice had sought to restrict women's claims to power by emphasizing biological difference, she believed that a new generation of women would "come to view our physicality as a resource, rather than a destiny." Rather than feeling trapped by the constraints of their bodies, they should embrace their differences. "In order to live a fully human life we require not only *control* of our bodies (though control is a prerequisite); we must touch the unity and resonance of our physicality, our bond with the natural order, the corporeal ground of our intelligence."[8]

This book locates and links moments from that "corporeal ground" that offered the potential to empower and unify American women in the 1970s and 1980s. While ideology and politics threatened the stability of feminist groups from within and without, there remained the possibility of "converting our physicality into both knowledge and power." Building on the movements and activism of the sixties, women in the 1970s were in an ideal position to challenge conventional thinking about the female body. Not only should women have access to information about their bodies, they argued; they should also help to *create* this knowledge.

The following chapters reveal the ways in which women challenged, expanded, and reinvented constructions of the female body and in particular reproductive health. "Nowhere are women more aware of and less patient with the 'system' as in the field of their own reproductive functioning," a Maryland midwife declared.[9] Frustration, impatience, and growing confidence in their ability to present an alternative, woman-centered approach to reproductive issues galvanized a growing group of American women in the 1970s and 1980s. As feminism grew more divisive, with politics, race, class, and sexual identity threatening to become insurmountable barriers, women's health appeared to be a cause that could unify disparate groups of the population. As the founding members of the Boston Women's Health Book Collective declared in their original edition of *Our Bodies, Ourselves*, "learning about our womanhood from the inside out has allowed us to cross over the socially created barriers of race, color, income and class, and to feel a sense of identity with all women in the experience of being female."[10] This claim turned out to be somewhat presumptuous, but it also created new possibilities and expectations for the relationship between women and their bodies.

What follows, however, is not a simple tale of enlightenment and progress. In the context of women's bodies and women's health, the notion that the "personal is political"—that sex and reproduction lay at the root of women's oppression—carried great weight. Individual women's stories, whether about their first pelvic exam, their experience with birth control or abortion, or their experience with childbirth, took precedence as a legitimate aspect of knowledge construction. As one reader of *Our Bodies, Ourselves* explained, "I think the book helped me internalize the idea that lived experience is as important, if not more so, than clinical or scientific 'knowledge.'"[11] Privileging individual experience over scientific analysis allowed for a more democratic, less hierarchical approach to learning about female biology—something potentially revolutionary.

But this privileging of experience, and the assumption that it provided incontestable evidence of a universal "sisterhood," ultimately stymied women's health activism. For one thing, the assumption that female biology was a central concern for all women, regardless of class, race, politics, or sexual orientation, became an issue. Attempts at creating a universalist notion of shared oppression reflected a certain lack of sensitivity toward different needs and perspectives. For another, feminist theorists cringed at what they believed to be the romanticization of female experience as something pure or innate. As a result, feminists grew wary of talking about "women's experience."[12] They challenged the privileging of women's stories (such as those central to *Our Bodies, Ourselves*) as being naïve.[13] Further, they argued that there is no "authentic experience" which can be divorced from the discourses that constructed it. Thus, while the women's health movement was still struggling to achieve recognition as a legitimate social movement, it was already being derailed in scholarship.

By the second decade of women's health activism in the second wave, new challenges and opportunities altered the playing field. Recognizing that they needed to earn a seat at the bargaining table to change the ways in which women's health was researched and regulated, activists developed recognized "insider" credentials as professionals (becoming physicians, consulting lobbyists, testifying at hearings, and gaining certification to deliver babies, to name a few). By doing so, however, they undermined their very notion of "difference." They appropriated the language of scientists, turning to a more traditional type of expert—those whose credentials were listed after their names rather than coming from any "authentic experience" as women. This process resulted in greater inclusion for women (both as researchers and as research subjects). But it also distanced these activists from their lay followers, who sometimes found their compromises or professional development to be indicative of selling out rather than furthering the cause of women's self-empowerment.[14]

This professionalization resulted in a mixed legacy for women's health. On one hand, it allowed for greater recognition and potential impact within organized medicine, thereby generating more legislation and regulation on women's health research and practice. On the other, it weakened the movement's ideological basis—albeit slippery to begin with— by undermining the notion that knowledge and power are rooted in the biological body. Rich's hope that every woman would become the "presiding genius" of her own body has only been partially realized.

:   :   :

Five chapters track the ideas, expectations, and pitfalls encountered by advocates of women's health in particular settings. Chapter 1, "Transforming Knowledge: The Making of *Our Bodies, Ourselves*," investigates how one particular groundbreaking book provided readers with an alternative knowledge base on women's health. Long before the Internet, this book provided women with information about their bodies that was difficult to find elsewhere. "I think that I learned more about my anatomy than I had ever known," reader Bethany Davis recalled.[15] More than just a source of information, however, *Our Bodies, Ourselves* promoted the revolutionary concept that experiential knowledge based on personal stories is a crucial component of women's health. With the help of reader responses, the authors created (and revised, and expanded) a text that allowed for a feminist reconceptualization of biology. Yet the book also contained the seeds of division that would limit the extent to which its promoters could truly revolutionize health care.

Chapter 2, "Reexamining the Pelvic: The Pelvic Instruction Controversy of the 1970s," addresses feminist pedagogy and medical education by tracing the rise and fall of the Pelvic Teaching Program created by feminist health activists at Boston's Women's Community Health Center in 1976. This program introduced Harvard medical students to a new view of a woman's body by transforming the model "patient" into the role of instructor. These feminist practitioners used their own bodies as teaching tools to offer a more compassionate, sensitive approach to a procedure traditionally fraught with tensions. It also promoted the idea that knowledge production should begin with a woman's individual subjective experience rather than with that of the physician. But the failure of the experiment over the course of three protocols revealed the problems inherent in a model of care based entirely on the subjective experience of the patient, in part because it excluded all male medical students.

Chapter 3, "Learning from the Uterus Out: Abortion and Women's Health Activism in Chicago," turns from feminist ideology and pedagogy to practice. In Chicago, health feminists worked first underground, providing abortions before their legalization in 1973, then on the ground, establishing clinics, referral services, and activist organizations in the name of reproductive rights. The evolution of feminist health activism from a subversive illegal service to a vocal and visible network of women reveals the movement's heartfelt commitment to transforming health care. But it also demonstrates the fractures and fatigue activists encountered as their efforts were repeatedly attacked by Reagan-era conservatives and by liberals who could not agree on political strategies and priorities.

Chapter 4 investigates the role of health feminists in regulating birth control. "Bodies of Evidence: Depo-Provera and the Public Board of Inquiry" analyzes the 1983 U.S. Food and Drug Administration Board of Inquiry hearing held to determine whether Depo-Provera should be approved for use as a hormonal contraceptive in the United States. It reveals the role of women's health advocates in restructuring scientific inquiry and contraceptive regulation. By the 1980s, these activists were more adept at negotiating with political insiders. But there was a price to pay, as they were forced to compromise their position on subjectivity and science. Though they had collected individual testimonials of women who had been injected with Depo-Provera, they learned that they could not use them to challenge notions of objectivity at the hearing. Just as Elizabeth Blackwell discovered in the late nineteenth century, these health activists found that formal networks of power "relegated more subjective and informal modes of knowing to the marginal and the feminine."[16]

The final chapter, "Choices in Childbirth: A Modern Midwife's Tale," tells the story of Fran Ventre, a midwife who "developed a special place in the modern midwifery movement" because of her ability to bridge the divide between lay midwives and certified nurse-midwives.[17] The two fields of midwifery had different origins, training, and philosophy about birth, including whether it should take place in the home or the hospital. The philosophical divide between the movements helps to explain why proponents of natural childbirth have not been entirely successful in demedicalizing the process or empowering mothers to be.

Instead, choices in childbirth have largely been reduced to requests for cesarean sections and epidurals.

: : :

It is a pivotal moment for writing about the history of women's health. After thirty-odd years, critical distance and aging activists provide fertile ground for new scholarship. In her thought-provoking article on feminism, history, and health-care policy in the United States, Susan Reverby begins to lay out a research agenda for historians of the recent past, suggesting, among other things, that we need to investigate how women's bodies were "experienced, imagined, and represented" and to "determine whether the voices of women patients . . . affected those who made policy."[18] My work is in part a response to her challenge, and part of a new trend in historical scholarship that integrates the histories of women's health, American culture, and medicine in its approach to understanding the late twentieth century.[19]

1 Transforming Knowledge: The Making of *Our Bodies, Ourselves*

In the spring of 2005, Simon & Schuster published *Our Bodies, Ourselves: A New Edition for a New Era*. "It's hard to believe that thirty-five years have passed since we first gathered around our kitchen tables to create *Our Bodies, Ourselves*," the founders of the Boston Women's Health Book Collective remark in the introduction. "What we couldn't have foreseen then was that our book would help create a women's health movement and radically change the way many people think about health care. Nor could we have known that the book's great success would generate a need for an ongoing women's health organization in which, over the next three decades, some of us would remain active as board or staff members."[1]

The collective authors are not alone in their belief that the book had an enormous impact on women's health and the feminist movement. Many other women vividly recall reading *Our Bodies, Ourselves* for the first time in the 1970s. "It felt biblical," remembers Joanne Williams, when she discovered the book in a Denver bookstore in 1974 at the age of twenty-seven. "I remember just sitting down with it and almost reading it completely through the first night of the weekend I had it."[2] Historian Estelle Freedman remembers that her best friend from childhood sent it to her in 1972 or 1973, when she was twenty-five.

"The best women's health reference book I've ever seen."—Julianne Moore

OUR BODIES, OURSELVES

 The Boston Women's Health Book Collective

A NEW EDITION FOR A NEW ERA

FIGURE 1 Cover of *Our Bodies, Ourselves*, 2005 edition. Photograph courtesy of the Boston Women's Health Book Collective. Reprinted by permission.

"I immediately sat and read through the book and felt a shift in my worldview," she recalls. "Some of my housemates asked what I was reading, and there was clearly a sense that it was subversive in some way!"[3] By 2005, the message of *Our Bodies, Ourselves* appeared more conventional than subversive, in large part because of its long-term success, measurable by the number of similar self-help texts lining the shelves of popular bookstores. A new generation of women has been raised with new expectations and awareness of female bodies and health, as mothers and mentors passed along the book's message.

Yet the story behind the book reveals that its significance goes beyond its status as a cultural artifact of 1970s feminism. The book's message was revolutionary not only for its attack on the medical establishment, but also for its creation of an alternative knowledge base structured around personal stories. *Our Bodies, Ourselves* legitimized the notion of experiential knowledge as a central component of health. In other words, every woman's body contained the seeds of knowledge crucial to defining her own well-being. Consider one woman's assessment of the book's influence: "I think the book helped me internalize the idea that lived experience is as important, if not more so, than clinical or scientific "knowledge."[4] *Our Bodies, Ourselves* was both a practical guide and a theoretical tool; an encyclopedia of information about women's health, and also a dictionary that introduced a new vocabulary to define women's health.

In essence, the book allowed for a "feminist reconceptualization of biology" that privileged individual women's experiences over clinical research.[5] As this chapter demonstrates, *Our Bodies, Ourselves* provided the tools for women readers to challenge medical decision making and to seek alternative structures of care based on the notion of experiential knowledge. But the book also embodied some of the contradictions and complexities that would stymie the burgeoning women's health movement. Two conflicting "truths" competed for the reader's attention: first, the singularity of being female (a shared identity based on female biology), and second, the plurality of individual experiences (every woman's experience is different and just as valid as every other woman's, because each individual is the authority over her own body). In short, *Our Bodies, Ourselves* contained within its pages a feminist paradox, an urgent contradiction debated continuously by feminist theorists, concerning the nature of womanhood.[6]

Yet Simon & Schuster continues to release updated editions of this popular book. Given the inconsistencies and divisions within feminist thought and feminist organizations, how has *Our Bodies, Ourselves* remained a vibrant source of information about health and sexuality to female readers over the past thirty-five years? The formation and development of the Boston Women's Health Book Collective in the 1970s, as well as the group's relationship with its readers, help to explain its longevity.[7] Even before the collective's formation, however, many young Americans were ready to challenge the status quo.

The 1960s

Women's health emerged as a major social and political issue in a turbulent decade. A new generation of Americans expressed its dismay that the wealthiest, most powerful nation in the world could not adequately provide for or protect its own citizens, and sought alternative solutions. Two best sellers published in 1962, Rachel Carson's *Silent Spring* and Michael Harrington's *The Other America*, drew attention to the destruction and poverty on U.S. soil that had been largely invisible to most middle-class Americans. Echoing the antiestablishment sentiment of these books, collective protests caught the public eye beginning in the early 1960s. Students for a Democratic Society (better known as SDS) issued its manifesto of New Left activism, the Port Huron Statement, in 1962.[8] The following summer, more than 250,000 civil rights protesters marched on Washington for freedom and jobs in the largest political demonstration in U.S. history up to that time. In 1968, radical feminists staged a series of dramatic protests, such as crowning a sheep at the Miss America pageant to protest the sexual objectification of women. In the final year of the decade, five days of rioting in New York's Greenwich Village fueled the gay liberation movement. During this unsettled period, no issue was left unexplored, no political structure unchallenged. By its end, a postwar climate of confidence had been replaced by one of cynicism and doubt. This included disillusionment with the medical profession.

Science and medicine had enjoyed unprecedented authority and power in post–World War II America, when medical care became one of the nation's largest industries.[9] But by 1970, medicine, along with other social institutions, had suffered a "stunning loss of confidence."[10] Beginning in the mid-1960s, according to David Rothman, the practice of medicine became thoroughly transformed within just a decade. An intrusion of outsiders, including academic scholars, government officials, lawyers, and judges, completely altered the doctor-patient relationship and brought "new rules to medicine."[11] Exposés on patient experimentation and unethical treatment challenged the notion that the physician had the patient's best interest in mind.[12] In this social climate, only outsiders, presumed to be objective, could effectively regulate and monitor a doctor's decisions. As they brought these concerns to light, popular agitation ensured that patients' rights would join the broader spectrum of civil rights. Patients, particularly African Americans, gays and lesbians, and women, were easily exploited as human subjects and therefore required their own bill of rights.[13] The doctor had become a stranger and a potential enemy, and patient trust virtually disappeared along with house calls by the 1960s.[14] Empowered by a new language of bioethics to replace bedside ethics, patients became wary consumers who sought protection *from* doctors rather than *by* doctors.[15]

A number of new health programs emerged in the 1960s to address what many were pronouncing a national health care crisis. Congress approved Medicare and Medicaid programs in 1965, and by the following year President Lyndon Johnson's Office of Economic Opportunity championed legislation that included funding for neighborhood health centers.[16] These facilities were designed to improve access to health care, particularly for the poor. Johnson became the first president to establish federal funding of family planning (excluding abortion) and maternal health programs.[17] In addition, hundreds of free clinics opened in the late 1960s, providing treatment that was less expensive or hierarchical than traditional health-care services.[18] For some, however, these measures did not begin to scrape the surface of what they believed to be an even more fundamental problem in American society: sexism.

Of all social movements, the women's health movement had its most direct roots in women's liberation. By the late 1960s, women inspired by the civil rights movement and its demand for equal citizenship created a new wave of feminist activism.[19] Though a fragmented movement—historians refer to several branches of feminism, including liberal, socialist, radical, cultural, and multiracial[20]—its unifying characteristic has been the claim that the personal is political. By challenging the divide between the two, feminists asserted that the most private aspects of their identity—relationships, sexuality, health, and family life—were indeed political issues.[21] Ideas and personal stories, rather than goals or strategies, united a broad range of women who came to identify themselves as feminists. Women's liberation, according to Sara Evans, depended "on the ability of women to tell each other their own stories, to claim them as the basis of political action."[22] For many, these stories and their political implications emerged through "consciousness-raising," a process in which the sharing of personal stories led to a "click"—a sudden recognition that sexism lay at the root of their struggles. Coined by early members of New York Radical Women, consciousness-raising became "an intense form of collective self-education."[23]

Thus, at a time when medical authority was already undermined, when activists sought protection for human rights, and when feminists argued that deeply personal issues had political consequences, renewed activism in women's health appears almost inevitable. Female bodies, argued health feminists, had been subjected to male medical authority;

women could not achieve full equality without the right to reclaim their bodies. Physicians were overwhelmingly male (in 1970, 7.6 percent of physicians and 7.2 percent of OB-GYNs were female), and, according to critics, paternalistic, condescending, and judgmental.[24] In addition, they had medicalized reproductive issues and turned women into human guinea pigs, argued activists at hearings on abortion, Depo-Provera, and childbirth.

Women's health activists used a wide range of strategies to increase women's control over their own bodies, including advocacy, education, and the creation of alternative health care organizations.[25] By 1974, more than twelve hundred women's groups were providing health services in the United States, according to a nationwide survey, though many of these were short-lived experiments. Other groups worked through legislative channels to ensure health protection and services, from abortion to the regulation of contraception by the U.S. Food and Drug Administration.[26]

As women became increasingly active consumers in the health-care industry, they sought out accurate, easy-to-understand information on women's health. The first and most comprehensive book to provide knowledge about women's health and sexuality was the Boston Women's Health Book Collective's *Our Bodies, Ourselves*.[27] From its origins as a 130-page newsprint manual in 1970, this comprehensive book on women's health was by 2005 an 832-page treatise (complete with a companion Web site) that had sold four million copies and had been translated and/or culturally adapted into eighteen different languages. This success was not inevitable; internal divisions and outside conflict in the early years threatened the stability of the collective and its publications. Yet despite the group's "growing pains," a passion for and commitment to women's health enabled it to persevere.

Writing Our Bodies, Ourselves

In May of 1969, Emmanuel College in Boston hosted a female liberation conference. This in and of itself was not so unusual: "women's liberation" activism had erupted in major cities beginning in 1967, and had introduced consciousness-raising as a formative process by which women could explore the political aspects of personal life. But what made this particular weekend conference significant was a two-hour workshop on Sunday afternoon called "Women and Their Bodies." The twelve participants, some of whom had never before been in any kind of women's group, shared stories of frustration and anger about their experiences at the doctor's office. Calling themselves the "doctors group," they resolved to continue meeting after the conference, with the idea that they would create a list of "reasonable" ob-gyns in the Boston area. (By reasonable, they meant doctors who listened to the patient; respected her opinions, and explained procedures and medications.)[28]

They quickly discovered, however, that they were unable to put together such a list—and, more important, that the women who had attended the workshop shared a desire to learn as much as possible about their bodies and their health. So they decided on a summer project. Each group member would research a topic of personal importance about their bodies and take the information back to the group. Members would then share personal experiences related to this topic. "In this way," they later explained, "the textbook view of childbirth or miscarriage or menstruation or lovemaking, nearly always written by men, would become expanded and enriched by the truth of our actual experiences. It was an exciting process."[29] By incorporating personal experience into the narrative, they began the process of transforming medical knowledge into something subjective, political, and empowering.

The following winter, the "doctors group"—now calling themselves the Women and Their Bodies Group—offered several evening workshops in the Boston area, each lasting ten to twelve weeks.[30] For the first session alone, over forty women signed up to learn what this group had uncovered over the summer and fall in its quest to learn more about women's bodies. The group had intended to offer a formal presentation at each meeting, followed by discussions, but the participants were so engaged and energized that the sessions quickly turned into a total-discussion format. Workshop leaders handed out note cards and asked participants to write down the experiences they had volunteered in the discussion. The content of some of these note cards was later transcribed into the personal narratives that became a central part of *Our Bodies, Ourselves*.[31] Many readers reacted strongly to them. "Including the personal anecdotes and individual feelings about all these issues—now, that was very powerful," remembers Judith Baker.[32]

As the number of topics and papers increased over the years, the Women and Their Bodies Group decided to publish them in an inexpensive newsprint volume. "They are not final. They are not static," explained the authors, who now called themselves the Boston Women's Health Course Collective. "They are meant to be used by our sisters to increase consciousness about ourselves as women, to build our movement, to begin to struggle collectively for adequate health care, and in many other ways they can be useful to you."[33] In December 1970, the alternative New England Free Press published 5,000 copies of *Women and Their Bodies* at a cost of $1,500, selling the volume for 75 cents. In April 1971, the press published 15,000 more copies, reduced the selling price to 30 cents to make it affordable to a larger number of women, and changed the book's title to *Women and Our Bodies*, then finally *Our Bodies, Ourselves*.[34]

FIGURE 2 Cover of *Our Bodies, Ourselves*, 1973 edition. Photograph courtesy of the Boston Women's Health Book Collective. Reprinted by permission.

After eleven printings and 225,000 copies, the collective decided to publish a revised expanded version with Simon & Schuster under the name of the Boston Women's Health Book Collective. This was one of the most difficult decisions the group ever made, and the first that was not by consensus, but by vote. Ultimately, it decided to go with a commercial press because it wanted to get the book out as quickly as possible to women in more places, women who would not have had access to the Free Press edition: "We feel a tremendous sense of urgency. . . . We want the book to reach women who don't ordinarily come in contact with movement publications," the BWHBC explained. "We have a sense of the women's movement becoming larger and more unified than it is now."[35] With the aid of a lawyer, it successfully negotiated a contract that "proved to be nothing short of phenomenal," included complete editorial control, and offered bulk discounts for women's clinics.[36]

The distributors and copublishers at the New England Free Press were, not surprisingly, opposed to the BWHBC's decision. "We at the Free Press feel strongly that 'Our Bodies, Our Selves' should continue to be distributed through the Movement where it will help build a socialist women's consciousness," they wrote at the end of the eleventh printing. "Women are now getting the book from political people and organizations they trust. This makes the book part of a personal process of political education. Selling the book through capitalist distributors in bookstores or even supermarkets will only impede that process." Both the collective and the publishers thanked those who had written letters supporting their side of the controversy. The publishers claimed that most responses "have supported our position in this matter, which is heartening." However, the BWHBC disagreed, stressing that letters it received "give us a good sense of who the book is reaching so that we're not just talking among ourselves." One college student in Oberlin, Ohio, supported its decision, explaining, "I can tell you that you are doing all of us a service by publishing so a wider audience can be reached. If any book is important to have widely read, it's yours."[37]

"Where do we go from here?"

As the nature of the BWHBC's tasks changed by the mid-1970s, so did the group dynamics, raising questions about its collective nature. Formed in the context of the Women's Liberation Movement (with many members coming out of the socialist feminist group Bread and Roses), the BWHBC functioned primarily as a consciousness-raising group.[38] Apart from the Simon & Schuster matter, it made decisions by consensus, sharing memories and fears along with strategies and solutions. Like many feminist collectives, it made a conscious decision to create a "leaderless, structureless" group to encourage discussion and support.[39]

The commercial success of *Our Bodies, Ourselves*, however, which stunned its authors, brought new demands: public relations, money management, book distribution, international publishing rights, and text revisions. BWHBC members began to question whether the original group structure could survive these changes. "The initial success of our wonderful book has passed," Joan reflected in the fall of 1974, "and we are personally and collectively trying to answer the question—where do we go from here?"[40] Although the group commonly disagreed on a number of issues, it shared a concern that the BWHBC was disintegrating. "Our fear is that the group will fall apart without our agreeing to that," Nancy, Joan, and Ruth wrote later that year. "Obviously we don't want that to happen. Okay, what are we going to do (because we gotta do something)!!!?"[41]

Over the next two years, fear and frustration generated a dialogue among members about the past, present, and future of the BWHBC. As they moved beyond their initial goal of teaching and publishing *Our Bodies, Ourselves*, they questioned their commitment to feminism, women's health activism, and one another. Factions within the collective, individual needs, outside obligations and interests, and time constraints all affected group dynamics. Given the number of women's groups that did not survive these kinds of internal divisions, it is not surprising that the BWHBC suffered its share of struggles. Yet the ways in which it characterized its particular fears about the group's future help to explain how it survived. Most members felt they had too much invested in the project to give up. Nancy, for one, expressed her eagerness "for us to all come together and hug and fight and get on with another stage in our growing."[42]

Though the group was used to disagreements and conflicts, these appeared to intensify in the summer of 1974. Many of the women lamented the lack of a clear working structure. Meetings were poorly attended and rarely started on time. "It's hard for us to say this because it scares us," three members wrote. "Therefore we hold on to our old group process—however haphazard—because it seems better than nothing. Or it has seemed that way, but it's clearer to us that it's more frustrating than effective now." These three attributed some of the problems to the growing number of tasks that the collective faced. "The problem is, how can we maintain ourselves as the casual and loving collective we are, take care of each of our individual needs, and still accomplish professional tasks which demand lots of time and energy?"[43] Determining the boundaries between emotional and professional support proved challenging at times.

Similar concerns emerged during the following summer. "I feel out of touch," Jane wrote. "Do other people feel this way?" Continuing the "where do we go from here?" questions, she asked, "What do we each want to do outside of the group and within the group? Do we all want to do one thing or several things? . . . Are we as involved in the group as we were when we were working on the book?" For Jane, the group, beyond the book, was crucial. "I want the feeling of process to continue. I want to feel I am growing as a person within the group. I want to feel the joy of really contacting all of you when we are together."[44] How could the BWHBC move forward in a way that benefited members individually and the group as a whole? Was the success of the collective based on providing emotional support, professional success, or both?

Herein lay the problem. No one could agree on which aspect was most important: individual needs, group needs, or professional goals. By 1976, the BWHBC had fractured further over what its professional goals should be. The drama centered on the development of the "parenting

FIGURE 3 Founders of the Boston Women's Health Book Collective, circa 1975. From left to right, standing in back row: Wendy Sanford, Paula Doress-Worters, Joan Ditzion, Judy Norsigian, Jane Pincus, Norma Swenson, Nancy Miriam Hawley; seated in front row: Pamela Berger, Ruth Bell-Alexander, Vilunya Diskin, Esther Rome. Photograph by Phyllis Ewen. Reprinted by permission.

project:" a goal on the part of four members to write a book about parenting on behalf of the collective. As these four began to meet separately and form their own agenda for the book (to be entitled *Ourselves and Our Children*), other members felt alienated and became wary of the breakdown in communications—exactly what Jo Freeman had warned about in her 1970 critique, "The Tyranny of Structurelessness." She pointed out that in actuality, there is "no such thing as a structureless group"; any group that exists for a long enough period of time will "inevitably structure itself in some fashion." Instead, the idea of structurelessness becomes a "smokescreen for the strong or the lucky to establish unquestioned hegemony over others."[45] This is exactly what happened in the Boston Women's Health Book Collective.

Judy articulated it first in April of 1976. In a letter to all members, she expressed concern about the group's "lack of a more 'formal' communications mechanism." She realized that for months she had been completely unaware of the parenting group's plans. "I think that three, or four, or even five of us cannot really duplicate the process that was such an important part of doing *OBOS*."[46] Others chimed in, stressing the need for accountability, given that the new book would claim the name and spirit of the original. Could a subgroup of the collective speak for all of them? "How much control should the nonparenting people in the *OBOS* collective have over the project, which is being presented in their name?" Wendy asked. "If others in the group do not agree with some of our process and content, how can the disagreement be dealt with in the most positive way?"[47]

Those not involved in the parenting project felt concerned that they did not express their reservations earlier in the process. They had been excluded from meetings during the fall, winter, and spring of 1975–76. Addressing the parenting group, Wendy wrote, "I realize that you felt that when others came sporadically to meetings, it was hard to get down to work. Also, in our collective only the four of you felt deeply committed to the project and had the time to put into it. At that point, however, I wish we had all had the wisdom to see that this might cause problems." The result was, in Wendy's words, "an unfortunate inside-outside dynamic which left several members of the larger group feeling left out."[48]

But Norma felt that the "sense of split, the we/they of which Wendy wrote so sensitively, has actually been a reality for a long time." She believed, in fact, that the parenting project was "simply a manifestation" of a larger shift in focus, as the work energy of the BWHBC drifted away from its original goals. The problem, as she articulated it, was that the group was *so* close, it was difficult for individual members "to realize the

precise ways in which our work energies have diverged, almost irrevo-
cably." Trying to balance individual needs, emotional needs as a group,
and professional needs as a group was proving to be quite a challenge.
Norma continued:

> For me personally, the business of looking at the reality (and
> unreality) of the splits, in both group work energy and direc-
> tion and personal career direction, VERSUS the personal rela-
> tionships in our group as a support group and a personal group
> of the most intimate kind, is our very first task. If we can do this,
> really look at it and see it the way it is, I think we can solve the
> rest of our problems; because I think re-affirming our solidar-
> ity as a group has been the source of our ability to solve other
> problems in the past. After all, even when we were unanimous
> in committing our work energies to women's health, we were far
> from unanimous at all times on the precise form that commit-
> ment should take. It took time to work out.[49]

An open acknowledgment of the inevitable challenges involved in collective work undoubtedly helped repair some of the damage, and ultimately
reaffirmed the BWHBC's commitments to collective politics.

However, although members attempted to encourage and support
one another, they also feared that these conflicts, however lovingly
expressed, signaled the decline of the collective. In the same letter in
which Norma expressed her love and commitment to the group, she
also warned against the dangers of letting their affection blind them.
She perceived the collective as a family, but believed it to be "inherently
impossible for a family to be both encouraging to the growth of everyone in it and still at the same time produce work with which every member can feel deeply identified."[50] Could the collective mature in such a
way that all members continued to feel fulfilled? Could the passion for
parenting that some members felt be translated into an effective sequel
to *Our Bodies, Ourselves*—even if not all members shared that vision?
What would it mean if the end product did not speak for everyone in the
collective?

For those concerned about the direction the parenting project had
taken by 1976, more than just a new book was at stake. "The process by
which the book was (is) being produced is contrary to, is a denial of the
collective group spirit which we have so clearly articulated, and on which
our own processes and our very reputation is built," Norma explained.
Three or four authors were simply not enough; the real power that the

book could have had "was missed because we were not really attempting to reflect a broad reality." As pioneers of the women's health movement whose work had resonated with so many readers, the BWHBC had an obligation to continue speaking to as wide an audience as possible. Norma warned, "if our book fails to do that it will not simply be too bad; it has the power to disillusion and disappoint literally millions of people, their faith in the women's movement, in our collective, in the power of the collective process, in the courage of people to really confront their social reality—the implications are enormous."[51]

Joan, a member of the parenting group, felt it was important to acknowledge the challenge that they faced. She wrote, "We all have to agree that the *OBOS* project was a magical event and probably will never be reproduced by ourselves or anyone else. In developing our book we developed a tool for consciousness raising that has touched the hearts and minds of women all over the world." However, she continued, it raised expectations in intimidating ways. "Clearly this is a hard act to follow and it is realistic to assume that no project that we develop will have as great an appeal and impact as *OBOS* did."[52]

Indeed, Joan was right. *Ourselves and Our Children* created some interest when it was published by Random House in 1978, but did not enjoy the broad appeal—or sales—of the first book. Their editor noted by April of 1979 that sales were "sluggish": approximately 130,000 copies sold in the first five months.[53] Reviews were mixed; while the *Library Journal* declared it "the definitive book on parenting," others found it far less innovative than *Our Bodies, Ourselves.*[54] For some readers, the book's emphasis on the roles of fathers as well as mothers diluted the empowering feminist political ideology they had come to expect after *Our Bodies, Ourselves*. And while the parenting group continued to meet into the 1980s with the intention of revising *Ourselves and Our Children*, they never completed the task, and the book is now out of print. Despite this letdown, the BWHBC persevered and continued to debate the role of parenting in its long-term goals. One member even proposed a new book, *Our Bodies, Ourselves, Our Children*, suggesting a desire to effectively merge the two projects.[55] Judy commented, "Given how little built-in overview and communication between the groups there has been, it's amazing that things have gone as well as they have."[56]

By creating something new and controversial within the collective, the parenting group also generated a debate about what had been so unique about the first book. "*OBOS* was not a book that we 'made' happen," Wendy reflected. "It was part of a large groundswell movement,

FIGURE 4 Cover of *Ourselves and Our Children* (1978). Photograph courtesy of the Boston Women's Health Book Collective. Reprinted by permission.

much larger than us. We were in some sense privileged to be there at the right time, although who we are certainly played a vital role in its getting put together and shared in such an effective way."[57] Norma agreed. "We have often said with genuine pride and humility that any women could have written our book, it just happened to be us," she wrote to the group. "Terrific as we are, I have a strong need to believe that, because it implies that we are accountable to the feelings and experience of that wider world of women out there, that we are simply a filter or a reflecting pool for those other women's lives."[58]

That sense of accountability, which shaped the concerns about the parenting project, was not limited to the authors of *Our Bodies, Ourselves*. In their desire to reflect that "wider world of women out there," they had welcomed their audience into the conversation. For the early editions of the book, the writing was directed by the twelve members of the BWHBC, but included other voices. "Many, many other women have worked with us on the book," they explained in the 1973 preface. "A group of gay women got together specifically to do the chapter on lesbianism. Other papers were done still differently. . . . Other women contributed thoughts, feelings and comments as they passed through town or passed through our kitchens or workrooms. There are still other voices from letters, phone conversations, a variety of discussions, etc., that are included in the chapters as excerpts of personal experiences."[59]

Including as many voices and stories as possible turned out to be crucial. One of the outside authors, Susan Bell, later wrote about the challenge of translating medical information into lay language. The BWHBC authors themselves were outsiders to the medical field; their role was to understand and interpret the information in a way that would speak to as many women as possible. When revising the chapter on birth control in 1984, Bell had to attempt "to see from and speak to the perspectives of teenagers, single women, women of color, poor women, women with disabilities, and women without health insurance (and so forth) without falling into the trap of believing I could 'be' simultaneously in all, or wholly in any, of these subjugated positions."[60] The feminist paradox was rearing its ugly head, challenging any theorist to articulate universal claims about female biology and still acknowledge the presence of multiple perspectives.

How, then, could Bell attempt to speak for such a broad spectrum of women? "One way out of this trap lies in positioning, opening up the process of knowledge construction to diverse perspectives by being attentive and responsible to other people," she acknowledged.[61] The BWHBC could not claim to represent all women, but by including their stories, it could speak to a more diverse body of women. In her study of the impact of *Our Bodies, Ourselves* on global feminism, sociologist Kathy Davis noted that "it was the method of knowledge sharing and not a shared identity as women which appeared to have a global appeal."[62]

Reader Responses

Letters from American readers clearly indicate that while not all women identified with the tone or content of every chapter of *Our Bodies, Ourselves*, the book still had enormous appeal. Written at a time when feminists stressed the power and importance of consciousness-raising, it confirmed that women's liberation depended on such knowledge sharing. As the authors declared, "knowledge is power," and personal stories are a crucial aspect of that knowledge. *Our Bodies, Ourselves* offered a level of intimacy that encouraged readers to respond to its text. At the suggestion of the authors (who solicited feedback for book revisions in magazines such as *Ms.*) or of their own accord, over two hundred women wrote to the BWHBC in the 1970s and 1980s to share stories, seek advice, chastise, or praise. They commented on what was helpful in the book, what was vague, what made sense, and what was missing, on subjects ranging from dental care to diaphragms. These letters leave many questions unanswered; names and addresses have been blacked out, and most do not reveal the writer's economic, racial, or educational background.[63] Viewed as a whole, however, they suggest both the appeal of *Our Bodies, Ourselves* and the expectations it engendered. Because readers strongly identified with the book (or at least the idea behind it), they believed their own experiences should be represented or accounted for in the text. The emotional expressiveness of their letters reveals their desire to participate in redefining women's health, from locations across the United States. Indeed, reader input helped shape revisions of the book and explain its longevity.

The responses from readers also tell us something more broadly about the development of feminist ideas and communities.[64] Women did not have to be actively involved in an organized group of feminists, or even in a consciousness-raising group, to participate in the movement. Since many women did not have access to these groups (demand far outstripped available resources), they turned to reading *Our Bodies, Ourselves* as a consciousness-raising resource. Literary scholar Lisa Hogeland argues that feminism can be understood as a form of literacy, a set of "reading and interpretive strategies that people who identified themselves as feminists applied to texts and to the world around them."[65] Feminist community was a "fantasy" that could be explored in complete geographic isolation.[66] "If not in a group," she argues, "then presumably one experienced the collective speaking of women's experiences in the activities of reading and writing."[67]

Certainly that was the case with *Our Bodies, Ourselves,* where read-ing was often described as a revelatory experience—as a "click" that drew women out of isolation and into a widespread dialogue about fem-inism and health. "When I realize how similar my feelings are to some of the letters in your book, it is indeed reassuring," one reader confided.[68] Establishing connections by reading personal accounts enabled readers to experience consciousness-raising at their own kitchen tables. They did not have to join a feminist organization or a self-help group to recognize their own oppression in the stories of others. "I was overwhelmed by the support I felt in all the information you gave me," another reader wrote. "What I felt then as skepticism about the women's movement vanished and my lonely farm-housewife lifestyle became a step in a steady pro-gression of changes."[69] One particularly enthusiastic reader declared, "Let me tell you I love your books! They make me feel great reading them—like I'm really a part of something bigger than myself!"[70]

By its very formation, then, *Our Bodies, Ourselves* encouraged read-ers to respond to its contents. It provoked passionate letters filled with heartfelt personal accounts of infections, miscarriages, depression, and disability. Some responses were humorous while some were angry. Some readers wrote in the name of sisterhood while others were simply scared. Together, their letters reveal that readers were active agents who identi-fied women's health as a crucial component of feminism. From Maine to Montana, those who read *Our Bodies, Ourselves* transcended tradi-tional geographic and organizational boundaries of feminism, simply by reading and reacting to the book.

What Does Vaginitis Have to Do with Feminism?

In April of 1981 Frances[71] telephoned Jane Pincus at the BWHBC in search of a cure for recurring vaginitis, noting later in a letter that Pincus had "tried in earnest" to help her. Frances believed that a women's health organization would have a solution. But the information Frances received from the collective proved to be inaccurate. Pincus had sug-gested a nonsulfa antibiotic preparation called Furacin, also mentioned in the 1979 edition of *Our Bodies, Ourselves.* Frances then called her doctor to ask for a prescription for the medication, which he provided. Much to her dismay, she learned from the pharmacist that it had been off the market for years; he then suggested Betadine or Vagisec. When she called her doctor again to ask his opinion of these two preparations, Frances recalled, he said he did not care which she tried. Frances was clearly frustrated with her doctor, but she was frustrated with the collective as well. "Though you tried hard," she assured, "it seems that the materials available to you are either out of date or weren't properly researched by someone!" Of the three medical advisors she sought out—Pincus, her doctor, and her pharmacist—only her pharmacist had accurate information, she believed. But in a hastily typed postscript, she updated her story. Even the pharmacist had "lied" to her—Vagisec had no antibacterial properties and was therefore useless in treating her condition.[72]

Though Frances's experience might have led to disenchantment with the women's health movement, instead it made her more intent on contributing to the cause. She did not bother complaining to her doctor; according to her, he did not care. In her opinion, the pharmacist was a liar. But she noted the compassion and earnestness of Pincus, and the importance of the movement: "Believe me the only hope for women lies in feminist organizations like yours." For this reason, medical knowledge and accuracy were all the more important. "So PLEASE, be careful in the information you dispense because no one else is, not in the medical industry, anyway."[73] Her motive for writing the BWHBC was not simply to chastise, but to correct a potentially damaging error, and it worked. The next edition of the book, *The New Our Bodies, Ourselves* (1984), omitted the Furacin reference.

Brenda was another woman "trying desperately to find a cure for vaginitis." Not knowing where else to turn, she had contacted the collective in March of 1979 in the hope that it could put her in touch with one of the female gynecologists quoted in the book. So far, she had had no luck with physicians; the first was "sarcastic" and "ridiculed the fact that I was concerned about the problem." So she never went back to his office. "I pity everybody who still goes and sees that particular man. (And I frankly hope he gets an itch one day!)" Her second doctor prescribed Flagyl, and though she had a bad reaction, she was told to finish taking the pills, and the nausea stayed with her for over two months.[74] Then in September of 1979, Brenda wrote Judy Norsigian at the collective with a positive update. She had found a new doctor—"a gynecologist from the Old World, with a great bedside manner." He suggested wearing cotton underwear, using gentle detergents, and eating yogurt, and so far, it was working. "By voicing my concern to others, I was shocked to hear how many people had had (or were having) similar problems, and that they didn't know who to turn to also, or were equally irritated and depressed by their doctors' impatience."

Brenda's comment calls attention to a common desire among women for dependable and sympathetic physicians. "Perhaps the problem *is* very common, but the patient suffers enough living with it day after day, for a 'dumb' doctor not to have sympathy. As I told one of the doctors I dropped, '*I* itch; you don't.'"[75] When asked by a feminist scholar in 1973 why women were so angry about current medical treatment, Marcia Storch, an OB-GYN, answered, "the personal touch is gone."[76] Because they were no longer making house calls by the 1960s, physicians lacked firsthand knowledge of a patient's environment. Those who spoke of distrusting doctors in the 1970s criticized them as "distant, arrogant, and uncaring."[77]

"Remember me?" began a letter to the BWHBC from Mary, another vaginitis sufferer. "I'm the law student who's written you several times about having vaginitis for more than two years."[78] She was writing to share the good news that her problem was finally going away, to explain how, and to share some of the things she had learned. Mary had been suffering from vaginal irritation since the first time she had had intercourse. Since then, she noted, "I have taken (and inserted, and applied, and douched with . . .) an incredible number of drugs in an effort to get some relief from this problem." Like Frances and Brenda, Mary had found her doctors to be unsympathetic. The collective referred her to the Elizabeth Blackwell Clinic in Philadelphia, where she finally found relief. The clinic physician recommended exercises rather than drugs. "He says I don't have good control of those muscles, and they tighten up very easily," making intercourse "painful and abrasive." Though skeptical, Mary took his advice, noting that it had taken some time and faith "to translate these exercises into a different experience of intercourse." For the first time ever, she began to enjoy sex, and to itch "less and less."[79]

Delighted, Mary explained her reason for writing. "All this may seem very simple to you, but really, this is the first time anyone has approached my problem in this way. No other doctor knew or cared why the problem had gone on so long." Instead, she continued, they had prescribed drug after drug. Knowing that other women had similar stories, Mary wanted to get the word out. "Forgive me for sounding like I'm on a soapbox, but if I can help other women before they have to go through some of the things I did, I'll at least have gotten something useful from the experience." A two-page, single-spaced typed list of issues and advice followed her remarks, including her experience using various remedies, dealing with pain, and interacting with a gynecologist. Betadine douche: "Maybe it's okay for some people, but it burned me out. . . . The doctor, when I complained about the horrible sting, said that meant it was working. Bullshit." Acigel: "I don't even like to think about using this drug." Intravaginal creams: "If it stings, forget it!" Her closing words underscored the agenda of the women's health movement. "Doctors simply don't know everything, and if their answers sound like bullshit to you, it's probably because that's what they are. So be assertive, ask questions, and be impatient!"[80]

What is striking about these three examples is their criticism of routine gynecological care. The women's frustration arose from the fact that even a simple, mundane disorder such as vaginitis lacked a common procedure or even diagnosis. According to the director of women's health sessions at the St. Mark's Clinic in New York City, vaginitis failed to interest physicians "because it is neither dramatic nor life threatening, and it is very hard to 'cure.'" Yet it was also a problem that concerned many women: the clinic regularly held a tremendously popular "vaginitis night" in the early 1970s that resulted in its being "swamped" with patients.[81] As Sheryl Ruzek notes, in 1978 there was widespread dissatisfaction with conventional gynecological services, "even among women not actively involved in either the women's health movement or the larger feminist movement."[82]

Negative Responses: "It matters to me what your book says"

While many women wrote the BWHBC to express appreciation for the encouragement *Our Bodies, Ourselves* provided or to share advice (as Brenda did), others wrote out of anger when they did not find the support they had come to expect. Encouraged by the text itself to "demand answers and explanations from the people you come in contact with for medical care,"[83] some readers interpreted this to include not only doctors, but also the authors of *Our Bodies, Ourselves*. As a result, the members of the BWHBC found themselves becoming mediators between organized medicine and women. They faced the difficult task of going into enemy territory—the medical establishment—and attempting to divorce medical "facts" from their assumed misogynist context. But as these reader responses attest, the boundaries between the two were never entirely clear. Nor was the exact role of BWHBC authors in bridging the gap between organized medicine and female patients.

A series of letters exchanged between Sarah and *Our Bodies, Ourselves* coauthor Norma Swenson in 1979 demonstrates the BWHBC authors' struggle to translate medical knowledge effectively for their readership. It began in February when Sarah wrote, "I have trusted you and learned much from your book in the past. But having spent the last year trying to conceive a child, and coming up with nothing, and then a class 3 Pap smear, the cause of which has not been terribly easy to find out, the last thing I need is a statement like the one I tripped over on page 147."[84] She was referring to the discussion of D&C (dilation and curettage) in a chapter on medical health problems. Sarah's abnormal Pap smear indicated the possibility of cervical cancer, and her doctors recommended a D&C and possibly a conization (removing a cone of tissue from the cervix during the procedure to biopsy). She returned home and immediately picked up her copy of Our Bodies, Ourselves to learn more about the procedure. The 1979 edition concluded the discussion of D&C by stating that conization "may lead to complications in future pregnancies."[85] Her reaction to that sentence was so powerful that she described it to the BWHBC in not one, but two different letters. Already feeling cheated by the time she left the doctor's office, she stated that she "got to the line [in the book] that said conizations might lead to complications in pregnancy. New paragraph. You didn't tell me *what* complications. *The* book didn't tell me; it just added another layer of mystery and innuendo. I hate veiled warnings, vague threats—just tell me what the options are, or the facts. I know enough to worry, but not enough to answer my own questions. . . . Before you and your book there was nothing, but still."[86] She demanded that the collective take responsibility; she ended her letter by stating, "Your part in the trauma of the last few days will long be remembered."[87]

For Sarah, the one publication she thought she could rely on had failed her. This was a serious charge; her trauma stemmed not only from her bout with an irregular Pap smear and the threat of cervical cancer, and not only from the medical response, but from the book's "vague threats." Could *the* book possibly be considered part of the enemy, part of the problem rather than the solution? Concern about cooptation and "selling out" was common among women's health advocates by the mid-1970s as feminist health was becoming a lucrative business.[88] Many opposed the BWHBC's earlier decision to leave the New England Free Press and publish with Simon & Schuster, for example. Sarah's letter suggests an attempt to shore up the boundaries between feminist women's health and what she and others believed to be a misogynist medical establishment.

Coauthor Norma Swenson responded carefully, sensitive to the charge. "We are really sorry that you found our section on conization in relating to pregnancy upsetting and unhelpful." She admitted that there was no way of knowing who had written the passage, but accepted full responsibility. Without knowledge of authorship, culpability had to be shared by all members of the collective. Swenson made it clear that the authors faced quite a challenge when discussing and analyzing medical treatment. "One of the problems we constantly stumble over as we try to research medical practice," she explained, "is that habits of treatment and prognosis get established with very little real evidence. . . . In sharing this kind of information with women, we want to be sure to include as much as we can of what is known, while at the same time leaving women some room to question and challenge the dogma about themselves and their conditions." However, according to some readers, too much room remained. "I wouldn't have sensed how unhelpful our sentence was if you hadn't shown us," Swenson acknowledged. "I'm not sure how to fix it, but you can be sure we'll make some modification next time around. We'll also try to do more research."[89] Indeed, the statement was omitted in the next edition and replaced with a more specific description of what the potential complications are and why they happen.

Sarah was clearly moved by Swenson's response, calling it a "generous" letter. In the "relative calm of early summer," she was able to reflect on her experience. "I don't blame anyone for that open-ended response; I just wish it hadn't been written," she noted; then added, "except that there are definitely good points to this correspondence." The dialogue, which Sarah now cast in a positive light, had begun directly with the text of Our Bodies, Ourselves (because Sarah believed it did not speak adequately to her), and had expanded into a warm exchange of ideas and explanations. "I probably wrote initially partly because it matters to me what your book says," Sarah explained. "By writing it you stuck your and our necks out, and I want us to look good, since efforts like these are still scrutinized so closely."[90] Like other readers, she perceived Our Bodies, Ourselves as a broader collective in which the book's readers as well as its writers all shared responsibility for the outcome.

It may seem surprising that feminist readers would direct their hostility toward the BWHBC rather than what they believed to be misogynist medicine. Yet Amy Farrell locates a similar trend in the relationship between the readers and editors of Ms. Magazine during this time. As Farrell argues, readers "forged strong yet volatile ties" with the magazine in that they identified with it, but also insisted it "live up to its promise as a resource for the women's movement."[91]

In the case of women's health, an erosion of trust in the medical establishment created critical consumers. These consumers were all the more willing to critique those feminist texts that claimed to speak for all women; they saw it as crucial that their particular perspective or experience was included in such a text. Indeed, the most common complaint of readers of Our Bodies, Ourselves who wrote to the collective had to do with their sense of exclusion. Readers expected to find themselves described within the book's pages, and expressed confusion, disappointment, frustration, or anger if they did not. Although the women's health movement had the potential to cut across racial and class boundaries, argued feminist scholars Barbara Ehrenreich and Deirdre English in 1973, it would become only "'some women's health movement' unless the diversity of women's priorities were taken into account."[92] Over time, readers ensured that such diversity was reflected in *Our Bodies, Ourselves*.

Surprisingly, one of the most fundamental categories of exclusion—namely, race—does not emerge from the letters.[93] Yet many women have voiced their concern in other venues about the book's limited treatment of race and, more generally, the ways in which white women had paid scant attention to the specific health needs and perspectives of women of color. Sheryl Ruzek noted in 1978 that the women's health movement remained "largely white and middle class—especially in leadership and in focus."[94] African-American health activist Byllye Avery recalled that "white women had no idea about certain issues affecting black women."[95] For this reason, she spearheaded a national grassroots project on black women's health, with the support of the National Women's Health Network.[96] Winifred Breines, a sociologist and former activist in Boston, notes the racial tensions between white and black socialist feminists in that city during the 1970s, a stone's throw away from the BWHBC.[97] At the collective itself, racial tensions erupted in the 1990s; in 1997, four staff members resigned, arguing that the organization refused to "grapple honestly with racism and issues of power with respect to the women of color within the organization."[98] Sociologist Kathy Davis notes that these were "turbulent years" for the BWHBC as it struggled to address diversity and experienced tensions similar to those of other predominantly white feminist organizations.

Though readers of *Our Bodies, Ourselves* did not address race directly in their letters to the collective, they touched on issues that had certainly affected, and been affected by, women of color—namely, reproductive health and sexuality. Readers adamantly expressed their views as to how these particular issues should be portrayed in the book. Their concerns challenged some basic assumptions about feminism and health, forcing the authors to reconsider their stance on a number of issues.

Greta wrote the authors to critique their portrayal of sterilization. She had decided to stop taking the Pill because she wished to be "in total control of my body as to what I eat, smoke, [and] drink." Though she found the section on birth control helpful, she still was not satisfied: "The one section which I continually skipped over was entitled 'When you are through with having children—sterilization.' I glanced at the pictures of tubal ligation and thought, 'That's not for me.'" But then she recalled the experience of a single, childless female friend who had expressed her relief and satisfaction with having undergone a tubal ligation. "It struck me that the title of this section in your book suggests that married or single women who have never had children don't, shouldn't, or mustn't have tubal ligations."[99]

In the 1970s, voluntary sterilization was the most popular form of birth control for white women and men.[100] But it was also a controversial procedure, one that proved to be divisive for feminists, because it was sometimes practiced coercively on poor women and women of color. Its contentious history as a eugenic procedure complicated the position of feminist activists who sought control over reproduction.[101] As Rebecca Kluchin argues, "women's race, class, and ethnicity clearly shaped their sterilization experiences, which in turn influenced their ideas of reproductive freedom." Organizations such as the Committee to End Sterilization Abuse and the Committee for Abortion Rights and Against Sterilization Abuse sought to protect women by promoting a series of guidelines in 1974 and 1977, respectively, to protect women from forced sterilization.[102]

While the BWHBC included a discussion of sterilization in the birth control chapter of *Our Bodies, Ourselves* from the beginning, the authors were aware that it was a complex issue. "Black women in the South are all too familiar with the 'Mississippi Appendectomy' in which their fallopian tubes were tied or their uterus removed without their knowing it," they wrote.[103] But for women like Greta, sterilization was a safe and effective method of birth control for women of any age, and thus an important aspect of reproductive choice. She suggested that in the next edition, "tubal ligation might be referred to as an alternative method of birth control rather than a step to be taken presumably after having had children already."[104] Consequently, in the 1984 edition the authors completely rewrote the section on sterilization (no longer entitled "When You Are Through with Having Children"). They warned younger women that "nearly one-third of the women who were sterilized at one point in their lives regretted this decision later on, particularly if they were under thirty years old when sterilized. Some women turn to sterilization in desperation because there is no suitable form of contraception for them." But they also took into consideration the opinions of women like Greta. "For some women, however, the choice to be sterilized is a positive wish to avoid pregnancy forever. Some have already had children; others decide they never want children."[105] Significantly, they also included a separate section on sterilization abuse in a new chapter on violence against women, and included the addresses of anti–sterilization abuse organizations (including the American Civil Liberties Union and the Committee for Abortion Rights and Against Sterilization Abuse).

Just as readers forced the BWHBC to reconsider the politics of sterilization, they also challenged feminist assumptions about the liberating effects of abortion. While most readers believed reproductive choice to be an essential component of the women's health movement, they also reminded the collective that every experience is different and that one-sided generalizations could be hurtful. "I have gone through a harrowing emotional experience," Melissa wrote to Wendy Sanford at the collective in 1980. "I decided to write this letter after reading your section on abortion in *Our Bodies, Ourselves* and not finding adequate information or emotional support for a person in my condition." As a "firm supporter of the women's movement," she was writing to offer constructive criticism in the hopes that her suggestions could be "implemented in the revised edition."[106]

Melissa desperately wanted a baby. But she and her husband learned that they were both genetic carriers of Tay-Sachs, meaning that their offspring had a one-in-four chance of developing the disorder and dying in early childhood. "In my particular case I did not want to have the second trimester abortion for the reason of *not* wanting a baby, as the women in your chapter on abortion did," Melissa explained. An amniocentesis revealed that the developing fetus would indeed develop Tay-Sachs. "Therefore, while my choice for an abortion can technically be considered 'elective,' I very much wanted this baby, which was to be my first, and was extremely upset to find I would need an abortion."[107]

Melissa would have consulted the revised and expanded edition of *Our Bodies, Ourselves* (1976, 1979), which included an extensive chapter on abortion. There she would have learned about the history of abortion laws and practice, the antiabortion movement, medical techniques for terminating pregnancy, and how to find an abortion facility. She also would have come across a section on "feelings about being pregnant," which included only one first-person account of these emotions. "When I found I was pregnant, I was frightened and angry that my body was out of my control," the account described. "I was furious that my IUD had failed me, and I felt my sexual parts were alien and my enemy. I felt I was being punished for my femaleness."[108] This was certainly not representative of Melissa's feelings and may have made it difficult for her to read on.

But her sense of exclusion did not end there. Perhaps because she could not have the abortion until twenty weeks into her pregnancy (when the disease could be detected), Melissa was also experiencing some of the physical and hormonal symptoms of a pregnant or postpartum woman. "Today I turned to *Our Bodies, Ourselves* to try to find some answers, and to see how other women in my position have felt," she wrote.

> Why were my breasts so sore? What could I do about them and how long would it last? Had other women who underwent similar abortions felt the same physical pains, weakness, and tiredness? How did women feel who had wanted the baby, but were forced by circumstances beyond their control to have the abortion instead? Did these women, like me, feel as if they had given birth but then had no baby to show for it? How long would the 'mourning' process last over a fetus which was not considered living? I had and still have so many questions.[109]

But the abortion chapter did not address any of these issues; instead, Melissa found she was forced to read about physical questions in the chapter on pregnancy, despite the fact that the symptoms are common after an abortion as well. "I must admit," she continued, "it makes it more depressing having to look in that section when I don't fit in that optimistic, happy section." While some women noted that reading *Our Bodies, Ourselves* made them feel less alone and more connected with other women suffering from similar problems, Melissa felt even more isolated by reading the book. Her experience clashed with those described in both the abortion and the pregnancy chapters. "I felt that for once, at a crucial time, *Our Bodies, Ourselves* had let me down." She asked Sanford to consider the physical and emotional feelings of women like herself, who "make up a substantial minority when you consider Tay-Sachs, Down's syndrome, neural tube defects, and other biochemical and chromosomal diseases." Sanford needed to be "sensitive to this issue and give it the attention it deserves."[110]

On behalf of the BWHBC, Wendy Sanford responded carefully to the criticism. "I feel very much humbled by your letter of August, and I appreciate the time you took to help us make the abortion chapter of *Our Bodies, Ourselves* more careful and compassionate," she wrote. Reflecting her commitment to the collective process, she explained that "it is letters like yours that help us make the book better, but it is always a sorrow for us that someone suffered for what we did or didn't say." Like Swenson's response to Sarah's experience with conization, Sanford's letter alluded to the fine line the authors had to tread in the book. Lack of information, or misinformation, unintentionally excluded and sometimes traumatized readers. "In this case," Sanford acknowledged, "it was both factual information that was missing *and* sensitivity to the emotional experience of someone who was not happy or at least relieved to end the pregnancy."[111] She promised to improve the abortion chapter in the revised edition. Indeed, the 1984 edition included an entirely rewritten chapter, by authors who had not contributed to previous editions. The chapter had a section on aftercare that discussed the physical and emotional response to abortion, as well as a first-person account from a woman who "very much wanted to be a mother" but learned from the amniocentesis that she would have a Down syndrome baby and did not feel emotionally or financially equipped to raise such a child.[112]

Disabling diseases affect women as well as their potential offspring. The disability rights movement led to greater awareness and discussion of the subject in the 1970s. This, in turn, prompted some readers to criticize the limited discussion of women with disabilities in *Our Bodies, Ourselves*. Jane sent the authors a postcard in 1977 urging them to change how they refer to people with disabilities in the 1976 edition. "People who have epilepsy, asthma, diabetes, etc. often do not enjoy being defined as the disease they have. In other words, they ARE NOT epileptics, asthmatics, and diabetics. They ARE people with many abilities and a few disabilities. They are people *with* epilepsy, asthma, diabetes. They are NOT the disease itself."[113]

Another reader had difficulty identifying with the sole first-person account of a woman with a physical handicap included in the 1976 edition. "In a disabled and disfigured body, I am 'desexed' by both society and myself," this account read. "Always I've asked, 'Am I a person despite my physical handicaps?' Now I ask also, 'Am I a woman?'" Inappropriately positioned under the heading "Growing Up," her narrative was left to stand on its own, with no wider contextualization of disability issues.[114]

Mary-Elyn pointed out this limited representation of disability issues in her letter to the BWHBC: "while her feelings are reflective of many disabled women, they are not 'typical' of everyone." Without other examples, readers would be left with the "impression that this is the only way disabled women see themselves," and would continue to view them "in stereotypic images." It was therefore crucial to "actively seek more input from disabled women and add it when the book is revised. In that way, you both humanize and sexualize disabled women and you give disabled women the opportunity to learn what other disabled as well as non-disabled women are thinking and feeling about their bodies and themselves."[115]

Once again, Wendy Sanford responded to the criticism, but this time, her answer went directly into the revised edition of *Our Bodies, Ourselves*. "Many of us in the Collective had never known women with physical disabilities," Sanford explained, so members consulted with a local self-help organization while preparing the 1984 edition. "Our meetings with the Boston Self-Help group began to change both how we see disabled women and how we see ourselves."[116] As a result, *The New Our Bodies, Ourselves* incorporated the stories of women with disabilities in various chapters on health and sexuality.

"Only about 1/3 of the book applies to me"

The issue that the collective struggled with the most in addressing reader correspondence and text revisions during the early years of *Our Bodies, Ourselves* was lesbianism, an issue that divided many feminists in the 1970s.[117] So many women wrote letters in response to the lesbian chapter that *The New Our Bodies, Ourselves* gave special thanks to the hundreds "all over the country telling about their experiences and asking for advice, news, contacts, support."[118] Although many respondents were enthusiastic about the chapter, they also pushed for more material. "What I most wanted to comment on was the assumption of heterosexuality throughout the book," Barbara wrote. "There is a way that even though lesbianism is acknowledged as an option for women, it is still ghettoized in the one chapter and male-female relationships become the norm throughout."[119]

In the New England Free Press edition, homosexuality was addressed in slightly more than one page of the sixteen-page chapter on sexuality. By the 1973 Simon & Schuster edition, it was the subject of an entire eighteen-page chapter, "In Amerika They Call Us Dykes," and written by women involved in the gay liberation movement. Conflict between the BWHBC and the lesbian authors of "In Amerika" was apparent in the chapter introduction. "We had no connection with the group that was writing the rest of the book . . . and in fact we disagreed, and still do, with many of their opinions," the lesbian authors wrote. The collective clarified its position with a footnote linked to the chapter's title: "Since the gay collective insisted on complete control over the style and content of this chapter, the Health Book Collective has not edited it. Because of length limitations, however, the gay collective has had to leave out much material that they feel is important."[120] In meeting minutes and memos from the mid-to-late 1970s, BWHBC members made it clear that they were not happy with the chapter's title and some of its content. Based on reader feedback "from both gay and straight women," they recognized that the chapter "gives only part of a picture," and that it needed to be "balanced out in some way (with input from older women, poor women, women with a longer experience of living a gay life, etc.)." They also felt that the title was problematic; Wendy Sanford argued that "someone who isn't a lesbian and who is fearful might feel pushed away." She suggested alternatives, including "Loving Women: Lesbian Life" (which eventually became part of the chapter title in a later edition, with different authors), but the gay collective insisted on keeping the original wording.[121]

Internal meeting notes reveal that by 1978 there was a great deal of frustration over how to integrate material on lesbianism into the next edition of *Our Bodies, Ourselves*. When the collective attempted to revise the chapter, its original authors rejected the changes, and asked for more space (sixty manuscript pages instead of thirty-five). After a divisive meeting with them, one collective member proposed stopping the writing process entirely until the disputes were resolved, despite the upcoming revisions deadline imposed by Simon & Schuster. Some resented that although "the gay women haven't been part of our process, we spend our precious hours talking about the gay chapter." Finally, at midnight on March 28, 1978, the BWHBC resolved to limit the gay chapter to fifty manuscript pages and to explain in the revised edition that "they weren't with us writing other chapters and they feel other chapters don't reflect them."[122]

But readers continued to complain. "I'm a Lesbian, which means that only about 1/3 of the book applies to me," Maggie wrote in 1982. "Now I'm sure you've had it suggested many times before that the rest of the book should integrate lesbianism more thoroughly," she chided. "These things should be obvious in 1982—every section except 'In Amerika' assumes the heterosexuality of the reader." Even "In Amerika" had problems, however. Although it was "very influential" in her coming out, and was "probably the most well read piece of Lesbian literature in the English language," it was "completely out of date now," Maggie maintained. She was sorry to see it go (note her assumption that it would not make it into the next edition), because it exuded the excitement of the beginnings of an important movement: "It would be hard to find someone to write a new one who would seem, like these Lesbians did, to be sharing something new which they were just putting together themselves for the first time."[123]

Maggie's assumption was correct; "In Amerika" did not make it into the next edition. It was replaced by "Loving Women: Lesbian Life and Relationships," which was authored by the "Lesbian Revisions Group." None had worked on the original piece, though "it provided crucial support and inspiration for several of us when we first came out as lesbians." Instead, they had written a chapter "quite different in focus and tone from the original one, using briefer stories so as to make room for more topics." This time around, the BWHBC authors' footnote linked to the chapter title was more conciliatory: "Although this edition of *Our Bodies, Ourselves* includes lesbian voices throughout, the collective decided also to have a separate chapter for a more careful focus on issues and information which specifically affect lesbians."[124] *The New Our Bodies, Ourselves* thus incorporated the suggestions and concerns of lesbian readers. However, it and later editions also revealed tensions within the text, underscoring the most basic challenge to the women's health movement: there simply was no universally shared perspective on women's health.

: : :

When the Boston Women's Health Book Collective urged women to gain control of their bodies beginning in the 1970s, it was also, in the words of scholar Catharine Stimpson, assigning "extraordinary moral weight to the body."[125] Along with the collective's authors, the women readers of *Our Bodies, Ourselves* contributed to that assignment by articulating highly specific ways to reclaim their bodies. They became part of a widespread network of women determined to rethink the relationship between mind and body. Their stories challenge us to consider the role of ordinary women in shaping the development of the women's health movement. Since the first "Women and Their Bodies" workshop in 1969, participants in the movement, broadly defined, have struggled to make knowledge about women's health accessible to all women. What they discovered early on was that even within a small group of white, Boston-based feminists, perspectives and experiences could differ radically. Attempting to make all decisions by consensus and include all women's voices proved impossible. But the commitment to try, to see themselves inextricably bound as a family in which everyone's individual needs would not always be met, resulted in a more powerful and accessible book.

Our Bodies, Ourselves was influenced not only by the formal collective, but also by readers who participated in a dialogue about women's health. By challenging the writers of the book on a number of points, readers influenced the way in which its authors, in the words of one of them, "translated science to the people." Confrontational letters to the collective reveal readers' expectations and assumptions about how women's health should be portrayed, as well as their desire to have their perspectives included. By demanding greater inclusion and diversity within the text, these readers ensured that *Our Bodies, Ourselves* would continue to be read by generations of women. These exchanges between the collective's authors and readers reveal how knowledge of women's bodies and health was reconstructed from a diversity of personal perspectives beginning in the 1970s. The conflicts expressed in letters underscore the inherent tension between two equally valid truths: the singularity of being female and the plurality of individual experiences among women. By the 1980s, this tension would contribute to a decline in the transformative nature of women's health activism. Nonetheless, *Our Bodies, Ourselves* continued to prosper decades after the second wave.

2

Reexamining the Pelvic: The Pelvic Instruction Controversy of the 1970s

We are under siege from the consumerists, environmentalists, women's liberationists, civil rights and other special interest activists yet to be organized.
—**Martin Stone, presidential address, American College of Obstetricians and Gynecologists, 1979¹**

As the Boston Women's Health Book Collective gathered, updated, and revised literature on women's health in the 1970s, other groups set out to put these ideas into practice by establishing feminist health centers. By 1976, there were approximately fifty women-controlled clinics operating in the United States. Though few in number, they were "vanguard organizations that were fertile soil" for many innovations in the women's health movement.² In particular, they provided an alternative space for women to obtain reproductive health services and play an active role in taking care of their bodies. Many of these clinics opened just after the 1973 Supreme Court decision in *Roe v. Wade* that legalized abortion during the first trimester of pregnancy; consequently, the facilities included pregnancy termination among their services.³ Also central to their goal, however, was routine gynecological care, which women's health activists believed could and should be provided in a women-centered, women-controlled environment.

The Women's Community Health Center, the only freestanding clinic in Massachusetts owned and controlled by women, opened its doors in 1974, not far from BWHBC headquarters. With a five-thousand-dollar grant from the collective and the proceeds from sales of plastic speculums and from benefit performances by local feminist singers and poets, the clinic's organizers rented space, installed phone lines, and put one of their members on a salary.[4] In its first few years of operation, the WCHC was run by a collective of thirteen to eighteen women ranging in age from 23 to 52. Though all its members were white, the collective stressed its diversity in sexual orientation. "We are lesbians, heterosexual women, celibate women," it declared in 1977, "all working to allow each woman the right to define her own sexuality." As with many feminist health groups, it stressed how women's health could unify women from different backgrounds. "Our diversity provides different perspectives, but our shared political base is the empowering of women through self-help so that we can control our own health care, our bodies, and our lives."[5] It defined self-help, a mainstay of feminist clinics, as simply "valuing what we learn from our bodies and experiences and sharing this information in groups."[6]

Thus, the WCHC's philosophy, like that of the BWHBC, was based on promoting experiential evidence as an alternative to clinical knowledge. Women, by their very nature, were the experts of their own bodies. As historian Michelle Murphy argues, "The central epistemological principle of feminist self-help, as with radical feminism more generally, was that all knowledge production should begin with women's experiences."[7] Self-helpers believed that women's experiences, not clinical research produced by physicians, represented the most empowering, most liberating source of knowledge.

It was not a far leap from claiming that women are the authorities over their own bodies to demanding a complete overhaul of traditional medical education in the United States. As part of that reform, members of the WCHC engaged in a one-year contractual experiment with Harvard University's Medical School, in which they created a Pelvic Teaching Program as part of the school curriculum. Although the experiment ultimately failed, it generated intense reflection within the women's health community over the appropriate role of women's bodies in medical training, and who is best authorized to make use of those bodies in a learning environment.

The WCHC did not realize that its concerns were part of a larger debate surrounding the study of routine gynecology. The controversy began in the 1970s, when gynecologists, medical students, patients, and feminists struggled over who had rightful claim to examining the female body and how, exactly, it should be examined. Traditionally, the pelvic exam had been under the jurisdiction of gynecologists, particularly after the introduction of the Pap smear as a routine screening technique in 1943. But by the 1970s, a new political and social climate forced a reexamination of the pelvic, prompting the president of the American College of Obstetricians and Gynecologists to declare the profession "under siege."

The subject of pelvic exams as a source of shame and secrecy became fodder for feminists, who began to view unpleasant memories of the procedure as indicative of sexist medicine. Women's health activist, journalist, and former Harvard Medical School student Ellen Frankfort opened her best-selling exposé, *Vaginal Politics*, with a description of her own first experiences in the stirrups. "Surely, these first penetrations—embroidered by feelings of shame and humiliation (I was naked, he was dressed; I was lying down, he was standing up; I was quiet, he was giving the orders), experienced in bare surroundings amid strange smells—taught me that both the doctor and anything done in the framework of disease are exempt from the usual taboos."[8] In the supposedly sterile environment of the doctor's office, traditional standards of propriety did not apply, and until the 1970s there was no language other than medical jargon to describe what was taking place. As the nurse practitioner Cortney Davis writes, "What happens to a woman in the privacy of a medical exam room has always been a secret between that patient and her caregiver."[9]

Yet a climate of consciousness-raising, popular disillusionment with medicine, and retrenchment within gynecology eroded this silence during the 1970s, influencing the way both patients and practitioners interpreted the nature of the pelvic exam. This chapter explores the explosive sexual politics surrounding the rise of pelvic teaching programs in that decade. Changes within medical education, combined with the increasing emphasis on self-help (particularly in resources such as *Our Bodies, Ourselves*), resulted in a widespread debate about the proper training for and practice of pelvic exams. Despite the failure of the WCHC's Pelvic Teaching Program to institutionalize its proposed method of learning, its brief existence created the potential for reexamining the relationship between bodies and medical knowledge.

Until recently, the pelvic has received little historical analysis—those who study the history of women's health are more likely to investigate abortion or breast cancer, for example, than a routine gynecological procedure.[10] Yet the stories from the previous chapter attest to the significance of this procedure to many women. The pelvic offers a fascinating window into the dynamics of the relationship between doctors and patients, as well as the blurred boundaries between sexuality and medicine. Though the procedure itself is routinely performed on healthy women in a supposedly sterile environment divorced from outside context, it is in reality loaded with context and meaning. As Terri Kapsalis argues, "Cultural attitudes about women and their bodies are not checked at the hospital door."[11] Doctors, patients, and students bring certain assumptions, varying levels of discomfort, and attitudes about sexuality that affect how they interpret and experience the procedure.

Many of those receiving or training for performing a pelvic for the first time have clear memories about how this initial experience affected them. "Since I experienced my own exams as a humiliating procedure, I feared inflicting the same humiliation on another person," former Harvard Medical School student Ellen Rothman recalled.[12] She and her classmates were forced to confront their personal feelings in the hospital setting. "For the first time we had to extricate ourselves from our sexual associations, cultural values, and personal beliefs about genitals and transform them into a purely clinical experience," she remarked. These memories suggest the difficulty of divorcing the procedure from sexual connotations, which made it a particularly contested aspect of gynecology beginning in the 1970s.

A Changing Specialty

It was not only feminists who were concerned about the state of gynecological care. Changes within OB-GYN and medicine more generally also affected the teaching of the pelvic exam. Though obstetrics and gynecology were formally consolidated as a specialty in 1920, by the late 1940s the profession had expanded to include "caring for women's entire reproductive system in all its physical and psychological aspects."[13] Obstetrician gynecologists now assumed the role of marriage counselor, for example, looking not just for bodily abnormalities, but behavioral ones as well. Historian Carolyn Herbst Lewis notes that performing a premarital pelvic exam—which became more common in the 1950s and 1960s—allowed these doctors to "communicate their definition of healthy marital heterosexuality" to their patients.[14] To ensure that young brides were ready for the wedding night, they used the pelvic exam as a form of sex instruction. A woman who feared the procedure would most likely fear sexual penetration as well. Doctors therefore "hoped to pre-empt any emotional or physical trauma that might be inflicted by a less-than-tender wedding night."[15] Guiding young women through the mechanics of sex to ensure marital stability, they established their position as moral arbiters during the postwar era. By doing so, of course, they underscored the link between the pelvic examination and sexual practice.

As a result, they found themselves in a delicate situation. Linking healthy heterosexuality with marriage and femininity, they stressed the importance of vaginal penetration and vaginal (as opposed to clitoral) orgasm. Thus, it was important for them to highlight the role of penetration in sexual stimulation. But while interested in measuring sexual response, they did not want their own actions to be perceived as sexual. According to Lewis, doctors could avoid any uncomfortable scenario by encouraging not arousal per se, but compliance. By making the patient relaxed and receptive, a doctor hoped to ensure that she would experience pleasure later, not while in the stirrups.[16]

By the 1970s, the cultural authority gained by the OB-GYN profession in the postwar period was on the wane. Both insiders and outsiders found much to criticize about the medical specialty. Traditionally associated with surgery, gynecology was now attempting to associate itself more with specific diseases of women. Whereas specialists in the 1950s approached women's reproductive health within a larger context of physical and psychological well-being, those practicing in the 1970s "rarely noticed women at all amidst the specific and discrete diseases she [sic] offered."[17] Leadership within the field switched from clinicians to researchers, and the field became more specialized. In 1968, the American College of Obstetricians and Gynecologists made specialty board certification a requirement for membership, thus pushing out generalists.[18] But this shift reinforced the notion that OB-GYN was not a clearly defined field, suffering from "frontier skirmishes" with surgeons, endocrinologists, and pediatricians. Many medical students chose what they believed to be more prestigious specialties than OB-GYN.[19]

A changing student body also challenged traditional medical education and specialization. Medical historian Kenneth Ludmerer notes that even the typically conformist medical student population did not survive the 1960s and '70s unscathed. Medical students engaged in political protests, demanded that their schools respond to the local community's health needs, and promoted educational reform. They challenged universities to reevaluate everything from tuition to curriculum. Some focused particularly on issues of race and gender; Boston University students organized a Student Committee on Medical School Affairs to "investigate allegations of institutional racism and sexism."[20] Students at other universities insisted on having a voice in institutional affairs, and some became voting members of faculty committees.[21]

Student demographics changed alongside with student demands. Affirmative action programs and minority recruitment resulted in a "substantial increase" in minority medical students, from 3 percent of the student population in 1969 to 10 percent in 1974.[22] In the 1970s, the proportion of women medical students grew dramatically as well, from 10 percent to nearly 28 percent.[23] Title IX of the 1972 Higher Education Amendments Act threatened to penalize schools that practiced sex discrimination in hiring or educational policies, a boon for female applicants to medical schools. As historian Naomi Rogers points out, the young women who applied to medical schools in the 1970s were not all feminists—indeed, in the early 1970s, many radical feminists urged women not to attend medical school but to work outside the system to transform it. But publications like *Our Bodies, Ourselves* and feminist health conferences certainly "embolden[ed] many women contemplating medical careers."[24]

Increasing numbers of female students, however, did not immediately transform medical education; if anything, their presence was initially met with resistance. Whether feminist or not, in the 1970s they were mocked by male students and teachers as "women's libbers."[25] Many suffered harassment and ridicule, a problem publicized by Harvard Medical School's first female dean, Mary Howell, who in 1973 published *Why Would a Woman Go into Medicine?*, a scathing attack on the treatment of women at U.S. medical schools. She resigned her post two years later, citing the university's unrestrained exercise of power.

In 1979, Harvard hired its second female dean, Carola Eisenberg, who remained in charge of student affairs until she left in 1990. Eisenberg exercised a greater influence over Harvard's female medical students. "I really became an advocate for women," she recalls. "I helped them organize the first women's groups, for instance." She notes that the school "is always so full of incredibly successful, ambitious men that for women to make it is still much harder."[26] Female students remember her as one of the very few women mentors they had during their medical training. Author Janet Bickel counts herself as "among the thousands who are grateful for the mentoring of Dr. Carola Eisenberg." She notes that in the 1970s, "women residents as well as students discovered in Carola a much needed beacon of sanity and support as, despite dramatic increases in the numbers of women trainees, the 'gender climate' remained decidedly chilly."[27] Eisenberg, a psychiatrist by profession, invited female medical students and residents to her home, where they would share horror stories of poor treatment by male faculty. This support, albeit limited, emboldened female medical students and residents to challenge some of the more traditional aspects of medical education.

How to Teach the Pelvic

With new competitors at the bedside and retrenchment in the OB-GYN field, some medical educators were receptive to new strategies for teaching the pelvic exam. Up to this point, most medical students learned how to perform the procedure on hospital patients (both conscious and unconscious), if at all. Starting in the late 1960s, gynecologists proposed alternative methods, including live models and plastic dolls. In 1971, Ortho advertised the use of the Gynny Pelvic Teaching Model in *The New Physician*, a journal published by the Student American Medical Association. "Help your medical students get a head start on pelvic examinations right in the classroom," the advertisement read. "With this learning experience, students will examine their first patients with increased confidence."[28] On the adjoining page, five medical students—all white, all male, and the two closest to the camera wearing wedding rings—digitally manipulated Gynny dolls that were lying supine on a lab table. The photograph is striking in its laboratory-like display of disembodied female pelvic parts penetrated by the hands of young married men in white lab coats (presumably unavailable and clinically detached). The assembly-line arrangement of the dolls suggests the complete dissociation of patient from doctor, while the male hands (rings and all) placed directly between each doll's truncated legs suggest that perhaps Gynny was the "medical correlate to inflatable sex dolls."[29]

The downside to plastic models was their lifelessness. While the mannequins may have relieved student anxiety, they could not provide feedback. Educators in other branches of medicine had begun experimenting with the use of live models in 1963, referring to them as programmed, simulated, or professional patients because of their ability to mimic the characteristics of a real patient. Teaching third-year neurology students at the University of Southern California, Dr. Howard S. Barrows introduced the programmed patient as a "technique for appraising student performance."[30] Borrowing a young female art model with acting ability from USC's art department, Barrows trained her to take on the role of Patty Dugger, a fictionalized patient who had multiple sclerosis. He found this method to be a "most effective evaluative tool."[31] Others, however, resisted the idea, believing that it would debase the doctor-patient relationship. A reporter for the *San Francisco Chronicle* hinted at

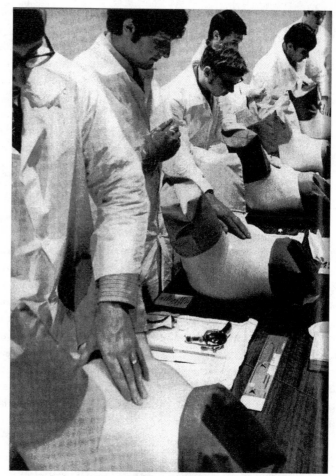

FIGURE 5 "Help your medical students get a head start on pelvic examinations right in the classroom. The GYNNY Pelvic Teaching Model lets your students learn the fundamentals of 15 gynecologic procedures under your supervision. With this learning experience, students will examine their first patients with increased confidence." Advertisement from Department of Educational Services, Ortho Pharmaceutical Corporation, published in *The New Physician*, November 1971, p. 700.

the sexual overtones of such an idea, writing that "scantily clad models are making life a little more interesting for the USC medical students."[32] In this particular scenario, Barrows's programmed patient posed not for a pelvic, but for the nonsexualized neurological exam—and yet she was sexualized nonetheless.

Despite this resistance, some gynecologists believed that Barrows's technique could be beneficial for their profession as well. Many medical students had trained on poor patients in city hospitals. Not only would a live model save hospital patients from (in one physician's words) "repetitive, inept examinations by inexperienced students who may have never before performed a pelvic exam," but she would also reduce student anxiety and result in a "more controlled educational experience with improved cost effectiveness through a reduction in physician faculty time."[33]

In 1968, Dr. Robert Kretzschmar developed an experimental program for teaching the pelvic in the Department of Obstetrics and Gynecology at the University of Iowa, based on Barrows's new technique. "We saw this as a potential tool for correcting the inadequacies of traditional medical education by freeing the real patient from the time and embarrassment involved in pelvic examinations by a beginning student," he wrote, "and by structuring the educational setting with a voluntary, cooperative, 'professional patient' to examine in a less threatening situation."[34] Kretzschmar's motivation for his controversial new program stemmed from his ten-year study of nationwide OB-GYN pelvic training methods, which yielded disappointing results. Though plastic models had helped some students learn the basics, that training technique could not adequately prepare them for their first encounter with a live patient. Most students, he found, performed their first exam on a real patient, under the guidance of a faculty member. This "triangular setting" of patient, instructor, and student was unsatisfactory. Instructor and student could not communicate effectively in front of the patient while she was "exploited." There was very little feedback, and "little or no emphasis was placed on the interpersonal skills necessary to do a quality pelvic examination." While problems with learning and communication existed in many clinical areas of medicine, Kretzschmar believed that "gynecology presents perhaps the most challenging doctor-patient encounter because of the sensitivity of the subject, the sexual overtones, and the anxiety to be coped with by both student and patient."[35]

Initially, Kretzschmar employed a nurse clinician as a simulated patient, with no training or experience in that regard. A physician instructor would give a pelvic examination on the nurse, and the students would repeat the exam. The nurse then evaluated the differences between doctor and students, but remained hidden behind a drape to provide anonymity. Therefore, her feedback to the students was necessarily limited. In 1972, Kretzschmar revised the program to "enhance communication between student and patient" by hiring two "professional patients," or gynecology teaching associates.[36]

Susan Guenther, one of the two GTAs, explained how she had helped to transform the program. "Although we were hired as evaluators, we began to develop the teaching program almost immediately. While learning to perform a pelvic examination, I suddenly realized how unpleasant an experience this simple procedure is for most women—and that there is no excuse for it." She became aware that the problem was not just poor skills on the part of students, but the method itself. "Armed with a newly found feminist consciousness and graduate studies in education, Stephanie and I designed the gynecology teaching associate (GTA) instructional program and persuaded Kretzschmar that trained nonphysician women could teach gynecological examination skills more effectively than physicians."[37] The idea, though still controversial, gained popularity, so that by the end of the 1970s, at least half of all medical schools utilized pelvic models.[38] Indeed, medical studies conducted in the 1970s and more recently suggested that such programs improved medical students' pelvic examination skills and attitudes.[39]

But turning to a live model raised concern. Dr. Kretzschmar remarked that the most frequently asked question by doctors was, what kind of woman would participate in such a program? Some speculated that such women would be motivated by questionable needs, such as financial or sexual—specifically, that the models would be exhibitionists, using the pelvic exam to "serve some perverse internal sexual gratification."[40] Given that USC's art-turned-neurologic model raised eyebrows, it is not surprising that pelvic models generated apprehension. This concern was probably exacerbated by the fact that initially, some programs employed prostitutes as pelvic models, including those at the University of Oklahoma and the University of Washington.[41] At the University of Oklahoma, prostitutes posed as university hospital outpatients beginning in 1973. During the exam, they provided feedback to students. "Frequent comments included: 'poor introduction,' 'too serious,' 'too rough,' and 'forgot to warm the speculum.' According to the associate director of the program, the prostitutes served well as 'university hospital outpatients' and seemed sincere in their interactions with the students." But at twenty-five dollars per hour, they were expensive and "not articulate enough to provide the quality of instructive feedback necessary for an optimal educational experience." And they were diseased: both of those used in the program had cervical erosion with class 2 Pap smears, and one tested positive for gonorrhea.[42] The use of so-called inarticulate, diseased prostitutes to train students in routine gynecological care raised questions about the nature of the procedure itself. The medical school paid these women for their services, using them, as a more traditional client would, for their sexual organs. Such an association would certainly challenge the program's attempts to separate the pelvic procedure from a sexual act.

Kretzschmar and his colleagues presented a very different type of woman as a pelvic model, reassuring medical educators that there was nothing suspect about the training. Dr. James Blythe was a fellow at Iowa who was asked to participate in the program in its early years. "My first question, as I suspect yours may be, was, 'What kind of woman lets four or five novice medical students examine her?' And the answer was that the women did a very good job, they were selected very carefully by Dr. Kretzschmar, and they did participate actively in the students' learning."[43] Kretzschmar stressed that all GTAs at Iowa were working toward or had received advanced degrees in the behavioral sciences, received six to eight weeks of training, and were paid at the rate of teaching assistants at the university. They agreed to work as GTAs because they were "dedicated to education" and preferred to "work within the existing system" rather than at a feminist health clinic. "They try to teach and reinforce good doctor behaviors early in medical education, seeking through their efforts not only to instruct medical students but also to effect better health care for women," he pointed out.[44] GTAs were selected for their teaching and communication skills, because they, not the physicians, would eventually be instructing medical students in the pelvic examination.

It was an added benefit that these instructors would be female; as Kretzschmar explained, a GTA is "able to add her sensitivity as a woman."[45] One physician noted that Kretzschmar had "dramatically altered the methods of instruction" by training these "devoted women who are a unique type of educator."[46] Another noted that he found it "a humbling experience to recognize that four young women were better teachers than I."[47] In these descriptions, the pelvic model is neither oversexed nor political, but someone for whom sensitivity, teaching, and communication come naturally. Here, a pelvic model is simply a natural extension of traditional feminine values rather than an assault on those values.

The Pelvic Teaching Program

The evolution of the Pelvic Teaching Program at Harvard Medical School, however, reveals a more complex relationship between physicians, models, and students. The women who participated in the program resisted stereotyping, and from the start expressed ambivalence about participating within the medical system rather than challenging it. As a result, the Harvard experiment failed, revealing the tensions between physicians and feminists about sexual vulnerability, the exploitation of women, and medical education. This conflict heightened the already extant tension over how to teach the pelvic.

In 1975, a group of female medical students at Harvard, disappointed by the school's gynecological training, approached the Women's Community Health Center about creating a pelvic examination teaching program for Harvard students.[48] Frustrated with the current teaching methods (including the use of anesthetized patients, prostitutes, and plastic Gynny dolls), they believed that the "time was ripe for women to assume a more active role" in pelvic instruction.[49] The WCHC agreed to provide pelvic models and created a formal organization called the Pelvic Teaching Program, or PTP. From 1975 to 1976, members of the PTP were contracted by Harvard to teach second-year medical students how to perform a pelvic exam. Over this time period, the PTP developed three very different protocols based on teaching experiences.

When medical students approached the WCHC in search of pelvic models, they got a mixed reaction. On one hand, it could be a way to reach out to sympathetic female medical students and to change the way the medical establishment approached women's bodies. On the other hand, it could be counterproductive; it might actually "strengthen the medical system by teaching physicians how to 'manage' their 'patients' (by changing their behaviors without changing their power in doctor/patient encounters)."[50] This ambivalence, even among those involved, influenced the evolution of the program and its ultimate demise by the third protocol.

In the first protocol, participants received twenty-five dollars per session as pelvic models. In each session, four to five students performed a bimanual pelvic exam on the model while instructed by a Harvard physician. Response to the first protocol was positive: physician instructors and students were pleased, believing that it "facilitated more efficient, comfortable teaching sessions."[51] The pelvic models, however, were not happy, because they found they had very little control over the teaching session. They wrote, "The students were pleased with the experience of having 'talking pelvises' to guide them, the physicians were pleased because the program enhanced their status within the medical community, but we were severely displeased." They felt exploited. Although they were paid, they believed that twenty-five dollars per session was "a condescending, patronizing sort of recognition. The unspoken agreement was that our bodies were valuable, but our information and skills were not."[52]

But it was an eye-opening, radicalizing experience. The pelvic models had hoped to bring feminist-self-help ideas into the clinic as part of the service they were providing. Stripped of their ideas along with their clothing, however, they realized that their conceptual framework of well-woman-oriented gynecological health from the WCHC was not welcomed. "We did not agree with their approach to health care," they wrote. "When we realized this, we began to discuss and implement ways to gain complete control over the program. We did not discard the pelvic model idea out-of-hand, but we unanimously decided to alter the program substantially."[53]

As a result, the WCHC instituted both internal and external changes to the program for the second protocol. It created an ongoing self-help group, consisting of five original WCHC members and six affiliated women for a total of eleven pelvic instructors. In a legally binding contract between the group and the medical schools, the WCHC stipulated that at least two pelvic instructors would be present per session, and that physicians, if present at all, were limited to the role of "silent observers." The pelvic instructors became the instructors of the session, rejecting the previous term *pelvic model*, "since it implied that we were passive recipients of the pelvic exam."[54] As with Kretzschmar's Iowa program, serving as both patient and instructor collapsed what had previously been an enormous boundary. A gynecology teaching associate at Dartmouth Medical School drew attention to this power dynamic a few years later, writing that "the usual doctor-patient relationship is reversed while the respective physical positioning is not."[55] Taking a more active role in the process challenged the most basic assumptions about hierarchy, status, professionalization, and power.[56]

Reflecting this new role, the pelvic instructors raised their rates from $25 to $50 per instructor per session, and required that at least one of the five students per session had to be female. Schools had to reproduce and distribute to medical students the WCHC's copyrighted manual, *How to Do a Pelvic Examination*, in which it presented "a healthy way to perform a well-woman gynecological examination with non-sexist, nonheterosexist, nonelitist assumptions."[57]

This "how-to" guide stressed the importance of cultivating a relaxed, trusting relationship with the patient, explaining that a doctor's attitude could make a "profound difference" on the experience. Physicians should monitor their mannerisms, language, and behavior from entrance to exit, including introducing themselves before beginning the exam and calling the patient by her last name. There should always be a female chaperone in the room to provide support. The patient should not have to put her feet in stirrups. She should be encouraged to try the speculum herself (which should be warmed), and offered a mirror so that she could see her cervix. "We encourage every doctor to have a mirror on hand—it is a really exciting experience to see one's cervix and vagina, especially for the first time."[58] In the right hands, the speculum had the power to reunite a woman with her reproductive organs in a way that feminists found empowering in a number of settings.[59]

Many of those involved in the second protocol were enthusiastic about the changes to the PTP. An associate professor of surgery at Harvard wrote the WCHC in January of 1977 to ask them to consider providing the PTP again, as "both the students and I thought that these sessions were extremely effective."[60] The assistant director of medical education at Mt. Auburn Hospital also requested the continuing involvement of the PTP in the Introduction to Clinical Medicine course, explaining, "We were most appreciative of your contribution to this course last year with regards to teaching of the pelvic examination. We would be most interested in your helping us again this coming year and would certainly be willing to sign a contract similar to last year's and pay the appropriate fee."[61]

An even stronger show of support came in the form of an article. Two male doctors who taught at Harvard Medical School published a summary of the Pelvic Teaching Program in the *Journal of Medical Education*, touting its success and offering it as a model for other medical schools to use. In particular, they stressed its potential to improve the decidedly one-sided relationship between the female patient and her physician, as feminists had shown that "women are relatively uninformed and passive in their gynecological care."[62]

The authors described pelvic teaching sessions scheduled during a three-and-a-half-month introductory clinical medicine course given at Massachusetts General Hospital in 1976. The course, also offered at other Harvard teaching hospitals, was required of all medical students, and was usually taken at the end of their second year. The pelvic teaching sessions were two hours long and considered optional, but only seven of the fifty-one students did not attend. Each session had two pelvic instructors and five students, as stipulated in the second protocol. Sometime before the session, students were given the "how-to" manual to review before the first class. At the beginning of the session, the instructors introduced themselves and explained the goals and methods of teaching, then both described and demonstrated the actual exam (totaling about thirty minutes). Each student then performed the exam on one of the instructor-models while being supervised by the other; the remaining students observed the procedure. Training included practicing introducing oneself to the patient, soliciting questions, and describing procedures, as well as performing them.

The authors of this journal review measured student and physician-observer reactions by anonymous evaluations (completed by about three-fourths of all participants), noting that "the use of nonphysician instructors was not challenged by the students, and physician-observers concurred that the teaching was excellent." One student remarked, "I enjoyed the establishment of the doctor/patient relationship as a two-way street. . . . I think it is always beneficial to get some feedback from a patient about any aspect of the physical exam." Another student found the instant feedback reassuring in a procedure in which "I would otherwise have been anxious about hurting the woman."[63] One physician, whose role had been reduced to that of observer, noted that what was most refreshing and remarkable "was the concept of the physical examination as an information-sharing procedure—this was new to my clinical experience and appears quite useful, not only for encouraging relaxation but also as a method for promoting the patient's participation in her health care."[64]

But there were still problems. Many students demonstrated their uneasiness by making flippant or joking remarks about sex. This type of reaction was documented elsewhere as well. A gynecology teaching associate at Dartmouth noted that students sometimes appeared "emotionally overwhelmed by receiving guidance from a woman with her legs spread."[65] This was the same problem previously noted by Mary Howell, Harvard's first female dean, in *Why Would a Girl Go into Medicine?* She described the "men's club" atmosphere apparent in the "laugh-getting comments and pictures about female sexuality" that female students described being subjected to. This environment reinforced the assumption that "any man has the right to regard any woman—colleague or patient—as an object of sexual interest."[66] She saw this behavior as a response to discomfort with sexuality, but believed there needed to be "more constructive ways to deal with and overcome these discomforts." Medical schools should provide students with settings to discuss their feelings honestly, Howell continued. "It is probably no accident that instructors from OB-GYN departments are often noted to be among the worst offenders in discrimination. It may be that they are only demonstrating the end result of a medical education that offered little outlet for the resolution of these anxieties."[67] *Vaginal Politics* author Ellen Frankfort also noted the dangers of pent-up feelings for students. "Medical students have sexual feelings which respond to touching, seeing and probing naked bodies with titillation and guilt. This is to some degree natural and inevitable. What is not is the denial of these feelings. But never in medical school is sexuality acknowledged except in the form of coarse jokes, often about nurses."[68]

Though acknowledgment of sexual discomfort was avoided in medical education, it was of profound interest in psychiatry in the 1970s. Over a ten-year period, Dr. Julius Buchwald, clinical assistant professor of psychiatry at the Downstate Medical Center, New York State University, measured the emotional reactions of approximately seven hundred medical students performing their first pelvic examination. He found that fear of being judged inept and fear of sexual arousal (by either the student or the patient) were among the most common anxieties shared by students about performing their first pelvic.[69] Though he initially perceived fear of being judged inept as simply a reaction to lack of experience, "what began to evolve was the image of the experienced, wise, worldly, and sexually competent adult (the resident or attending physician) sneering at the floundering explorations of an adolescent (the medical student) who is striving to become a 'man.'" Buchwald interpreted the first pelvic exam as "a kind of initiation rite with clear sexual undercurrents."[70] This gendered interpretation (the reading of a pelvic as a *male* rite of passage), despite the growing number of female medical students, demonstrates how the powerful link between medicine and masculinity continued through the decade.[71]

For some, sexual discomfort seemed to be exacerbated by the assertive position that feminist instructors took in teaching the pelvic. That the Harvard pelvic instructors originated in a feminist health clinic (rather than in a graduate program, as at Iowa) made the PTP more susceptible to criticism. Some students resented the feminist approach that they characterized as "strident." A few of the female students were uncomfortable with the level of immodesty, one noting, "It seems that all of this is a bit idealized and could be misleading when one considers that many women expect or are 'conditioned' to a more formal and traditional approach."[72] These reactions suggest that the pelvic program at Harvard, much more so than at Iowa, challenged traditional assumptions about women's role in the stirrups. It was not just their presence as instructors that unnerved some students; it was their political intent of "seizing control of our bodies," which included, of course, their sexuality.[73]

Discomfort over the type of woman used as a gynecology teaching associate, or GTA, was not limited to students. In a letter to the editor of the *Journal of Medical Education*, four physicians chided the authors of the Harvard study for failing to credit Dr. Kretzschmar and the Iowa program with initiating the use of trained public models. They felt that the methodology employed in the Harvard program, by contrast, left "much to be desired."[74] The Harvard authors, they charged, "seem to have abrogated their obligation to administer instructional programs by relinquishing this responsibility to the Women's Community Health Center, Inc." They were not surprised at the negative reaction expressed by some of the students. "It is little wonder that some 'informal discussions after the session indicated occasional resentment by the male students of "women's lib" stridency on the part of the instructors.'" Once again, the concern is not over the use of pelvic models per se, but the type of woman used. "As Kretzschmar has emphasized and as others of us have found, the success or failure of this program depends entirely upon the choice of instructors. . . . Their attitudes should represent the attitudes of a wide segment of the female population." Thus, concern over what kind of woman served as a GTA included fear of not just an oversexed prostitute, but a women's health activist. The four physician authors felt that it was the responsibility of the university "to avoid subjecting students to personal crusades." The Harvard program was doomed to failure because of "inappropriate patient model choices," they concluded.[75]

Forming a somewhat uneasy alliance, members of the Pelvic Teaching Program agreed with these physicians that the approach was unacceptable—but for very different reasons, of course. They circulated a position paper to feminist publications in which they evaluated their experiences and set up a third protocol—one that signaled the demise of the PTP.

What was wrong with the present agreement? One of the top medical schools in the country had agreed to relinquish authority in the clinic to feminist laywomen in a move that had the potential to transform routine gynecological care. But the WCHC's experiences with this program caused its members to question its revolutionary potential. They believed that the program, as it stood, reinforced the existing hierarchical system. It was, in their words, "doomed to creeping liberalism, contributing to the support of a health care system that needs *radical* change." They discontinued the second protocol and "*strongly* discourage[d] other groups of women from participating in similar programs."[76]

For those in the PTP, contributing to traditional medical education could undermine their primary objective of promoting self-help. As PTP member Susan Bell explained, self-help meant "empowering women through sharing knowledge and skills, demystifying and demedicalizing health care by reclaiming areas of health which have been defined as medical problems, looking at the politics of the medical system as a whole, and challenging this system."[77] If women were not feeling empowered, if the process was still hierarchical in nature, then the group was not achieving what it had set out to do.

The only possible solution, the PTP members believed, was a radically different approach to pelvic training based on "reciprocal sharing," which they explained in a third and final protocol. Participants would learn to both examine and be examined—which meant that the new program would be limited to women. "Men cannot share in pelvic exams or directly in women's health experiences," they argued. According to one member, there was another reason to exclude men: many of the GTAs felt exploited or embarrassed by the male students in teaching sessions. This way, they could focus on women and feel more comfortable.[78]

The third protocol also changed the structure of the proposed group of students to challenge the hierarchy of learning; "medical students should learn from the outset to share information with those who receive their services." If medical students learned their skills alongside future patients and other health-care workers, they would have to confront elitist attitudes about knowledge. Finally, the new program would be extended from one to four sessions and the fee raised to $750. The revised PTP was the only approach, its members argued, "which will not oppress women but will instead assert the principles and practices of the Women's Self-Help Movement."[79]

Not surprisingly, all teaching hospitals affiliated with Harvard Medical School rejected the third protocol. As one medical director explained, "I understand your desire to teach in a self-help fashion, but cannot help but believe that male students need this help as much or more than their female counterparts. . . . Your exclusion of male students in an otherwise worthwhile venture, I believe, simply reverses past inequality and diminishes the chances of helping male physicians to become aware of women's health needs from the woman's viewpoint."[80]

Up until the third protocol, the structure of the Pelvic Teaching Program at Harvard resembled simulated patient programs at other medical schools, such as Iowa. Surprisingly, the PTP was unaware of these other programs, having only investigated how Harvard had been teaching the pelvic exam. As PTP member Susan Bell argued, "what seemed to the feminists, at times, as risky and dangerous at Harvard, had already become institutionalized in other medical schools." Though their politics were already apparent to most, they became hard to ignore by the third protocol. Bell believed that "it was with the third protocol that the women were not only devising a better program, but were also explicitly challenging commonly held assumptions about medical care and explicitly stating some of their own political goals."[81]

As the PTP evolved, the distance between medical educators, at least some medical students, and the pelvic group widened. This is not surprising, particularly given the demands of the self-helpers in the program, which by the third protocol had become virtually impossible for Harvard to accept. A woman who identified herself only as gynecology resident "Elizabeth B." complained that the third protocol "was set up in such a way that they knew it would be rejected and they'd be removed from that part of the struggle." She was responding to an article that Susan Bell (program member turned sociologist) published about the PTP in *Science for the People* in 1979. "It's like going into a factory with a full blown program for socialism and demanding that the union bureaucracy and the rank and file subscribe to it completely or you'll not work with them," the resident declared. "It's sectarian."[82] Bell retorted, "In point of fact, the third protocol was aimed at directly challenging the elitism and the power of physicians as *providers* of care, as *definers* of the role of medicine in society, and in *relationship to* the majority of employees in the medical system by teaching medical students rudimentary skills in a politically responsible way."[83] The resident, she pointed out, had ignored the presence of a clear-cut hierarchy between female patients, medical students, and the medical profession, and thus had missed the point. What the self-helpers hoped to do with the third protocol, Bell explained, was "to initiate a dialogue with representatives of the medical education establishment . . . and to create an arena of discourse in which to debate them during teaching sessions."[84]

But by the end, the experience yielded something of a surprise for the WCHC feminists as well. They had become involved in the PTP because they believed it would make Harvard's pelvic training less exploitative of women. They believed that the program would ultimately empower women by increasing medical students' awareness of the pelvic's exploitative potential. What they did not predict was how that exploitative potential would affect them personally.

Personal reactions to the program were recorded in an interaction between female medical students and a PTP instructor, who took notes on the meeting. As things were beginning to unravel between Harvard and the PTP in March of 1977, two students met with the instructor to attempt a resolution. But what they revealed suggested that a resolution would never come. She learned from the students that "the docs were thirsting for some reason to criticize us and cut us down. The new proposal was the excuse they were looking for. Apparently they are extraordinarily resentful and scornful and this feeling is being passed onto many of the students." The students then asked for her side of the story. She recalled, "After I explained our position (I included some personal anger and feelings of exploitation and rape), they were very sympathetic." They pleaded with her to reconsider, believing that the group "should somehow step between the powerless anesthetized women who are currently receiving pelvic exams and the medical students." But it was too late to turn back, and the conversation with the students made her realize that the group had not gone far enough in articulating its position. Though it had written a "position paper" (published in the journal *Women and Health* and the newspaper *Sister Courage*, with a similar statement in the newsletter *HealthRight*), this member felt that the group's published statement "does not adequately address the issues of sexism, exploitation and rape," which she felt was evident at the time. "When looking at our own individual by-session evaluations and the student evaluations, I realized that a large portion raised these issues." Overall, she concluded, "when I look back at the program I most strongly remember a sense of being used."[85]

What had gone wrong? The instructors had reached across the aisle to facilitate a shift in the medical treatment of women's bodies, creating a new model of female reproductive anatomy that was accessible to all women. The pelvic examination was no longer a secret affair or a sexual rite of passage for male medical students, but a procedure that required sensitivity and dexterity. Somehow, though, in the process, the PTP members began to realize the complexity of this shift. Far from feeling empowered as pelvic instructors, they felt used.

Others articulated similar concerns. Performer, scholar, and health educator Terri Kapsalis worked as a GTA in Chicago-area medical schools in the late 1980s. She notes the "pink-collar" nature of the position, comparing it to the role of an airline stewardess. "Like the stewardess," she writes, "the GTA is costumed with a smile, a well-defined script, and a uniform."[86] In 1991, she became a health worker for the Chicago Women's Health Center (the only feminist health clinic still in operation in the United States), where she had been fitted for a cervical cap. She never worked as a GTA again.[87]

A GTA at the University of Toronto revealed in an interview that "some friends actually felt like I was prostituting myself. When I first started the program, I didn't feel like that at all, but by the end, that *was* how I felt . . . like I was working on the street." Her colleague added, "We started realizing how this program was tied up with sexuality. We both started feeling like we were in the same position as prostitutes, and then we started saying, 'Yeah, we are. We are. We're doing exactly the same thing. We're being paid. It's just a little more legitimate because it's down on paper somewhere; we're getting a cheque from the University of Toronto." Like the members of the PTP, they felt that the program "valued our bodies, but never our skills or knowledge."[88]

Ultimately, the GTAs' offering their bodies to medical students served to both challenge and reinforce traditional assumptions about medicine, sexuality, and the female body. On one hand, by unveiling their bodies and demanding that students, physicians, and patients talk about sexual discomfort in the examining room, feminists raised awareness about inappropriate sexual behavior. Physicians and medical students could no longer view the pelvic patient as passive, ignorant, or compliant. On the other hand, in their efforts to assert control over the procedure, the GTAs (perhaps unwittingly) sexualized it. The very act of voluntary exposure suggested the presence of desire. As feminists and scholars have noted, "The feminist quest to enhance knowledge about women's bodies and their sexual experiences had as its goal the enhancement of women's pleasures."[89] Feminists decried the "myth of the vaginal orgasm," emphasizing the importance of sexual self-determination and the legitimation of their own sexual desires.[90] Within this context of sexual assertion, how to desexualize the pelvic exam became, ironically, a challenge. For those who feared whether there was "sex after liberation," these words and actions assured them that yes, female sexuality was alive and well.[91] But it was certainly different. The days of the gynecologist as sex counselor, guiding a compliant vagina into healthy heterosexuality, were over. What stood in place of this old scenario was less clear. For pelvic models, sexual liberation also brought confusion; what seemed like good, assertive feminist behavior could ultimately end up feeling like prostitution.

More recently, pelvic exposure has become an established part of public culture through the work of Annie Sprinkle and Eve Ensler. Exprostitute/porn star/sexologist/multimedia artist/"utopian entrepreneur" Annie Sprinkle began performing her Public Cervix Announcement in 1991, where she invited the audience to view her cervix with the aid of a speculum and a flashlight. Why? "Many of you have never seen a cervix before," she explained. Her male assistant offered the flashlight to each viewer, while Sprinkle held a microphone to project each viewer's reaction. After an intermission, she ended the show with a "sex magic masturbation ritual."[92] Is the Public Cervix Announcement pornography, or is it consciousness-raising? Does her viewing demystify the cervix, or does it merely sexualize and objectify women's bodies at an even deeper level? The tension between these two possibilities remains unresolved.

In 1996, Eve Ensler published *The Vagina Monologues*, a series of short stories about women's experiences with their vaginas. Based on her interviews of two hundred women, it is already considered a "feminist classic" that is regularly performed on college campuses. But some scholars who were active in the women's health movement back in the 1970s are concerned about the "unproblematized tension between a celebration of the pleasures of the body and the politics that underlie the play and the movement it has spawned." Sociologist and former PTP member Susan Bell and historian Susan Reverby see the connections between the seeming empowerment of the first vaginal self-exam and that of discovering the *Vagina Monologues*.[93] But in both cases, there remains a disconnect between an individual sense of liberation through exposure and the public interpretation of the meaning of exposure. As a result, the pelvic examination remains a contested site.

Even today, discomfort and confusion over how to distinguish between emotions, sexual attitudes, and clinical objectivity flood the classroom as well as the examining room. "For patients, genital examination carries with it powerful personal and cultural expectations, often negative in nature," declare the authors of a study on pelvic examinations published in *Academic Medicine* in 2003. "For physicians, similar forces are at play during and after medical training, and physicians may never acquire the skills necessary to perform a sensitive and thorough examination."[94]

Concern about sensitivity was heightened by a study also published in 2003 in the *American Journal of Obstetrics and Gynecology*, which revealed that 90 percent of medical students surveyed practiced gynecological exams on anesthetized patients, often without their consent.[95] While some defended the practice as essential and argued that consent was implied, others reacted with horror. A professor at the Cleveland-Marshall College of Law views this practice as a form of offensive contact—more specifically, sexual battery. "Defining the offense as a sexual one is understandably distressing to physicians, who have gone to great lengths to define pelvic (and mammary) exams in nonsexual ways," she writes. "But medical practice cannot abstract itself from the culture in which it operates."[96] Despite decades of dialogue, the question of how pelvic exam training is best conducted remains unresolved.

Perhaps this tension is best illustrated by the production of a documentary film, *At Your Cervix*, written, directed, and produced by several GTAs from New York City. The purpose of the not-yet-completed documentary is to "break the silence around the unethical ways in which medical and nursing students learn to perform pelvic exams," the producers explain. They claim that most of the 90 million women in the United States receiving the exams think they are supposed to hurt. The film follows the work of GTAs training future physicians and nurses on the "nuances" of a comfortable pelvic exam. In the pilot, the camera appears to be inside a vagina, on the end of a speculum, tracking the faces peering into the opening in search of her cervix, as if the viewer of the film is the subject of the gaze, the cervix itself. This forces the viewer to consider the subjectivity of the pelvic exam, as well as the limited exposure of the cervix. The producers describe *At Your Cervix* as a "mandate to change the expectations that surround the pelvic exam so that it becomes an empowering experience for women."[97]

Like the members of the PTP thirty years prior, these GTAs-turned-filmmakers hope to raise awareness and expectations about gynecological self-help. They believe that their film tells a story that "will dramatically affect the quality of these oft-dreaded exams, a story that will transform breast and pelvic exams into opportunities women actually welcome to discover more about their bodies, and about their sexual and reproductive selves."[98] Whether the speculum still holds the potential to raise consciousness as it did in the 1970s remains to be seen.

: : :

For those at both ends of the table, those receiving and those giving a pelvic exam, a number of factors contributed to how the experience has been interpreted. Beginning in the 1970s, many of these factors, particularly issues of sexuality and gender, were laid out for the first time. As a result of the women's health movement, an increasing number of female medical students, and changes in medical education, the experience for many women has changed. Despite the ultimate failure of the Pelvic Teaching Program at Harvard University's teaching hospitals, the Women's Community Health Center drew attention to what had previously been a muted subject. The center's demands forced both patients and practitioners to question the nature of the pelvic exam and how it was taught. They also made the Kretzschmar GTA model appear, in comparison, to be a more acceptable solution for many medical schools, 90 percent of which now use this model.

Though the pelvic examination controversy represents only one pedagogical issue of medical education, its appearance alongside the emergence of feminist women's health clinics and the growth of a female medical student body underscores its significance. More was at stake than a question of procedure; the debate encompassed wider issues of caring and compassion within medical education. Could a male doctor (or medical student, or nurse) adequately empathize with a female patient while performing a pelvic? Were women, by their very nature, more apt to relate to the vulnerabilities of a patient? Would they therefore make better doctors, and transform the health-care industry? Or would they succumb to feminine weaknesses that would limit their ability to make decisions?

Dr. Eisenberg, Dean of Student Affairs first at MIT and then at Harvard, reflected on these questions in an address at Johns Hopkins Medical School in 1978. Her comments underscore the ideological tensions of emphasizing female biological difference. "The 'difference' argument—whether it is offered as a rationalization for the status quo or as a justification for change—is a two-edged sword," she argued. "It begins with an observed or assumed difference which is then used to justify closing, or as a warrant for opening, doors." But it is not an effective measure of how an individual will perform.[99] Nonetheless, she did believe that women had much to contribute to the practice of medicine and praised women's tendency to show emotion, arguing that it could be done "without compromising professional identity" or strength.[100] In fact, she had done this herself, by responding to the president of MIT's request to help him "humanize this place" by becoming a dean.[101]

While Eisenberg sought to humanize medical education from within, others, such as the PTP members at the Women's Community Health Center, came to believe by the mid-1970s that working within organized medicine would undermine their political and pedagogical goals of self-help. They were not alone. A group of health feminists in Chicago discovered in their work both underground and on the ground that alliances with organized medicine could unravel their own personal and political ties.

3

Learning from the Uterus Out:
Abortion and Women's Health Activism in Chicago

Like many major cities, Chicago found itself under siege in 1968. As the site of the most violent and contentious presidential convention in U.S. history, it remains embedded in historical memory as a symbol of the chaos, despair, and political conflict in the sixties. Largely absent from this historical memory is the role of the student health workers and community health activists in that city who attempted to heal the wounds of the sick and injured. They cared for those protesting in Chicago's streets as well as the uninsured of its working-class neighborhoods, creating free community clinics where the poor could receive basic health care.[1] Also largely absent is the work of health feminists, who drew on the community clinic and student health models to revolutionize gynecological care and reproductive rights. What makes their stories different from—and just as vital as—those of the Boston Women's Health Collective or the Pelvic Teaching Program is their focus on place. Theirs was a purpose not solely ideological or pedagogical, but also practical. They wanted to create new spaces outside organized medicine in which women could learn about and heal their bodies. Women needed information, care, and the ability to control reproductive decisions. They needed a place to go to receive this information and care. Women's health activists in Chicago sought to make that happen. What they found, however, was that theoretical and political struggles over abortion plagued their practice. Within a decade, fatigue would replace idealism, and many of these new places would disappear.

Feminism and the Chicago Women's Liberation Union

It is difficult to associate protest in 1968 Chicago with anything *but* the Democratic National Convention. Yet a few months after that event, at a YWCA retreat center outside Chicago in Lake Villa, nearly two hundred radical women from thirty cities convened a very different sort of protest, one that symbolized the role that feminism was to play in American activism over the next two decades. The organizers envisioned the meeting as a commemoration of the 120th anniversary of Seneca Falls, the 1848 convention that officially launched the American women's rights movement.

While Seneca Falls yielded a unified Declaration of Sentiments regarding women's rights, the 1968 Women's Liberation conference produced division. It was to be the only national conference of radical women in the United States, one that had the potential to generate a national network, but instead sparked contention.[2] This conflict was exacerbated by the food running out well before the conference was over, since twice as many women showed up as had been expected. Nonetheless, it was a historic and significant gathering of women, including some whose diverse philosophies would become well known in radical feminist circles: Ti-Grace Atkinson and Shulamith Firestone, who proposed "extrauterine gestation" in test tubes as a strategy for liberation;[3] Dana Densmore, who proposed celibacy; and Ann Koedt, who presented the "myth of the vaginal orgasm." Nancy Hawley, future member of the Boston Women's Health Book Collective, came from Boston with two friends who were members of the radical organization Students for a Democratic Society. Pregnant and with a child at home, Hawley undoubtedly cringed at some of the sentiments of her radical "sisters" who decried motherhood and pregnancy as oppressive. It was these varying attitudes toward sexuality, reproduction, politics, and strategies that mired the conference in factionalism.[4]

Yet not all attendees left the conference disillusioned. While Heather Booth, a member of SDS, remembered "lots of arguments" there, she also recalled that it yielded "political breakthroughs" and "wonderful warmth."[5] She came to Lake Villa with other politically active Chicagoans who were members of the "West Side group," one of the first, if not the first, women's liberation group in the nation.[6] Angered by their treatment in the New Left, they resolved to "turn the world upside down," and they brought this same revolutionary mentality to the conference.[7]

Less than a year later, these same women founded the Chicago Women's Liberation Union, the "first and most successful women's union in the country," according to historian Alice Echols.[8] The CWLU created a mass base for women's activism in Chicago by reaching out to already established women's groups and "providing a forum for additional groups to develop."[9] From 1969 to 1977, it organized women's liberation groups into "chapters" or "work groups," based on geographic location and function. At its peak in the early 1970s, it included some five hundred dues-paying members and about twenty work groups and chapters.[10] Work groups included a feminist graphics collective, the Chicago Women's Liberation Rock Band (probably the first of its kind), the Liberation School, and the Health Evaluation and Referral Service (which would outlive the CWLU). The rock band performed and even toured from 1970 to 1973, discovering along the way that not every woman was a born musician after a disastrous opening performance in Grant Park that included twelve singers and four guitarists. After paring down the group to seven performers, the group incorporated feminist lyrics to popular songs and mocked the gestures of male rock stars that were offensive to women. The Liberation School offered courses in anything from car repair to women's bodies, based on the material in *Our Bodies, Ourselves.*[11] While the work groups and projects varied widely, they shared a similar goal. As the CWLU explained in its newsletter, "Our primary purpose is to attack sexism. . . . Sexism exists everywhere in this society—for example, on the job, in family roles, and in the laws. We are fighting for changes in ourselves and other individuals, and in the institutions and policies that set up our lives in sexist patterns."[12]

Ending sexism, however, proved to be a challenging goal; gradually, the enthusiasm and creativity, along with the wide variety of work groups, began to crumble. A decentralized organizational structure along with internal conflict resulted in the CWLU's dissolution in 1977.[13] Even the Chicago Women's Liberation Rock Band folded, suggesting that positive lyrics and an all-woman atmosphere still could not transcend personal politics. But one cause did survive beyond the CWLU's demise: that of reproductive rights. This chapter analyzes the emergence and evolution of abortion as a feminist issue in Chicago in the 1970s and '80s. During this time, pregnancy termination changed from an illegal, underground procedure, to a symbol of female liberation, and finally to a divisive obstacle to coalition building. Chicago women's health activists transformed the realities of abortion in their city through a number of different venues: the Abortion Counseling Service (better known as Jane), the Emma Goldman Women's Health Center, the Abortion Task Force, and the Reproductive Rights National Network. In the process, however, they were confronted by growing dissatisfaction from both the Right and the Left as they attempted to place abortion in the wider context of reproductive rights. They also used abortion and its increasingly public role in media and politics to address broader issues of race, class, and women's health. Thus, abortion presented health feminists with both an opportunity and a challenge: drawing attention to women's health and reproductive concerns through the issue of abortion had the potential to either unify or splinter the movement. In the end, it did both. Competing agendas and conflicting visions about how best to secure and protect reproductive freedom in the midst of repeated attacks from the Right constrained activists' efforts. And for those activists and theorists opposed to grounding feminism in the female body, abortion's failure to unify the movement came as no surprise.

No single chapter can track the varieties of abortion activism during the period shortly before and after *Roe v. Wade*. States varied in their responses to and implementation of the 1973 Supreme Court decision that upheld a woman's right to an abortion during the first trimester of pregnancy. While feminists increasingly came together to protest restrictive abortion laws and later attempts to dismantle *Roe*, they were not the first to demand reform. In response to greater suppression of abortion practices during the 1950s, physicians and public health workers who had witnessed the injuries and deaths to women from illegal abortions sought legal changes. An increasingly repressive climate, then, triggered a widespread reaction from those who saw the repercussions to women's health. According to historian Leslie Reagan, abortion rights activism "arose out of the deteriorating conditions of abortion and the frustrations of both women and physicians." Though most states had outlawed abortion by the late nineteenth century, it was generally accepted as an "open secret" well into the twentieth. "The social movement to decriminalize abortion," Reagan continues, "drew upon and brought into the open a longstanding acceptance of abortion."[14]

Abortion reform activism changed in the hands of feminists, who began in the late 1960s to perceive abortion as not just a medical or public health issue, but a "collective problem for all women."[15] Abortion, according to the Jane member and biographer Laura Kaplan, was a touchstone. If women could not make decisions regarding their own bodies, then other gains were "meaningless."[16] Feminists introduced new tactics, including abortion speak-outs, in which women shared stories of illegal abortions and their anger over their lack of rights to control their bodies. The *Village Voice* reporter and future feminist Susan Brown-miller remembered her introduction to the women's movement in 1968, when she first encountered a women's group talking about abortions. "Saying 'I've had three illegal abortions' aloud was my feminist baptism, my swift immersion in the power of sisterhood. A medical procedure I'd been forced to secure alone, shrouded in silence, was not 'a personal problem' any more than the matter of my gender in the newsroom was 'a personal problem.' "[17]

But abortion was not an easy topic, especially for a group of white, urban activist women interested in building coalitions across race, class, religion, and politics. Whether one identified more with socialist femi-nism or radical feminism could be just as divisive as being white or black, rich or poor. Socialist feminists identified patriarchy with capitalism, arguing that women would always be oppressed in a capitalist society. Any solution to the problem of abortion, therefore, would have to be placed within the wider context of critiquing capitalism (for example, ensuring that health services were free and accessible to all women). Radical femi-nists identified more with emphasizing the universal experience of being female, focusing more on tearing down patriarchy than reforming it.[18]

Many socialist feminists emphasized how racism affected reproduc-tive rights. For example, in 1970 black women were twice as likely to have been sterilized than white women, sometimes having to choose between having their tubes tied and receiving a welfare check. For these women, access to reproductive health services had to be matched with protective regulations (such as waiting periods for sterilization) that would protect vulnerable women from abuse. These different priorities made compromise and coalition building across race and class boundaries all the more challenging.[19] In certain contexts, feminists found themselves on opposing sides of policy decisions. For example, historian Rebecca Kluchin describes the "direct and irreconcilable conflict" in the mid-1970s between different reproductive rights groups over proposed new sterilization guidelines designed to protect women from abuse. Specifi-cally, the National Organization for Women and the National Abortion Rights Action League objected to a mandatory waiting period and a min-imum age for sterilization, reflecting their "privileging of abortion rights over other reproductive rights issues and their concern that if the gov-ernment could prevent women from receiving sterilization on demand, it could use this precedent to prohibit women from accessing abortion on demand."[20]

In Chicago, political division—between those women who identified more with socialist feminism and those who saw themselves as radical feminists—affected the rise and fall of a number of women's health organizations and clinics.[21] Many sought a more inclusive reproductive rights agenda that incorporated protective regulations along with access to abortion. This multi-issue position put them at odds with larger, increasingly professionalized, single-issue pro-choice organizations, such as NARAL, Planned Parenthood, and NOW, all of which placed a singular focus on the accessibility of abortion. It also made organizing at the local level nightmarishly difficult, and prevented any long-term or large-scale legislative reform, a problem encountered in many activist urban areas in the late 1960s and 1970s.

But unlike most cities harboring feminist activity, Chicago was home to Jane, the Abortion Counseling Service. Its emergence and transformation into a woman-run medical service empowered activists to create an alternative model of health care, one based on patient participation rather than hierarchy and power. After Jane folded, its members attempted to apply this model to other aspects of women's health care and abortion reform, but with limited success. They developed greater confidence in their ability to function outside a traditional medical model, but not without a cost. In retrospect, some self-reflective local activists concluded that the model "played some part in producing a knee-jerk reaction against professionals which cut the movement off from access to professional skills and probably from some women who could have worked with it."[22] Nonetheless, how Jane developed and took root is essential to understanding the tenor of women's health activism in Chicago. It speaks to that city's unique history in abortion reform, but also underscores a larger trend in the history of reproductive rights in the United States, as competing agendas and conflicting priorities weakened the possibilities of broader coalition building.

Jane: The Abortion Counseling Service

Heather Booth was active in civil rights and antiwar movements before making her first abortion referral. She began her studies at the University of Chicago in 1963; recalling the turbulence of the times, she said that "it was like the whole world was exploding." She became involved with the civil rights movement, and joined the Mississippi Summer Project in 1964, teaching at a Freedom School and registering voters. "I embraced [the movement] because it really reflected the values that I was brought up to believe in," she explained. "I was brought up in a Jewish household, and I was brought up to believe that there is right and wrong and good and bad, and in the face of injustice, you struggle for justice."[23] But like many young female college students involved in civil rights in the 1960s, she was stunned at the lack of respect for women's opinions. At a student meeting, one of the men told her to shut up. She left the meeting and helped to form the first campus women's liberation group, the Women's Radical Action Project (WRAP), at the University of Chicago in 1967.

Though she viewed herself as a radical feminist, Booth's involvement in abortion counseling began only accidentally, after a pregnant friend asked her for help. A few months later, she received another request. Booth began to realize that the need for access to a safe abortion was more widespread than she had known, and took on more and more calls. By 1968, pregnant and working on a master's degree, she found that she needed more help. "The amount of people who were coming through on this word of mouth was too great for me to handle alone," she recalls. "I tried to get in other people to help me."[24]

Jody Parsons, a young mother of two who was suffering from Hodgkin's disease and a frustrating abortion experience, answered the call. She had never viewed abortion as a cause women could rally around, fearing it was considered "seamy" and morally controversial, and would alienate women rather than bring them together. But after hearing Booth speak about abortion as a woman's right, she changed her mind. "It wasn't just the power of the doctor," Parsons reflected about her own abortion. "It was me, my existence as a woman, that left me vulnerable to this terrible oppression."[25] She signed on to the project, and would become a major figure in it. She, along with other interested people in Chicago, began meeting regularly to learn more about abortion.

As with the Boston Women's Health Book Collective, the more the group researched, the more it realized needed to be written about and learned. Very little information on women's bodies or abortion had been produced for lay readers. Despite the fact that most physicians knew little about performing abortions (since it was illegal in most areas except to save the mother's life), the activists discovered that the procedure itself is fairly simple. They named their group the Abortion Counseling Service of Women's Liberation, but they also wanted a code name to protect group members' identities and a woman's privacy when contacting them. When a woman left a message for the service, a member could respond with "This is Jane from Women's Liberation calling."[26] Over the next four years, over one hundred Jane members estimated that they helped eleven thousand women get abortions.

Judith Arcana phoned Jane in the summer of 1970. Separated from her husband, in the midst of an affair, and recently fired from her teaching job, she thought she was pregnant. "My life was coming apart very dramatically," she recalled. The woman who returned her call talked to her for a long time. "She asked me a lot of stuff about my life," Arcana said, "and I was in a mood to tell her, because I was changing in every possible way and trying to figure out a whole lot of stuff about myself and the world."[27] Much to Arcana's relief, she got her period. Though she no longer needed Jane's services, she realized she wanted to be part of the underground organization, which she later credited with transforming her worldview. "I was looking for the women's movement," she explained. "Coming out of all this turmoil, intellectual, political, the sociology of my own life, I was seeking some sense of self as a woman of the world which I had never had on a conscious level before." In the fall of 1970, she attended an orientation session at a church in Chicago's Lincoln Park neighborhood. Service member Ruth Surgal led the meeting, and warned these prospective members of the risks involved. Arcana was willing to take those risks, and so she began regular training sessions where she learned how to counsel women. "I learned about the emotional situations for women who go through abortions, I learned a whole lot of stuff about gynecology, and sat in on the counseling sessions, and then began to counsel myself."[28]

Arcana joined the Abortion Counseling Service during a time of transition. In the early years, Jane members provided counseling and referrals only. After discovering that the male abortionist they had hired was not an MD, Jody Parsons and Ruth Surgal sat through all the abortions with him, learning the skills themselves while comforting the women going through the procedure. They realized that performing an abortion did not require a medical degree. Slowly, they began to let other Jane members assist in abortions as well, with the goal that they would take over all procedures. This would not only train and empower Jane members; it would lower the cost and raise the number of procedures they could do at one time. Although New York had liberalized its abortion law that summer, legalizing terminations of pregnancies up to 24 weeks if performed by a licensed physician, there were still many women in the Chicago area who could not afford the $300 trip to New York. Nor could they afford the $375 fee that Jane currently charged ($350 of which went to the abortionist).[29]

Parsons finally informed the entire service at a meeting in December that its abortion provider was not a doctor. Many women in the room felt dismayed by the deception, and believed that Parsons and Surgal had been lying to them. A large number of members left the group and never returned. But others, such as Arcana, welcomed the opportunity. She pointed out that if the abortion provider could perform the procedure without a license, then they could as well.[30] "I was one of the people who was in the first round of folks who began doing the medical procedures," Arcana recalled. "One woman learned, another woman learned, and then they began to teach some of the rest of us." By the time Jane closed its doors for good, more than three-quarters of the women in the group had learned both counseling and medical skills, according to Arcana. "We were doing everything."[31]

As Jane changed from a referral service to a provider service, group members found themselves in an entirely different position. Those who chose to stay were fascinated about what they were learning, and it politicized many of them to a higher degree.[32] Since abortion was illegal, they had to learn by observation and practice alone, and in the process gained more general knowledge about gynecology, sexuality, and reproduction. "The first time I saw an abortion performed, I was filled with a sense of personal power as a woman at a very conscious level," Arcana reflected. "I thought, 'this is what it is.'"[33] She became aware that the service Jane was providing should include sharing this knowledge with the women it helped.

That sharing of knowledge was facilitated by a new publication. When Ruth Surgal was speaking about abortion in Michigan in the spring of 1971, she discovered a copy of *Women and Their Bodies*, the original version of *Our Bodies, Ourselves*. She was transfixed. "It was spectacular," she said. "The attitude presented in the book . . . was what we wanted people to hear. It talked about the fact that people had the right to information, and that it was useful to know how your body worked, nothing magical or mysterious." At thirty-five cents, it was also affordable. Surgal ordered boxes of the book, and from then on, every woman who got an abortion from Jane received a free copy. Jane members read it as well, and "learned more about their bodies from the book than they had previously known."[34]

The new information available to them through *Our Bodies, Ourselves*, combined with the hands-on experience of providing abortions, contributed to a newfound feeling of expertise among the members of Jane. Nonetheless, Surgal felt that the absence of any medical training impeded the group's ability to give complete care to all its patients. The following fall, she asked her doctor whether he would be willing to teach her and a few others how to perform a pelvic exam. Because of his experience as a resident at Cook County Hospital treating women who had come in after botched abortions, he was sympathetic. During a weekend, five Jane members came to his office to learn the mechanics of a bimanual pelvic exam. He demonstrated on one member, and then they took turns examining each other. Later, they trained other members of Jane. As yet, they were unaware of the emerging controversies and conflicts among medical educators regarding pelvic training. They also did not yet know that two feminist activists, Carol Downer and Lorraine Rothman, were promoting cervical self-exams at the Los Angeles Feminist Women's Health Clinic, calling it "self-help gynecology."[35] But later that fall, Jane members learned of the movement at a NOW conference in California. When Downer and Rothman announced a cross-country tour to promote self-exams in twenty-three cities, the Jane members invited them to spend a day sharing their ideas and expertise in Chicago.

It was a tense exchange. Despite the fact that both groups promoted lay abortions (Downer and Rothman taught both cervical self-examination and menstrual extraction, similar to vacuum aspiration abortion) and believed that experiential knowledge empowers women, each was wary of the other's methods and practice.[36] Downer and Rothman intended to generate publicity (including getting arrested), while Jane focused on secrecy. The visitors disapproved of the messy conditions under which abortions were practiced, causing some Janes to feel defensive.

But many also recalled the exchange with excitement, for they were taught for the first time how easily one could see her own cervix with a flashlight and a mirror. As one Jane remarked, "The first time I saw my own cervix, the first time I did a self-help with a group of women, which was in fact, the women I worked with in the service, I thought, 'this is the most extraordinary thing.' . . . It was big. It was very big."[37] The following week, they brought mirrors to work, offering to show their patients their own cervix. When most declined, they simply stopped asking, and showed it to them anyway.[38] Educating women about their bodies became central to their abortion provider philosophy. While some feminist philosophers (and even some health activists) would later criticize the cervical self-exam fad as merely a form of self-absorbed navel-gazing, Jane members used this knowledge as a way of transforming their practice, and a way of defending at the deepest level a woman's right to know her own body at a moment when she might feel the most

FIGURE 6 Cartoon from L.A.
Women's Center newsletter *Sister*,
July 1973.

betrayed by it. "I know we say biology is not destiny, and indeed it is not," Arcana noted. "But for me biology was the beginning of my education. I learned from the uterus out."[39] Such language underscores the emphasis on experiential knowledge as critical to feminist consciousness. Learning "from the uterus out" empowered Arcana in a way that mere words could not.

Not all were convinced that this type of process would result in a better (that is, less discriminatory) form of health care. Feminist theorists such as Donna Haraway and Joan Scott have challenged the notion that experience can be used as "uncontestable evidence."[40] Is a woman's own view of her body more accurate, more real, than that of a male physician's? "When women look at their bodies through a speculum," sociologist Kathy Davis explains of Haraway's position, "they unwittingly adopt the same objectifying medical 'gaze' that historically has been central to the medical appropriation of women's bodies."[41] In other words, their actions are simply replicating those they are seeking to displace. What about when lay health workers made their patients gaze at their own bodies? Was the process revelatory for those women as well, if it wasn't by choice? Perhaps some viewed it this way, particularly those who chose to join the movement after getting an abortion from Jane. Many were relieved to have any options at all, but if given an alternative, would pick a more clinical setting. One woman recalled an unpleasant abortion experience with Jane that involved a great deal of pain and what she believed to be unsanitary conditions. She remembered her surprise at the setting—a sparse apartment, a bedroom with a camping cot covered by a plastic liner, an abortion provider with long hair wearing a flannel shirt and jeans. Sometime after *Roe v. Wade* she had another abortion, performed by a physician, and in comparison found her experience with Jane to be "atrocious."[42] As a young, poor African American, she may have felt uncomfortable in a group run almost entirely by white women. Or she may have simply preferred a clinical setting, interpreting white coats and stirrups as indicative of better medical care.[43]

But members of Jane believed that they had made a big difference, not only in providing patients with something they couldn't otherwise get, but in getting them to think about the doctor-patient relationship and their bodily rights. "We provided our service in an unstructured and non-hierarchical way, so that the women who came to us in need were included in the process," Ruth Surgal declared. "We felt that patients had the right and the responsibility to make medical personnel answer their questions."[44] The group viewed the sharing of knowledge as a form of empowerment, regardless of whether such knowledge was asked for. Though Surgal described Jane as "unstructured" and "non-hierarchical," there was still a structure in place—it was just very different from that of a traditional medical setting. Similarly, the enforced sharing of knowledge *whether or not it was asked for* attests to the group's implicitly hierarchical structure, as it imposed its politics of self-help on its clients.

Surgal hoped that what Jane offered was a first step in changing the "mystique of medicine," making health care a partnership between patient and practitioner. But that required enlightenment, desire for knowledge, and a sense of entitlement to that knowledge. "We helped women feel better about having the procedure and about abortion in general," she believed. "In clinical and political terms, we turned their depression into anger."[45] Translating anger into action was yet another step, however. And because Jane had to remain underground, that was an impossible task. It would take other venues, and additional women, to grapple with the challenge.

The Politics of Self-Help: Women's Health Centers

On the night of the *Roe v. Wade* decision (January 22, 1973), members of Jane held an impromptu party to celebrate. Some, however, expressed sadness that this would mean the end of the Abortion Counseling Service. "What we Janes got was the most intense experience of our lives," Surgal recalled.[46] Jody Parsons saw that the service would be a "hard act to follow."[47] The women began to brainstorm about what directions their work might take, including creating a women's health clinic.

This was not the first time a group of Chicago feminists shared ideas about opening such a clinic. In October of 1970, the Chicago Women's Liberation Union had announced plans to open a feminist health center, to be called the Alice Hamilton Women's Health Center (named for Dr. Alice Hamilton, a research professor in industrial medicine at Harvard University who died in 1970 at the age of 101). The CWLU women noted their increasing concern over the quality of health care for women and children in Chicago. "In addition to constantly rising and often prohibitive costs, large numbers of women are embarrassed or afraid to bring 'women's problems' to a doctor," they explained, fully aware that they would need to justify the need for a health center restricted to women and children.[48] Given the presence of free clinics situated across the city, why should one specifically serve the women's community?

Feminists were not the only activists committed to changing health care in Chicago. The city provided a key organizational base for the Medical Committee for Human Rights, an organization of health professionals committed to overhauling health care in the United States. In the 1960s, local chapters of MCHR provided medical care for civil rights workers, picketed the American Medical Association for racist membership policies, provided free health clinics in inner cities, and campaigned for national health care. Dr. Quentin Young, a Chicago activist and founding member of the Committee to End Racial Discrimination in Chicago Medical Institutions, also served as national chairman of the MCHR in 1967–68.[49] Under his leadership, along with a fledgling organization, the Student Health Organization, volunteers flooded Chicago's inner-city slums to provide health-care education and assistance, but their efforts seemed to raise temperatures rather than lower them. Racial tension and continued discrimination plagued the project.[50]

The CWLU presented the Alice Hamilton Women's Health Center project as something far more radical than that attempted by the MCHR. "The crisis in medical care, not only for the poor and the aged, but for people in all segments of society, has moved many groups to develop crash band-aid programs to answer the immediate need," it disparaged. "Others, however, feel that a reorganization of the distribution, and a new understanding of the meaning of health care is needed."[51] The Alice Hamilton project sought to offer free health care in a feminist setting in which education, prevention, and child care were part of the total package of services.

Unfortunately, it was beset by problems from the beginning. As with many such projects, funding became a major challenge. One worker noted that fund-raising was difficult "because male directors have trouble understanding why women need a separate health center of their own, and because the CWLU is neither a geographical community organization nor a group of health professionals."[52] The center also found itself competing for funding and clientele with other inner-city clinics.

The largest problems, however, were political and geographic. Debates about where to locate the Alice Hamilton Women's Health Center generated larger ones about priorities. "I think one part of the problem was trying to create one single women's clinic to serve the 'women's community' as the other free clinics served the Black or Latin or white working-class community," CWLU member Elaine Wessel observed. "That was not a good analysis—to assume that because women are oppressed and ethnic minorities are oppressed, you can take a form that works for ethnic minorities and use it to help women." The model, she argued, did not apply, because the perception of a women's community was not as clear-cut. "There was the beginnings of a sort of self-conscious feminist community, but it has never been the kind of 'community' that has had a tight geographical base, which is one thing that the other clinics did have." Moreover, choosing one neighborhood for what was intended to be a citywide clinic accessible to all women was inherently problematic, especially because the CWLU did not address what ramifications a chosen location would have on potential clients (such as concerns about accessibility, child care, or going into a different neighborhood).[53]

Even if an ideal location existed, CWLU members struggled to define what their place would be within it. "I think what we were expecting was to be able to set up the clinic as a sort of 'free space' within the neighborhood where we could do our inter-racial thing, attract some people from the community, and not be bothered by the rest of the neighborhood," Wessel commented.[54] Her reflections underscore the ideological bind that health feminists were in, especially with their attempts to practice their philosophy in a particular place. Note the wording of the Alice Hamilton Women's Health Center's initial flier: "The center does not define any geographical boundaries and is open to all women of child-bearing age." It may not have defined any boundaries, but the boundaries, of course, still existed.[55]

Due to limited funding and organization, the CWLU compromised by opening two facilities, one on the North Side at 2150 North Halsted, and a second on the Southwest Side, at 5711 South Ashland Avenue. Many CWLU members lived near this second location, in what is known as the Back of the Yards community (named for the stockyards that once were there), and hoped to reach more working-class, Puerto Rican, Mexican-American, and African-American women. The two clinics were far from being all-inclusive, however. Each offered only pregnancy testing, and when each lost its lease, the Alice Hamilton Women's Health Center project officially ended, replaced with what was more appropriately named Pregnancy Testing, at various locations throughout the 1970s. Elaine Wessel remained with Pregnancy Testing after Alice Hamilton folded, noting the significance of providing women with this important service. "The chemical tests were fairly easy to learn," she explained. Like today's pregnancy tests obtainable at the supermarket, these earlier tests measured the level of HCG, or human chorionic gonadotropin, in a woman's urine. Wessel believed that they "succeeded in demystifying medicine (at least for women who were active in the pregnancy testing project)."[56] Although the testing project was not the all-encompassing enterprise that she and others at CWLU had envisioned, it was a step toward it.

The Alice Hamilton Women's Health Center project ended in the summer of 1971, one and a half years before the *Roe v. Wade* decision. But as Jane members brainstormed over future projects, attempting a new women's health center might have seemed more plausible than it had just a few years before. Abortion was now legal if performed during a woman's first trimester of pregnancy, and more and more free clinics had emerged in Chicago, thanks to the Medical Committee for Human Rights and other health advocacy groups. Jane members had witnessed firsthand how experiential knowledge had transformed a movement. Why not take that philosophy further?

One year later, in January of 1974, the Emma Goldman Women's Health Center opened its doors on West Loyola Avenue in the city's Far North Side. Most of the staff members came from the Abortion Counseling Service, bringing with them the same activist philosophy that had characterized their work in Jane. But they would not be performing abortions; instead, they would focus on preventive medicine. "We at Emma's are a collective of feminist paramedics involved in well-women health care," they explained in a flier. "Our role as feminist paramedics is a revolutionary one because we have taken it upon ourselves as women to learn skills previously monopolized by the professional medical establishment."[57] The wording of this flier indicates that the center's staff had appropriated not only the skills of organized medicine, but also the language. Specifically, their decision to call themselves "feminist paramedics" suggested that they viewed themselves as accredited medical professionals, despite their lack of licensing. The term also conjured up the notion of emergency service, reflecting both their previous roles as underground abortion providers, and their belief that preventive medicine was a critical component of revolutionizing women's health care.

Such terminology was clearly intentional, for part of the message of Jane and Emma was that experiential knowledge is just as vital as what is taught in medical schools, if not more so. "Each of us came to Emma's with varying degrees of skill," the members explained. "Most women have no previous medical experience; a few had prior training. Basically, the knowledge we have is knowledge learned from each other. We see ourselves as part of a large community of women who come together and share of their knowledge and experience."[58] If women could teach one another how to perform abortions, then they could certainly offer routine gynecological exams, pregnancy testing, VD screening, and other basic services. In addition, they provided abortion referrals, health education, and counseling. They viewed health education as a crucial component of their agenda, requiring patients to participate in group discussions and skill-sharing activities before receiving services.

Although the center did not provide abortions, it practiced the philosophy first introduced in the Abortion Counseling Service. "Traditionally, doctors have decided what is best for our bodies," it noted. "Now we are reclaiming our power to control." Women controlling their own bodies required not just access to abortion, but the ability to engage in preventive health methods. The best way to do that, Emma's staff argued, is through self-help. "The concept of self-help is essential to everything we do," they explained. "Self-help means that a woman can take responsibility for her life and make her own decisions." Providing women with the skills and knowledge to understand how their bodies functioned would enable them to take better care of themselves: "We are women aware of our bodies as healthy and we want to learn how to maintain our health as well as deal with sickness."[59] This post-*Roe* shift from pregnancy termination to well-woman care allowed members of the Emma Goldman Center to remain actively involved in educating women about their bodies, despite their lack of direct involvement in abortion services.

But maintaining the center proved challenging. As with the Alice Hamilton clinic, Emma Goldman suffered both financial and philosophical obstacles. Its reliance on donations rather than fees for services left the clinic plagued with financial problems. In addition, members were determined to function entirely as a collective, with all members sharing all the tasks and decision making. They could not agree, however, about the overall purpose of their work. Some believed that the focus should be solely on teaching self-help skills as a form of feminist consciousness-raising. Others wanted to expand services and incorporate physicians into the collective, and believed they could do so "without developing hierarchies or losing commitment to alternatives to the traditional medical model." They wanted to make the center more accessible to a wider range of women by reaching out to more poor and minority women. After a year and a half, the clinic temporarily closed its doors. Twelve women left the collective to create a new clinic, the Chicago Women's Health Center, in a storefront on Halsted and Armitage, along with two female MDs. Terri Kapsalis, who has worked at the center for the past eighteen years, remembers how "incredibly diverse" the neighborhood was when the center first opened.[60]

The following fall (1975), Emma reopened, with its staff explaining, "The group has gone through numerous changes and growing pains resulting last spring in a split in the group that left the Center understaffed and emotionally drained." But they appeared enthusiastic about a second chance. "EMMA GOLDMAN LIVES!" they announced. "Now we are once again excited by our new beginning." Those staff members who had chosen to stay remained committed to self-help rather than any expansion of health services: "As always we find ourselves primarily concerned with passing on to other women the information and knowledge that we have been able to acquire so that it may be used as a tool to develop strength and self reliance."[61] As before, the center provided well-woman health care along with pregnancy testing, birth control counseling, cervical self-exams, Pap smears, and fittings for diaphragms and cervical caps—and no doctors. In 1977, a young woman named Tanya McHale came in for a diaphragm fitting, fell in love with the center, and soon joined the staff. "It seemed like it was actually action from a particular political philosophy that was very appealing to me as a nineteen-year-old," she recalls.[62]

McHale was the last to leave the Emma Goldman Center, closing it in 1986 when its lease expired. "We had been kind of getting a progressively smaller number of people interested" in Emma by then, she says. Meanwhile, the shrinking staff had begun to collaborate with the Chicago Women's Health Center and even a group of young feminist OB-GYNs at Illinois Masonic Medical Center—a move that would have seemed hypocritical to Emma's founders a few years earlier. But the conflict that had divided the groups no longer seemed as important by the 1980s. "I think it was much more turf at that point, because the concept of whether physicians would taint the experience and whether we would end up back serving more of the medical system was very much a big part of the dilemma, the philosophical dilemma that occurred," McHale explains.[63] The Chicago Women's Health Center model—still a collective, but with the collaboration of trained doctors—won out. McHale joined and even served as director for eight years in the 1990s, until she decided to go to nursing school.

Abortion Task Force

Given Jane's underground history and philosophy, it is not surprising that many members turned to the creation of alternative spaces for women's health care when the group disbanded in 1973. Others, however, were critical of this reluctance to integrate their experience into reforming traditional medicine, especially now that abortion was legal. They chose a different path, creating watchdog services to monitor the growing number of legal abortion providers in Chicago. But they quickly discovered that attempting a singular focus on abortion generated discord, particularly when they tried to organize local communities where minority groups brought different priorities to the bargaining table. These groups required a more inclusive definition of reproductive freedom, in which access to abortion was just one of many components that would ensure a woman's right to choose when and if she would bear a child. These competing visions of reproductive freedom would affect the rise and fall of the city's first abortion task force.

Legalization of abortion created a new set of challenges. As Chicago health activists explained, "The 'problem' with abortion used to be that abortions were dangerous and illegal. Now the 'problem' is that abortions are hard to get and expensive."[64] Although most physicians expressed support for keeping abortion legal, very few attempted to integrate abortion services into routine medical care.[65] As a result, new, for-profit, freestanding abortion clinics became a main provider of abortions. Unlike clinics such as the Women's Community Health Center in Cambridge, Massachusetts (at the center of the pelvic examination controversy), most abortion clinics did not market themselves as feminist or promote the principles of self-help so central to feminist health ideology. Therefore, health activists questioned these clinics' motives as well as their treatment of clients.

The Chicago Women's Liberation Union created the Abortion Task Force in January of 1973, to investigate the quality of care at particular clinics and hospitals. In March, the group of five core members (some of which were former Jane members) began a survey of local abortion services. As it discovered, "These places are overcrowded, "often make us feel alone and awful and finally are too expensive."[66] Although hospitals could provide abortions, they were not meeting current demand. The Task Force found that while approximately 200 abortions were performed per week in Chicago, the three main referral services were receiving more than 400 calls per week. Only three hospitals performed a "sizeable" number of abortions, often limited to regular patients or clinic users. Prices were "extremely high, making it impossible for women who are poor but not on welfare and women without insurance to get an abortion."[67] By March, the group had created a flier to help abortion seekers, "If You Need an Abortion," that listed eight different abortion providers, with costs ranging from $125 to $430.[68] The women also distributed their findings to the media in a "Hospital Fact Sheet," arguing that "it is difficult for all women to get abortions at a reasonable cost and safely and with care because of the above items expressed in the chart."[69] Without accessibility, the victory of *Roe v. Wade* would be hollow.

For one year after the Supreme Court's *Roe* decision, the Abortion Task Force demanded that abortion in Chicago remain in the public eye. In addition to surveying clinics and hospitals, the group utilized direct action campaigns, and on March 8, 1973, even performed guerrilla theater in front of the American College of Obstetricians and Gynecologists, which had its headquarters in Chicago at the time. A transcript of this skit illustrates how the Task Force continued the antiprofessionalism rhetoric begun in Jane. Now, however, the rhetoric made it aboveground, no longer whispered in secrecy, but shouted in the face of organized medicine.

The cast included two readers, two actresses, a group of "women-who-want-abortions," a human chain to represent "establishment-restrictions," and musicians. The skit opened with the readers providing a history of abortion. "This is a story about women and their control of their bodies," began Reader A, underscoring the centrality and symbolism of the female body to the debate. "This is about abortion." Reader B continued, "Once upon a time only a few short years ago, abortions were illegal or very difficult to obtain anywhere in the U.S." As she provided statistics regarding the number of deaths from botched abortion attempts, a harmonica wailed and the actresses (placed closest to the audience) clutched their stomachs in pain. Despite the restrictions, women began to "fight this tyranny over their reproductive lives," continued Reader B. "Challenge after challenge was raised in the courts, women gave public testimony about their experiences, women set up their own abortion counseling services to help each other, women demonstrated in the streets." The actresses shook their fists at the human "establishment-restrictions" chain, then joined hands with the "women-who-want-abortions." As the readers described the events leading to *Roe v. Wade*, the "women-who-want-abortions" surged toward the human chain. Suddenly, with the coming of *Roe*, Readers A and B began a chorus/verse chant, each line punctuated by tambourine or harmonica.

> A: Of course, you can have abortions . . .
> B: . . . if you have a private doctor.
> A: Of course, you can have abortions . . .
> B: . . . if you stay, and pay, in the hospital.
> A: Of course, you can have abortions . . .
> B: . . . if you have $150 or $200 or . . .
> A: Of course, you can have abortions . . .
> B: . . . if you're less than 10 weeks' pregnant.
> A: Of course, you can have abortions . . .
> B: . . . if you can get through all the new restrictions, all the red tape.

During this exchange, the "women-who-want-abortions" repeatedly pushed themselves against the wall of establishment restrictions and fell back. Meanwhile, the two actresses were tied up in red tape, a metaphor that surely would not have been lost on the audience.

The "women-who-want-abortions" then turned to the audience and stated together:

> WE DEMAND THE RIGHT TO CONTROL OUR LIVES
> NOT AT THE MERCY OF YOUR KNIVES
> TO BEAR CHILDREN OR NOT MUST BE OUR RIGHT
> WOMEN! NOW ARISE AND FIGHT!
> WE HAVE THE RIGHT TO AN ABORTION.
> ON THIS LET THERE BE NO DISTORTION,

LET THIS BE EVERY WOMAN'S GOAL—
WE SWEAR, OUR BODIES, <u>WE'LL</u> CONTROL.

Then all members of the street theater joined together and sang:

YOU'RE NOT GOING TO KEEP US
DOWN ANYMORE,
NOW THAT WE KNOW YOUR GAME.
WE'RE ROUGH AND TOUGH AND ALL TOGETHER
NOW
AND ONE BY ONE YOU'RE GOING TO KNOW OUR
POW-ER.
YOU'RE NOT GOING TO KEEP US
DOWN ANYMORE.
NOW THAT WE KNOW
YES, NOW THAT WE KNOW
NOW THAT WE KNOW YOUR G-A-A-M-ME!

The skit drew attention to the Abortion Task Force, particularly its refusal to concede all decision-making power to physicians and legislators. Performing in front of ACOG, shouting "We demand the right to control our lives / Not at the mercy of your knives," the Task Force made it unmistakably clear that organized medicine was not an ally but an enemy of abortion rights.[70] The group's guerilla theater tactics drew attention to its cause and led, remarkably, to a meeting with a doctor and staff at ACOG. According to the Abortion Task Force, ACOG "assured us that they were doing what they could to sway a sometimes conservative medical community, suggested other meetings, and agreed with suggestions about their guidelines."[71] Thus, despite their confrontational approach, Task Force members achieved some success at keeping abortion in the spotlight and challenging organized medicine to implement *Roe v. Wade.*

For all the commitment and energy that members put into the Abortion Task Force, it did not last long; the group dissolved only one year later, in 1974. Ironically, what pulled it apart was its whole reason for being: abortion. As one member recalled, "many in the ATF did not really want to organize around abortion but rather around women's health services, especially because abortion was such a difficult issue around which to organize support in many black, Latino, and white communities."[72] Members were cognizant of the discord and of the need to develop a multi-issue approach to reproductive services, but they found themselves mired in the overly simplified abortion debate, whose definitions and limitations seemed beyond their control.

Why did people join the Abortion Task Force if they were opposed to organizing around the issue? This ambivalence is key to understanding why abortion did not, and could not, become a unifying force for health feminists—or any feminists, for that matter. Many were reluctant to engage in the debate, either because they disagreed with how politics and the media had flattened the complex issue of reproductive rights into the singular topic of abortion access, or because they were wary of losing support from politicians who were not pro-choice.

In Chicago, many feminists became involved in the abortion debate only after the passage of *Roe*. Though the National Organization for Women (formed in 1966) endorsed the repeal of restrictive abortion laws in 1967, the Chicago chapter was initially reluctant to take on the issue. Many NOW members found abortion to be too controversial, preferring to focus on economic inequity issues instead.[73] Madeline Schwenk, who had performed illegal abortions as a Jane member, joined the Abortion Task Force and chaired the NOW chapter's abortion committee. She struggled to get any other NOW members to work on the abortion issue, however, because "most of the other activists in the chapter were personally more interested in employment issues."[74] She urged local NOW members to write state legislators to support abortion bills, but got a limited response. "I remember going down to Springfield for some show of support on an abortion bill," she later recalled, "and I couldn't get anyone else in NOW to go."[75] Most of the legislators were steadfastly opposed to abortion reform, and many NOW members therefore saw little reward in lobbying.[76]

The legalization of abortion, however, created new opportunities for activists to tackle a broader range of women's health-care issues.[77] Leatrice Hauptman of the Abortion Task Force recalled that despite much divisiveness among members, all agreed that "we would talk about broader women's health needs" in their abortion work. All were interested in taking direct action against institutions (such as with their street theater), and viewed abortion as a potential avenue for accomplishing this goal. "Abortion was a concrete demand," Hauptman pointed out, "an issue that had a public presence; we could *use it for what it was worth* in the hopes of building a citywide campaign to win some reforms from institutions and to confront those institutions with organized power." Because of this opportunity, she explained, "we attempted to let our differences ride. We did attempt to work through them with presentations by members at group meetings on broader issues like union organizing in health institutions, [and] abortion and genocide in the black community."[78] But ultimately, their differences undermined their goals.[79] "Our energies to create one strong organization around abortion or women's health issues were very dispersed, and this overriding goal got lost," Hauptman wrote. Even their direct-action tactics failed to unite the group. "Our accomplishments in direct action were minimal and modest," she continued. "This is because our targets were often major medical institutions like Illinois Masonic, Cook County Hospital or the 16 hospitals on the North Side. To do good direct actions against these places requires a mass base. Because our conflicts as a group existed in the context of different styles of leadership, different timetables for direct action, and how we should use our membership, we never built that base."[80] As a result, the group disbanded after only one year.

Here is the irony regarding abortion in 1973: many activists believed that having won the constitutional battle to legalize abortion, they could move on to other issues. What they found, however, was that abortion provided them with a framework and an audience that was difficult to walk away from. As Hauptman figured, "we could use it [abortion] for what it was worth" to build a larger reform campaign. Ultimately, this strategy backfired, because increasingly vocal counterforces on both the Left and the Right—those demanding other reproductive freedoms alongside abortion, and those morally opposed to abortion—destroyed the potential for larger coalition building.

HERS

Despite the short-lived groups and continuing divisiveness within Chicago's feminist health network, one service organization managed to transcend much of this conflict. For seventeen years (1973—90), the Health Evaluation and Referral Service (HERS) monitored abortion and other women's health services in the city. The group was initially going to be called the Health Information Service (HIS), but to create a more appropriate acronym, members christened it HERS. Its mission was to empower women in two different ways: first, by providing them with necessary information that "enables women to become advocates for themselves and their families," and second, by bringing about "positive changes in the policies and conduct of health care institutions."[81]

Between fifteen and twenty volunteers (initially all laypeople) operated a 24-hour callback telephone service reminiscent of Jane and with advice from former members. They were trained to provide information on abortion facilities, family planning clinics, and later, mental health services. By the late 1980s, they received over five thousand calls per year.[82]

HERS also evaluated and monitored health services in the Chicago area to determine the level of safety, affordability, compassion, and education provided.[83] The top five recommended abortion clinics appeared on its brochure, which it hoped would provide an incentive for clinics to provide higher-quality services. Factors affecting the evaluation included price, payment flexibility, counseling, type of facility, staff and administration, and follow-up. HERS recommended three clinics without reservation, and two with reservation. The Midwest Population Center, for example, received a high rating for its low price ($65–$160, depending on the procedure needed and gestational age), its pleasant facilities, which evaluators found "conducive to discussion," and their assessment that "attitudes toward women are superior." In contrast, the Friendship Medical Center received a recommendation with reservations, in part because the two male directors of the clinic were "friendly, concerned, but somewhat paternalistic."[84]

In addition to recommending particular abortion services, HERS claimed responsibility for closing down at least one disreputable clinic. The group received complaints that a Michigan Avenue clinic was telling nonpregnant women that they were pregnant and needed a $150 abortion. As one of the original members, Mim Desmond, recalled, "Three of us went to the clinic with witnesses ('friends') to see what they'd tell us." The previous day, the women had been certified by a University of Illinois clinic as not pregnant. The director of the Michigan Avenue clinic informed each of them that they were pregnant. Posing as a physician, he "took the opportunity to examine one of the women 'to see if her breasts and abdomen showed signs of pregnancy.' We took this information to court, publicized it in the newspapers, and the clinic was closed down." Other successes "were smaller and less exciting, but important. Clinics have responded to our negative and positive criticisms by expanding waiting areas, and concentrating on good counseling in order to have us refer women to them."[85] HERS members believed that in their advocacy and referral work, the organization "had an impact and influence on health care which is far greater than the agency's actual size."[86]

The small size and budget of the organization—15–20 members, all but one volunteers, with a budget that never exceeded $60,000 annually—impeded its goals. Members were aware of these constraints early on. "In the year we've been doing the phone referrals," they wrote on a questionnaire, "we've become aware of a huge number of other things that we want to do." Mim Desmond reflected that HERS "had not had

the womanpower or the financing to expand as much as it would wish."
Part of the problem was that "a great deal of energy goes into maintenance—keeping the phone lines going and keeping referral information
up-to-date."[87]

Despite its small size and budget, HERS worked to broaden its sphere
of influence. In 1977, Desmond and fellow members attempted to channel their extensive referral work into a guide for local women. Together,
they published the "HERS Healthy Kit," a collection of sixteen color-
ful leaflets on health issues. The packet included four consumer guides,
nine fact sheets, a female anatomy chart, cartoons, and a personal gynecological record. Consistent with the philosophy of HERS, the kit was
"intended to help women better choose and use health care services."
Topics ranged from menstruation to the environment to childbirth. The
juxtaposition of practical advice to artwork and personal stories resembled
the format of *Our Bodies, Ourselves*. Some wording was identical (for
example, the environmental section is entitled "Our Environment, Ourselves"), as was the feminist message that "knowledge is power" when it
comes to understanding bodies and health.[88] One contributor acknowledged the group's debt to the Boston Women's Health Book Collective,
remarking, "We were inspired by *Our Bodies, Ourselves*, by the Boston
Women's Health Collective which reflects a unique approach to wom-
en's health. The KIT gives us a chance to share a comprehensive overview
of our resources with many women instead of giving pieces of information to individual callers."[89] The kit sold well, but it did not overtake the
group's call volume. Within three years, HERS had sold 3,000 copies of
the Healthy Kit, but had taken over 20,000 calls.[90]

What is most striking about the Healthy Kit is how little it had to
do with abortion. While HERS began primarily as an abortion referral
service, it had clearly moved beyond pregnancy termination, and was
instead trying to implement the feminist vision of well-woman health
care promoted at the Emma Goldman clinic and the Chicago Women's
Health Center. For example, one of the consumer guides was entitled
"How to Own Your Own Body," and juxtaposed one woman's negative
experience at the doctor's office to another woman's positive story. "I'd
hurried from work to get to the doctor's office on time," the first woman
wrote, "but then I sat for hours in the dreary waiting room, watching
people come in and out like a production line." Finally her name was
called, and she was ushered into an examination room. There, unclothed,
she waited another twenty minutes. After the doctor brusquely entered,
he put her feet into the stirrups and began inserting the speculum. "As
I lay there in awkward silence," she continued, "the sheet draped over

me, I suddenly felt totally in the dark about my own body. Was it really *me* being examined—or some strange alien thing?" In this narrative, the patient is completely disconnected from the physical experience of being examined. She is both disempowered and disembodied.

In contrast, the second woman described her first experience in a women's clinic. Here, the examiner (we don't know if she's a physician; she's addressed as "Barb") walks her into the room. "During the exam, Barb explained to me how I could relax my muscles so the speculum would slide in easier. Then she gave me a mirror, and after a few fumbled attempts I could see for myself what she'd just discovered—a redness that was a sign of a possible infection." Barb took a culture, and together, they went to study it under a microscope, where Barb told her that the little cells were indicative of a yeast infection. While the first patient had been charged thirty dollars cash, Barb gave this woman an envelope and suggested a fifteen-dollar donation, or whatever she could afford. Her reaction? "The whole experience had been very human."[91] The moral was clear: alternative women's health clinics empowered women to participate in the process of health care, and did so in an affordable manner. However, as the negative response from a Jane patient reminds us, not all women subscribed to the notion that affordable empowerment equaled better health care.

HERS members agreed that good health care depended on more than the creation of alternative health clinics, though not necessarily for the same reasons. They believed that change was necessary on both an institutional and a personal level. "We've begun learning about our bodies so they are no longer alien territory," they declared, and they recommended that readers do the same. "As you yourself move toward owning your own body, we hope you will find through this brochure, not only services and skills—but sisters—to help you."[92] Like the Boston Women's Health Book Collective and the Pelvic Teaching Program, HERS literature continued the assumption that physical self-discovery would lead to a shared sense of identity and community. Learning "from the uterus out," as Jane member Judith Arcana described it, reaffirmed a biological basis for sisterhood. This assumption, however, would become increasingly problematic for women's health activists over the next decade.

Going National: Reproductive Rights National Network

By the time the Healthy Kit emerged in feminist bookstores and health clinics, the political climate in Chicago and the United States had shifted, drawing greater attention to the abortion issue than it had since *Roe v.*

Wade. In 1976, Henry Hyde, a conservative Republican congressional representative from Illinois, introduced an amendment to the current bill providing funds to the U.S. Department of Heath, Education, and Welfare that would prohibit the use of federal money to pay for Medicaid recipients to have abortions.[93] More than ever before, class became central to abortion legislation. As Hyde explained, "I certainly would like to prevent, if I could legally, anybody having an abortion, a rich woman, a middle-class woman, or a poor woman. Unfortunately, the only vehicle available is the HEW Medicaid bill."[94] In 1977, the Supreme Court issued a ruling that permitted state abortion-funding bans. Access to safe and legal abortions was once again a major issue on the political landscape, as nearly all states—including Illinois—responded to this ruling by refusing to fund all but therapeutic abortions. The Republican Party adopted an anti-abortion plank as part of its platform in the 1976 election, and in 1980 achieved victory in the election of Ronald Reagan as president, who supported a constitutional amendment banning abortion.

The conservative ascendancy and its threat to the Supreme Court's decision in *Roe v. Wade* galvanized abortion reform activists, greatly expanding the movement far beyond what it was in the pre-*Roe* era.[95] New organizations formed and existing ones strengthened their support and resources. For example, the National Organization for Women and the National Abortion Rights Action League instituted more formal organizational approaches than ever before. They also became more narrowly focused on defending legal abortion as they found themselves on the defensive. As sociologist Suzanne Staggenborg explains, though NOW and NARAL continued their work in lobbying and litigation, "the political arena became the central battlefield of the abortion conflict."[96] Theirs became a single-issue campaign based on political action strategies. Here, "pro-life" and "pro-choice" became the rallying cries of political candidates responding to movement and countermovement demands that the personal was political.

For many feminists already involved in abortion reform, this more conservative, professional platform was not a welcome addition. NARAL's lobbyists and lawyers could not take the place of grass-roots activism, they believed. Nor could these individual professionals convey the complexity of reproductive rights. New Chicago-based organizations such as the Reproductive Rights National Network (R2N2, formed in 1978) and its affiliate, Women Organized for Reproductive Choice (WORC, formed in 1979), developed out of earlier women's health networks, but they specifically targeted the New Right and right-to-life movements as dangerous to women's health. Moreover, they believed that pro-choice organizations were too willing to compromise feminist principles and had allowed the countermovement to define the terms of the debate. As Marilyn Katz, one of R2N2's founders, recalled, "The debate on abortion was being framed narrowly and being framed by the Right, by reactions to the Right, rather than by the women's movement. . . . The real impetus [for R2N2] was to reframe the debate, to talk about the conditions which would be necessary for women to be able to make a real choice."[97] Feminist health activists in Chicago refused to abide by the limitations of the "pro-life"/"pro-choice" debate, demanding that the conversation take place within a larger context of women's reproductive health.[98]

As with Jane, the Reproductive Rights National Network began with the ideas of one woman active in Chicago's civil rights movement. Just as Heather Booth began abortion referrals because of her exposure to women's vulnerability while working for SDS, so Marilyn Katz witnessed the violent protests in Chicago in 1968 and became involved in the antiwar movement, specifically, the MOBE (National Mobilization Committee to End the War in Vietnam). She became the national political secretary of the New American Movement, formed in 1971, a socialist organization made up of former SDS members. In 1978, she convinced the organization to create a project on reproductive rights, which would become R2N2. Though some feminist activists were wary of creating yet another women's health organization in Chicago, Katz convinced them that a national organization centered on broader women's health issues would accomplish more and unify the movement in a way that former groups such as Jane could not. Many of these groups, including the Chicago Women's Liberation Union, the Abortion Task Force, and (obviously) Jane, had already dissolved, and lots of activists concerned about the repercussions of the Hyde Amendment and a growing countermovement were eager to channel their energy into a national movement. By the end of the year, R2N2 had organized approximately fifty different women's and left-wing groups nationwide.[99] The organization benefited greatly from the "availability of preexisting organizational bases," most important the Committee for Abortion Rights and Against Sterilization Abuse, formed in New York in 1977, which offered staff support, office space, and use of its membership network.[100]

Four times a year, Katz, along with activist-physician Pat Rush, edited a reproductive rights newsletter, in which they conveyed the importance of placing abortion within the wider framework of reproductive rights. "What is the meaning of the current attack on reproductive rights?" Katz asked in the introductory newsletter, published in February 1978. "We must look at the fight for abortion in the context of a total program for reproductive and social rights," she urged. Success would only be realized if activists "develop a position and coalition that reflects our broadest interests and allies."[101] With that in mind, she and other editors of the newsletter created a "Bill of Reproductive Rights" (later revised as the "Principles of Unity") to define the varied aspects of the movement "that must necessarily coalesce if we are to defeat the reactionary attacks on our freedom of sexual choice and our reproductive rights." They encouraged feedback from readers, seeing the initial bill as a the start of an important conversation, a "vehicle for talking to each other and to those we have yet to reach." Significantly, they also saw it as a way of gaining support from other community activists. The bill included ten different rights, from the right to abortion, to the right to safe and effective contraception, to the right to freedom from involuntary sterilization, to the right to free, quality day care, to the right to free medical care, to the right to "education about our bodies."[102] At a time when the women's movement was suffering from divisiveness and fragmentation, R2N2 sought to build coalitions even beyond those interested in women's health issues. Its Principles of Unity came far closer to echoing the Declaration of Sentiments produced at Seneca Falls, New York, back in 1848 than did the 1968 commemorative conference at Lake Villa, Illinois.

Two years later, the editors wrote of their partial success with coalition building along with the extent of their challenges in achieving their goal. "R2N2 has been able to demonstrate that a multi-issue approach to abortion can be a firm basis, not only for defending abortion rights but for a movement capable of fighting for all the economic and social conditions necessary for true reproductive freedom," they maintained. Despite this optimism, the editors were aware of the limitations they faced. "The women's liberation movement, from which we came, is fragmented and on the defensive. When the Network began, we felt that we were a component part of a strong women's movement that could give us, as we gave them, support. We have found, however, that our focus on reproductive rights has, at times, inadvertently cut us off from sectors of the women's movement." Consequently, they resolved to "make tighter links with women working on other aspects of women's liberation, expand the scope of our organization's focus, and see as one of our tasks aiding in the rebuilding of the autonomous women's movement."[103]

Yet R2N2's internal memos and meeting notes reveal the extent of the conflict that individual members felt and underscored the limitations of the group. "We don't have much of a feeling of growth in the women's movement or feeling of victory," admitted Mardge Cohen, a physician who would go on to found one of the first women's HIV clinics at Cook County Hospital in Chicago in 1987. "Abortion to me isn't the be-all of women controlling their lives—we need more than a pro-abortion strategy." A colleague agreed, asking, "To what extent is focusing on abortion just defensive?"[104] Like other reproductive rights and pro-choice groups, R2N2 did find itself responding to the strategies and tactics of the New Right rather than reframing the debate, as founder Marilyn Katz had envisioned. Dr. Cohen noted that the Right was "calling the shots—setting the terms of morality; we are on the way down instead." Another colleague stated even more darkly, "We will never win if we stick with abortion."[105]

The massive effort behind a nationwide abortion rights campaign did not improve this frustration, signaling a downturn in the group's enthusiasm and membership. From October 22 to 27, 1979, cities across the United States hosted National Abortion Rights Action Week, with demonstrations, rallies, petition drives, and health fairs. In Chicago, the newly formed local R2N2 affiliate, Women Organized for Reproductive Choice, took charge of organizing that city's events. WORC joined forces with NOW and NARAL to sponsor special forums, seminars, and a rally downtown. WORC coordinator Cathy Christeller noted that the group "very quickly developed an awareness of the strategic issues facing us" as the New Right was "zeroing in on abortion as their leading public appeal issue." Perhaps more disturbingly, the attempt at coalition organizing was disastrous. Problems began at the first official planning meeting, when NOW and NARAL staff announced they would not support any event except the rally. "From then on out we were on the defensive," Christeller noted. "The NOW staffperson let us know from the outset that she hated working in coalitions and basically didn't believe in them." Next, the National Association of Black Feminists walked out of the coalition, insulted by NOW members who apparently indicated that they were not interested in reaching out to minority women or groups for support, and did not feel a need to print leaflets in Spanish. There was continued divisiveness over the wording of leaflets for the abortion rights rally, as NOW insisted that the only wording it would support was "keep abortion safe and legal." "Our coalition delegates agreed under protest, and then were faced with the anger of our members who felt that we had 'sold out' our reproductive rights perspective," Christeller continued.[106] There was also major disagreement among the groups about who would be the rally's keynote speaker.

Perhaps such tension was unavoidable, but the members of the newly established WORC felt derailed by the coalition's inability to make progress. "What was the most aggravating about the coalition was that it took so much energy and produced so little results. The week was not a priority for either NOW or NARAL," Christeller concluded, noting that NARAL's main interest seemed to have been holding a $50-a-plate dinner at the Playboy mansion.[107] Other women's health groups across the country echoed WORC's disappointment that the effort had not appeared to have a "significant impact on their communities." Most groups who responded to a *Healthright* survey published by the Women's Health Forum in New York City said that abortion "is not a priority issue for women in their communities."[108]

Shortly after National Abortion Rights Action Week, membership in WORC started to shrink, peaking in 1979 at thirty members and dropping to seven or ten by the early 1980s.[109] Christeller noted, "We have to come to grips with the fact that large numbers of supporters have not materialized around reproductive rights. Women do not seem to feel any urgency about these issues, despite the legislative assault on abortion."[110] Abortion did not appear to galvanize a large groundswell of support, as abortion reform activists had assumed it would. Instead, it had become a liability for the movement. WORC member Pat Rush, who had decided to go to medical school because of the activism she witnessed in Chicago in 1969, remembered the transition from idealism to frustration within the organization. She went to medical school at Loyola University, worked at a free clinic, and began to think about how to transform the medical establishment. She took a position at Cook County Hospital and moved into a house with five other physicians, including Mardge Cohen, and all became involved in WORC. From 1978 to 1983, it was a daily part of Rush's life. Then, as she put it, "the whole thing just kind of collapsed." Reflecting later on what happened, she noted that "some people felt we could not in good conscience just promote abortion without talking about the other larger social context . . . it just couldn't hold together." When asked how she felt about the movement coming apart, she responded,

> Oh, it was devastating. Except that it isn't like one Sunday it's over. It wasn't like that. It was like less people came to meetings, and, let's say, people would always have different ideas; well, I think we should have a march here, or have a march there, or I think we should work on daycare, or whatever. . . . In the Hyde days [late 1970s], even if we would disagree, we would end up

doing something. As things kind of petered out, then what happened was if there wasn't an impassioned champion for doing
something, then we would just say let's meet again in a month.
And then let's meet again in a month, and then whatever. I think
many of us were depressed by it. Again, it was a tremendous
sense of loss.[111]

In an R2N2 abortion strategy meeting during the early 1980s, Mardge
Cohen articulated what she believed to be the reason why abortion was
not the touchstone for their movement. "In the 1960s and 1970s," she
noted, "the reason we won [support for abortion reform] was because
lots of people (men and women) were talking about control of life." They
had viewed making abortion safe and legal as just one aspect of a larger
agenda to empower women in every aspect of their lives, she explained.
"Abortion in fact reduces to talking only about control of body. In this
way we feel trapped."[112] Cohen captured the dilemma facing health feminists as they entered the 1980s. After more than a decade of emphasis
on naturalizing knowledge—"learning from the uterus out," as Judith
Arcana described—it had stifled them. What had begun in Jane as a revolutionary concept grounded in self-help had become by the end of the
decade a divisive, frustrating issue battled from the Right as well as the
Left. By the mid-1980s, most of the organizations discussed in this chapter had folded. Members were tired of trying to come up with new strategies, short on time, and low on cash. Those who had come of age in the
late 1960s "thought there was going to be a revolution any day," as Pat
Rush characterized the times. "We weren't thinking in terms of twenty
years."[113] Activists were now entering their thirties; some were having
children. In the meantime, a new enemy had emerged on the national
landscape, one that would further complicate the agenda and strategies
of health feminists: the injectable contraceptive Depo-Provera.

4 Bodies of Evidence: Depo-Provera and the Public Board of Inquiry

At 9:22 a.m. on January 10, 1983, Dr. Judith Weisz called the crowd inside the Hubert Humphrey Building in downtown Washington, D.C., to order. As chair of the U.S. Food and Drug Administration Public Board of Inquiry on Depo-Provera, she became the first woman and only the second scientist to officiate at an FDA hearing. "What I didn't know and I soon became aware of," she notes, "was what a political hot potato this really was."[1] Seated to her left was Dr. Paul Stolley, a professor in the Department of Research Medicine at the University of Pennsylvania, and to her right, Dr. Griff Ross, associate dean at the University of Texas Medical School in Houston. Behind her, scrambling to take his position, was FDA attorney Jess Stribling. "For Judith, it was a very memorable and special event that she felt and still feels very keenly about," Stribling says.[2] Weisz's task at the hearing was to determine whether Depo-Provera—trade name for Depo-medroxyprogesterone acetate—was safe for general marketing as a contraceptive in the United States. The FDA had already rejected the pharmaceuticals manufacturer Upjohn Company's application twice in this regard due to lack of evidence that the drug was safe, and Upjohn was now appealing the agency's latest decision. "Everybody kept [asking] me, 'Why are you spending this much time on this? It won't make any difference.' Well, it kept the damn thing off the market for eight years," Weisz declares—revealing only years later her distaste for the drug.[3]

The Depo-Provera Board of Inquiry proved to be a definitive chapter in the history of women's health activism. Its investigation centered on the safety of one of the most controversial forms of birth control, injected intramuscularly every ninety days to suppress ovulation. Although highly effective in preventing pregnancy, Depo-Provera's availability to and higher use among poor and minority patient populations before FDA approval generated concern among activists that the drug was a dangerous tool for population control advocates. Journalists reported women in developing countries lining up by the thousands for injections of the contraceptive, funded by international family planning organizations. One Namibian physician noted that during the 1980s, injections were "simply banged into black and colored women, without discussion, explanation or even permission."[4] These reports led to concern about racist population control policies, and also drew attention to poor scientific research methods. Clinical trials failed to follow up with patients who discontinued use of the drug and inadequately documented the risks and side effects, ranging from weight gain to heavy bleeding to

FIGURE 7 In Africa, promotion of Depo-Provera continues in the twenty-first century. A billboard in Guinea promotes the injectable contraceptive: "Depo-Provera—Efficacious, Reversible, Discreet. Contraceptive with a long duration." Photograph © 2002 Sara A. Holtz, courtesy of Photoshare. Reprinted by permission.

cancer. As a result, in the 1970s and 1980s the FDA repeatedly turned down Upjohn Company's requests to market Depo-Provera as a contraceptive in the United States. Not until 1992, after a long-term study by the World Health Organization suggested the overall risk of cancer to be minimal, would the FDA approve the drug for such marketing. Nonetheless, during these decades thousands of American women had received Depo injections to prevent pregnancy, either through clinical trials or through off-label use, since the drug was already FDA approved for the treatment of endometrial cancer.

Depo's widespread availability and use in the United States as a contraceptive before FDA approval triggered feminist indignation. In 1979 Belita Cowan, director of the National Women's Health Network, announced, "It is time for all of us to speak out, to expose the horrors of this drug, and Upjohn's role in promoting suffering and disease."[5] The NWHN, a Washington, D.C.–based lobbying group formed in 1975, created a Depo-Provera patient registry, generating media attention and consumer concern over the drug's safety and possible misuse. By the time of the 1983 FDA hearings, the network had galvanized consumers and public interest groups, who were increasingly receptive to the idea that women's personal experiences should revolutionize a flawed health-care system. The Board of Inquiry thus served as a significant stepping-stone for women's health advocates, who now found themselves in a more powerful position than they had in previous legislative debates regarding reproductive health. As Rosalind Petchesky argues, women made "real gains" in this regulatory process, as birth control marketers "have had to contend with a new political consciousness" in the form of feminist health activists.[6] Yet these negotiations also served as an ideological stumbling block, as feminists were forced to abandon their body politics—in particular the privileging of female experience over scientific data, at least in the scientific arena.[7] Wary of being cast as too "emotional" in their approach when testifying on a scientific panel, they began to replace stories with statistics, ultimately compromising their position as outside agitators.

This chapter is part of a broader intellectual conversation regarding the contested nature of drug regulation and organized medicine in American culture.[8] In the context of the women's health movement and the regulation of birth control, ideas about gender played a central role in negotiations between scientists, doctors, patients, activists, and pharmaceutical corporations. Female activists and patients confronted a regulatory structure reluctant to incorporate individual stories—particularly *women's* stories—into a scientifically rigorous risk-benefit analysis. As a result, they limited their personal testimonials to press conferences and women's health newsletters; in the scientific arena, they attempted to confront scientists on their own terms, yet still place women's bodies squarely at the center of the debate. Beginning with describing the formation of the historic Depo-Provera Public Board of Inquiry, this chapter then addresses the experiences of patients (those who filled out registries for the NWHN), the strategies of women's health activists who desired to testify at the hearing, and the controversial trials conducted particularly on women of color at the Grady Clinic in Atlanta. Taken together, these stories and strategies reveal the enormous complexity of regulating reproduction in the late twentieth century and thereby help to explain why, despite huge gains, the women's health movement was not ultimately more successful in revolutionizing reproductive health care.

The Public Board of Inquiry

Judith Weisz fondly remembers being asked to chair the FDA Public Board of Inquiry. "It was just wonderful that [FDA commissioner] Art Hayes appointed me," she recalls. "And I said to him, 'You appointed me because I'm a woman.' And he said, 'No.' I said, 'Does it help?' and he said, 'Maybe.'"[9] In truth, Hayes appointed her out of respect for her science, she says. Weisz was professor and head of the Division of Reproductive Biology in the Department of Obstetrics and Gynecology at the Hershey Medical Center at Pennsylvania State University, where Hayes had previously worked. Regardless of his reasoning, she eagerly accepted the honorable role.

At just over five feet tall, Weisz probably did not cut an imposing figure at the PBI. But she was resolute, a quality that emerged early in her dramatic life. Having fled Hungary three weeks before the start of World War II, she says that "the Holocaust and the reality of what we can do as human beings is very real, very close to me. . . . You must go on pushing what you believe in." After the war, as a young student at Cambridge University, she had a seminal encounter with a Hitler supporter whose opinion she was unable to change. "I said to myself at that point, 'I will not cease to try to explain and make my position clear. However, I recognize this exists and I will not let it deter me.'. . . And I think this is what I carry with me."[10]

Weisz took her role as chairperson of the PBI very seriously. In preparation for the hearing, she pored over the data with her assistant, Rita Shinnar, and "really analyzed everything that we could lay our hands on and tried to do it as scientifically as possible," she recalls. The more she

FIGURE 8 Photograph of Dr. Judith Weisz circa 1983, wearing the suit in which she conducted the FDA Public Board of Inquiry hearing.

read, the more horrified she was at what she believed to be an inappropriate use of Depo-Provera. But perhaps most upsetting was the manipulation of evidence. "I was appalled at the poor, poor science and the way that science was being used for political or emotional positions that the investigators had," she says. "There were no good studies. And it taught me something. . . . The potential of special interest . . . distorts the science; it is not the best possible science."[11] Weisz became determined to resolve the controversy surrounding the drug by "evaluating the scientific validity of the information available."[12] In her introductory remarks on that first morning of the hearing, January 10, 1983, she noted, "We realize this is a complex and emotional issue on which people have taken certain viewpoints and have taken them strongly."[13] But, she stressed, the objective of the hearing was to weigh scientific evidence, not to determine the implications of that science.

That task would turn out to be nearly impossible. Though Weisz's desire was to focus solely on scientific evidence to determine the future of Depo-Provera, she was keenly aware of the difficulty of separating the science from the society that produced it. The room was filled with special interest groups that had a vested interest in shaping the outcome of the hearing. Upjohn, the company that produced Depo-Provera, had appealed the FDA in 1978 in the hopes that a PBI would prevent consumer and feminist activists from participating in the hearing. The company hoped that the board would limit its attention to "expert witnesses": research scientists and clinicians who had studied the effects of the drug on animal and human subjects. "Upjohn believes it is essential that the issues in this proceeding be reviewed and decided by a panel of scientists, rather than a lay person," it explained. "The issues . . . are technically complex, require an understanding of sophisticated scientific concepts, and necessitate the comprehension and evaluation of a large body of scientific literature and other data."[14]

The FDA Bureau of Drugs initially balked at Upjohn's request, remarking that "the notion that only scientists and physicians can understand the issues in this hearing is patently false."[15] Consumer and health activists agreed. Feminist health activists in particular responded with outrage at the notion that they, as potential users of the drug, were not qualified to weigh the evidence. They interpreted this scientific hearing as just one piece of a larger conspiracy to silence their voices and inflict damage on their bodies. Along with the FDA's Bureau of Drugs, they did not believe that such a controversial matter could result in any sort of "objective" results, or that disinterested scientists could even be found to serve on such a board.

Despite these reactions, FDA commissioner Donald Kennedy granted Upjohn's request to hold a PBI. He believed that the use of qualified experts would "add another dimension to the analysis of the questions presented at the hearing." He also disagreed with the notion that a PBI should avoid controversial matters, explaining, "Determining whether a drug is 'safe' always involves a risk-benefit judgment. . . . I do not believe that the use of a PBI should be confined to proceedings in which there is no need to resolve a risk-benefit issue."[16] He did not realize in 1978 that it would take the FDA another five years of preparation to carry out Upjohn's request.

By the morning of January 10, 1983, all interested parties had had ample time to practice their lines and gather their props. The well prepared included Dr. Weisz herself, who knew that her objectivity was questioned. As she explains, "This is one of the reasons that I insisted that we bring in I don't know how many files. We had a whole big filing cabinet behind, as a backdrop."[17] For Weisz, appearance was nearly as important as actual preparation.

Women's health activists affiliated with the National Women's Health Network, who had learned from previous contraceptive controversies, also arrived at the PBI armed with evidence. They charged that Depo-Provera represented "another massive experiment like those of the Pill and DES, which have caused severe and unnecessary damage to thousands of women."[18] To document this "massive experiment," the NWHN had created a registry of women using the drug so that it could track the damages incurred. By the time of the hearing, the group had accrued 529 registrants and hundreds of additional letters, the majority of which attested to the suffering of users who were not prepared for the crippling side effects of the drug. Seated in the room that morning listening to Dr. Weisz's introduction was the *Our Bodies, Ourselves* coauthor and NWHN witness Judy Norsigian, who had taken the train down from Boston, her infant in one arm, a large box of these testimonials in the other.

On that same morning a few miles away, the NWHN held a press conference in the Senate Room of the Capitol Hilton Hotel. Standing in front of dozens of microphones and television cameras and flanked by flow charts, executive director Belita Cowan vowed to file a class action lawsuit against the Upjohn Company, and to launch a nationwide search for additional Depo-Provera victims to join the suit. The testimonial letters in Norsigian's possession at the PBI proceedings took center stage at this event. The writers' experiences with the drug were listed on the flow charts next to Cowan. Side effects such as blood clots, depression, menstrual irregularities, and breast tumors were categorized and quantified in bold colors. "Our nation's drug safety standards are being threatened," Cowan began. "If Depo Provera is approved as a contraceptive, it will be the first time in F.D.A. history that a contraceptive is allowed on the market which has failed the required animal safety tests. . . . Such a dangerous precedent could affect every future regulatory decision. It would affect every future prescription drug, and virtually every person in our country. We believe it would be a terrible mistake."[19] In a dramatic gesture, she held up the long list of side effects of Depo-Provera published in the *Physician's Desk Reference* in her left hand, and Upjohn's patient package insert, about the size of a postcard, in her right. No layperson viewing this would miss the suggestion that Upjohn was intentionally hiding pertinent information from patients.

But the most compelling aspect of the press conference, according to reporters, was the "tearful" testimonials of three victims of Depo-Provera, flown in from as far away as California to participate. It was

FIGURE 9 Belita Cowan, executive director of the National Women's Health Network, displays instructions for the use of Depo-Provera, an injected contraceptive, at a news conference. In her right hand are the brief instructions included in the contraceptive package for the consumer; in her left are instructions given to physicians. Photograph by AP Images. Reprinted by permission.

their pictures and stories that captured media attention. Thirty-six-year-old Sandra Martin had been given Depo-Provera during two different pregnancies and had not been informed that it was not FDA approved as a contraceptive or that any risks were involved in its use. Both of her children were born with structural deformities, and she suffered from severe depression, weight gain, and ovarian cysts. After experiencing terrible side effects from the Pill and then an IUD, Adele Butterfield agreed to try Depo-Provera as a contraceptive. "I distinctly remember asking [my doctor] what the side effects were, and he told me there were none." Six months later, she was extremely depressed. "I lost interest in everything: my boyfriend, sex, my child, and my job." Then she was diagnosed as having cervical cancer. "I feel as though a time bomb has been placed in my body. . . . I live in constant fear that the cancer will come back." Barbara Askinosie suffered from a menstrual disorder and was prescribed Depo-Provera's pill form, Provera, as a treatment. Shortly thereafter she developed mammary dysplasia. "I live in the shadow of these risks and the fear of one day developing breast cancer," she declared.[20]

Back in the Hubert Humphrey Building, there were no tearful testimonials at the PBI that morning, nor would there be over the next four days of the hearing. Yet there was certainly an awareness that media coverage might undermine the appearance of scientific objectivity in the proceedings. When a documentary filmmaker, Karen Branan, requested videotaping the hearing, the Upjohn Company balked. "The constant presence of cameras with the intended purpose of producing edited materials for a documentary film would turn a scientific forum into a media-based event," the company's spokesman declared. Branan had a bias, Upjohn believed, because she was a member of the NWHN, and was producing the documentary to "encourage women to organize around the Depo Provera issue." It felt that her position put the company at an obvious disadvantage in that "the film would undoubtedly emphasize emotional statements and evidence." Furthermore, Upjohn argued, certain witnesses might refuse to testify under such conditions, thus forcing the company to find last-minute replacements. Videotaping would also negatively impact the entire hearing because it "could have a chilling effect on the gathering of necessary evidence." In its statement, Upjohn articulated what was to be the biggest challenge for everyone involved—from the chairperson herself, to scientists, to corporate figures, to women's health activists: to leave emotion out of the proceedings. File cabinets and boxes of registry documents surely assisted participants in maintaining such professional demeanor, but, according to Upjohn, cameras might lead to a more complex scenario. "The presence of cameras for the purpose of producing such a film might encourage theatrics or emotional statements rather than the objective scientific testimony intended by the panel. As a result, the Public Board of Inquiry could be depicted in a manner that would emphasize the emotional rather than the scientific nature of the proceedings."[21] In this gendered analysis, "emotional" was equated with the women's health agenda, and tearful testimonials with something fundamentally feminine and thereby unscientific.

Initially, Weisz concurred and prohibited any videotaping of the PBI. "I do this reluctantly," she acknowledged two weeks before the hearing, "because I am not unmindful of the policy and obligation of the Federal Government . . . to conduct its public business as openly as possible." But she believed the taping would prevent the PBI from "fulfilling its purpose." The NWHN and Ralph Nader's Health Research Group immediately appealed her decision. Their appeal was undoubtedly strengthened by a letter to FDA commissioner Arthur Hayes from the bureau chief of CNN. "We cannot recall any occasion in which the FDA has discriminated against the television media," Larry La Motte wrote. "While such a decision may soothe some pharmaceutical manufacturers—it opens up a big can of worms with the television news industry and the general public it represents." La Motte's final sentence reveals the emotion with which he couched his appeal. "I *implore* you to give careful consideration to our point of view and to take note of our vigorous objections."[22] Such strong language undoubtedly led Weisz to realize "what a political hot potato," in her words, the hearing would become.

The appeal was upheld, and the hearing opened with one camera stationed in the room for its duration. Any witness, however, had the right to refuse being videotaped. Notably, on the first day of the proceedings, which were devoted to Upjohn, seven of the ten witnesses declined to be on camera, some more vocally than others. "Madam Chairman," stated Dr. Roy Hertz, research professor at the George Washington Medical Center, "I have declined to be videotaped because I think it detracts from the objectivity and scientific environment in which this very difficult matter is being evaluated."[23] Jess Stribling, the FDA attorney, recalls that the possibility of videotaping was "shocking and even abhorrent to three very gifted and able medical researchers who were not accustomed to doing their work in front of the camera." In his assessment, they were "afraid that it was going to turn into a grand mess, and become a sideshow."[24] Those most likely to cause a scene, they feared, were the feminist health activists.

The irony is that, according to Weisz, the only witness who "introduced an element of partisanship" into the proceedings was not a feminist activist, but a male supporter of Depo-Provera who opposed being videotaped. He introduced "a kind of pugilistic perspective," she remembers. "You know for him this was a game, in a way. And for me it wasn't a game. It couldn't be." She and the other members of the PBI felt strongly that they had to keep emotional outbursts under control. "I wanted the scientists to speak, to feel obliged to keep to the science, which we could critique. I can't critique all other things."[25]

Regulatory Revolution at the FDA

The last-minute debate over videotaping underscored the challenges of incorporating outsiders into FDA regulatory decisions. In fact, the agency had spent the previous decade transforming itself from a relatively powerless "cog in the Federal regulatory bureaucracy" into one of its most "important and visible components."[26] Under the direction of Commissioner Charles Edwards and General Counsel Peter Hutt, it spent much of the 1970s "trying to adapt its form and function to the new realities of greater public involvement, a more accessible government, and scientifically-based decision-making."[27] The FDA found itself much more susceptible to public interest, largely because of new legislation (such as the Freedom of Information Act) that opened up 90 percent of its files to the public.[28] Consumer activists and organizations such as the Health Research Group demanded information about the safety of products on the market. They also, as in the case of the Depo-Provera PBI, generated media attention as a way of drawing the public's attention to safety and regulatory decisions. They demanded not only greater access to information, but more involvement in making the decisions that affected public safety. They began to realize that, in scholar Barbara Troetel's words, "risk/benefit decisions were not necessarily scientific calculations but political judgments which they had a right to help make."[29] This certainly played a role in the expectations of activists attempting to keep Depo-Provera off the market.

But greater public accessibility was not the only concern that Commissioner Edwards addressed in the 1970s. He recognized that the FDA "needed to upgrade its scientific capabilities and draw upon the expertise of the nation's community of scientists and physicians."[30] He developed a system of advisory committees to make use of expert scientific opinion. He explained, "I think it is all terribly important, because the complexity of the decisions, both scientific and technological, that we make every day are only as strong as the science behind them. A regulatory agency like FDA must have scientific credibility."[31]

Commissioner Edwards appointed Peter Hutt, a lawyer for Covington and Burling, as FDA general counsel. In his three and a half years in that position (before returning to C&B), Hutt radically transformed agency procedures. In what came to be called "Peter's Preambles," he offered detailed explanations of all factors that contributed to FDA regulatory policy, alongside any official changes.[32] He was determined to make information available to all interested parties, something previously unknown to the FDA. Through his preambles, he offered a window into the formerly secretive world of food and drug regulation. As a lawyer, he wanted everything to be clearly structured and standardized.

The challenge was to incorporate this style of enforcement into a scientific setting. As a lawyer, Hutt wanted definitive yes or no answers to his questions regarding drug safety. FDA counsel Jess Stribling, Hutt appointee, heard that Hutt once met with the scientists at the FDA's Cancer Research Center and asked, "On all of the questions of safety I will have only one question for you and I want a yes or no—does it or does it not cause cancer?" Stribling found this to be "an interesting example of the difference between the lawyer and the scientist, but also the needs of a government agency making regulatory decisions." Hutt may have wanted clear-cut answers, but "scientists of their very nature always want more data, and they should. They are looking for truth . . . and so they tend to be exhaustive and color what they say with all kinds of conditions."[33] The end result of this difference in perspective was a giant discrepancy in how to define "good science." Despite Hutt's desire for a definitive answer, determining whether or not a drug should be allowed on the market was not a black and white issue. Instead, FDA regulators applied a *risk-benefit assessment* to evaluate whether a drug's benefit outweighed its risks. By the 1970s, as the author Philip Hilts points out, it was possible to "calculate what the hazards of a substance or action might be to society; a similar accounting of its benefit could be made as well. The notion was revolutionary."[34]

But it raised new questions. Who was qualified to make such an assessment? What factors should be included when determining a risk/benefit ratio? The complexities of such a decision emerged clearly with the debate in 1977 over whether to ban saccharin, a calorie-free sweetener that caused cancer in rats. The campaign to keep saccharin on the market included arguments about the more dire consequences that would occur as people returned to greater sugar intake. Ultimately, more people would be affected by obesity than by cancer, opponents argued. The extreme doses given to rats suggested to some that anything, in large enough quantities, will cause cancer. As one reporter noted, "Because the idea of a human being drinking 800 cans of soft drinks a day is grotesque, there is somehow a widespread disbelief in the validity of animal tests." In the case of saccharin, scientists failed to convince the American people that its risks outweighed its benefits; Congress prevented the FDA from banning the product.[35]

Thus, risk-benefit assessment involved more than a simple mathematical formula. By the 1970s, special interest groups demanded a role in regulatory decision making. Determining a drug's safety and efficacy became a negotiation between different actors who interpreted evidence in drastically different ways. Scientific experts and consumer representatives sat side by side more frequently as the number of FDA advisory committees grew over the decade, but that does not mean that they always worked harmoniously. Consumer representatives frequently remarked that they recognized the difference between having the opportunity to voice their opinion and actually effecting change. They were aware that industry, scientific, and pharmaceutical professionals viewed them as outsiders. Over the course of the decade, however, they became "more sophisticated in their lobbying techniques."[36] The result was sometimes even greater antagonism and conflict between those who supported the marketing of a drug and those who viewed it as unsafe.[37]

The Burden of Birth Control: From the Pill to the Dalkon Shield

Unlike saccharin, however, the debate over Depo-Provera tapped into an already explosive political issue. Reproductive politics, as Rickie Solinger argues, "has been and remains one of the most fiercely contested and most complicated subjects about power in American society."[38] Whether fertility is controlled externally, by coercive measures, or voluntarily, by individual choice and access to safe and reliable methods, radically alters individual meaning and experience. Poor women and women of color have had to negotiate economic and institutional constraints that blur the boundary between voluntary and coercive. As activist and scholar Loretta Ross explains, "our ability to control what happens to our bodies is constantly challenged by poverty, racism, environmental degradation, sexism, homophobia, and injustice in the United States."[39] Documented cases of sterilization abuse and unsafe testing procedures on women of color led many to see that what may constitute reproductive freedom for some women "is reproductive tyranny for others."[40]

The Depo-Provera controversy can only be understood within the history of hormonal contraceptives and the emergence of the birth control pill. As reproductive endocrinologist Carol Korenbrot noted, the politics of contraception changed dramatically with the introduction of biomedical technology. "What is new about contraception," she observed shortly before the PBI hearings, "is the promotion of the development of new biomedical contraceptives by scientists and physicians, national governments, private groups concerned with the rate of population growth, and the drug industry. Because of this," she continued, "the research and development of new contraceptives has become entwined in politics, both national and international."[41]

Emerging at the dawn of the sexual revolution, the Pill raised expectations that women were sexually available without the threat of unwanted pregnancy. By 1965, over six million women had taken oral contraceptives. Planned Parenthood noted that 70 percent of clients using its services for birth control chose to get a prescription for the Pill.[42] This form of contraception offered many advantages over barrier methods: it was highly effective, convenient, and entirely separated from the act of intercourse. It also did not require the consent or even awareness of a male sexual partner. Both physicians and female patients initially expressed enthusiasm for this new form of birth control.

Yet by the end of the 1960s, many had lost confidence in the Pill. The first, Enovid, contained approximately ten times the amount of progesterone and four times the amount of estrogen used in later doses. As a result, many women suffered from severe side effects, including blood clots and heart attacks. Working as a columnist for the *Ladies' Home Journal*, Barbara Seaman (who would later help create the National Women's Health Network) began receiving letters from her readers who were concerned about the risks of using the Pill. "I started finding out very early on that the patients taking the pill didn't agree with the doctors that it was perfectly safe and simple and wonderful," she wrote.[43] She followed up by interviewing other users, along with physicians and other health professionals, revealing a more widespread concern about the effects of the hormonal contraceptive. The resulting book, *The Doctors' Case against the Pill*, inspired Senator Gaylord Nelson to hold congressional hearings on the safety of oral contraceptives in 1970.

While Seaman's book had not initially garnered much attention, the hearings received "intense media coverage."[44] Nelson used many of the same physicians that Seaman had interviewed as expert witnesses for the hearing. But he did not ask Seaman—or any Pill users—to testify. For this he experienced the wrath of feminists who at one point interrupted testimony, shouting from the audience: "Why is it that scientists and drug companies are perfectly willing to use women as guinea pigs?" and "Why have you assured the drug companies that they could testify?. . . They're not taking the pills, we are!"[45] They were promptly dismissed from the room, but their outburst appeared on the evening news. This vivid scene was undoubtedly on the minds of Upjohn officials thirteen years later when they feared the presence of cameras at the Depo-Provera PBI.

One research scientist who appeared both in Seaman's book and in the Nelson hearings as a critic of the Pill was Hugh Davis, associate professor of obstetrics and gynecology at Johns Hopkins. "Never in history have so many individuals taken such potent drugs with so little information as to actual and potential hazards," he declared—a statement that would be NBC's evening news lead-in to the hearings on January 14, 1970.[46] Instead, Davis advocated use of a new intrauterine device, ostensibly much safer than hormonal contraceptives.

What he did not reveal in his testimony was that he was the designer of this new IUD, called the Dalkon Shield. Made from plastic, it was in the shape of a shield, with ten "fins" or "claws" intended to attach to the uterus to prevent expulsion of the device.[47] In 1971, the A. H. Robins Company introduced Davis's IUD as the "Cadillac of contraception"—modern, effective, and safe. One advertisement that Robins ran in several OB-GYN journals claimed the Dalkon Shield was "the only

IUD anatomically engineered for optimum uterine placement, fit, toler-
ance, and retention." It also claimed the device was highly effective, with
a very low pregnancy rate of 1.1 percent.[48] Due to a massive marketing
campaign, the Dalkon Shield quickly became the IUD of choice, captur-
ing 10 percent of the entire contraceptive market.[49] Robins distributed
4.5 million of the IUDs to eighty countries before sales were halted in the
mid-1970s; about half of these had been inserted in American women.[50]
Many of these women had turned to the Dalkon Shield because of the
recent Pill scare.

But some began to express concern about the widespread use of the
new device, as well as the touted efficacy rates. In 1972, Dr. Thad Earl, a
general practitioner in Ohio who served as a consultant to A. H. Robins,
informed the company that six of his patients in whom he had inserted
Dalkon Shields became pregnant with the device implanted. Five of these
women suffered from spontaneous infected abortions. Further reports of
spontaneous abortions (miscarriages), as well as large numbers of cases
of pelvic inflammatory disease, raised questions about the efficacy and
safety of the Dalkon Shield.[51] One woman wrote to *Ms. Magazine* in
July of 1975 to explain why she was part of a large lawsuit against A. H.
Robins. After suffering severe abdominal pains for three weeks and getting little help from several doctors, she landed in the emergency room
of a large hospital. "Had it not been for a cautious, young resident,"
she wrote, "I might not be alive today." He rushed her into surgery and
discovered that severe infection threatened her right fallopian tube. "I
hope as many Dalkon Shield wearers as possible will have their IUD removed—to be on the safe side. It seems to me, after my experience, one
can't trust the safety of such a product, or even the decisions and suggestions of a doctor about such a product."[52]

In 1974, the FDA implicated A. H. Robins in the deaths of four-
teen Dalkon Shield users. In addition, the agency acknowledged that
thousands of women suffered complications and injuries from all IUDs
(though it found the Dalkon Shield to be the most dangerous). In Barbara
Seaman's next bestseller, *Women and the Crisis in Sex Hormones*, she
entitled her section on IUDs "Pain and Perforation."[53] Those words
aptly described the experiences of some users who chose to write letters
about their experience to *Ms. Magazine*. One woman had recently had
an IUD inserted at a Planned Parenthood clinic. "I expected some initial
pain afterwards, but when it continued so severely the following day I
called them to see if I could have it removed immediately," she wrote. "I
was going through more pain than I'd ever experienced in my life and it

just didn't seem worth it to be putting my body through that." She was surprised with the response she received. "They just told me to put my feet up, take aspirin, put a heating pad on my abdomen and 'wait it out' (none of which helped, by the way). . . . The doctors are there to put in these devices but where are they afterward when you really need them?" she asked. "It frightens me to think how little control we have of our bodies in situations as serious as these. And can't something be done about it?"[54] A writer from Rescue, California, reflected, "It was a horrifying experience to know you are healthy yet you have to be cut open to have a foreign object removed. The emotional strain was as difficult to bear as the pain resulting from the first time I tried to straighten up after the operation."[55] Stories such as these undoubtedly raised concern among contraceptive users about the presence of a foreign object hidden deep within their bodies. Their emotional intensity and graphic details further established the power of patient testimonials to educate women about the hidden dangers of contraceptive use.

Depo-Provera Testimonials

By the time of the PBI on Depo-Provera, health activists involved in the National Women's Health Network had become far more astute in recruiting patient stories to illustrate what they believed to be the harmful qualities of the drug. They had also raised greater awareness and funds for women's health activism. The idea of creating such a network emerged in 1974, a brainstorm of Barbara Seaman and Belita Cowan, who believed that women's health should have a lobbying presence in Washington, D.C.[56] The organization was incorporated in 1976 with a twelve-member board of directors, and members consisted of both individuals and women's health organizations. The NWHN's budget, which was about $22,000 when the PBI hearings were first announced in 1979, was nearly $500,000 by the time they were held in 1983. During those same years, individual membership grew from under 3,000 to about 13,000.[57]

Through the NWHN newsletter and advertisements in women's magazines, the network solicited over 800 responses from Depo-Provera users interested in joining its patient registry. Though these responses are not necessarily representative of the larger patient population receiving Depo-Provera injections (with a clear bias toward those who were dissatisfied with the drug), they provide crucial evidence of how concerned women chose to interpret the drug's effects on their minds and bodies.[58]

Sheryll, for example, wrote the NWHN in 1984, "This letter is written to register myself as one of the Depo Provera guinea humans," suggesting that she saw herself as an unwitting subject. Her biggest concern, she explained in her letter, was that she had to watch her daughter face the same difficult choices about birth control that she had dealt with more than a decade earlier. Her daughter could not tolerate an IUD, failed with the diaphragm, and was currently taking birth control pills. "This is not progress," she wrote. "This is not the purpose of the FDA. . . . I think we are facing a national disgrace."[59]

Three weeks after having a hysterectomy to stop severe bleeding after a Depo-Provera injection, twenty-two-year-old Sara read about the NHWN patient registry in *Ms.* Though her anger was "clouding [her] senses," she vowed that her story was true. "Thank you for caring about this and me," she wrote from Buffalo, New York.[60] Nancy picked up the same issue of *Ms.* and decided to contact the network. "My experience you might not be interested in," she wrote from Delray Beach, Florida, "but I'd like to add my name to your list of unfortunate women who also received this drug." She proceeded to tell her story over four handwritten pages, documenting more than ten years of physical discomfort from endometriosis and her disillusionment with the medical profession. "I just want my story told to let other women know that if you need the help keep searching. There is someone out there who will believe in you and help you. . . . Thank you for letting me tell my story."[61] Like the readers of *Our Bodies, Ourselves* who shared their stories with the Boston Women's Health Book Collective, these women believed that their personal experiences could help to restructure the knowledge base about reproductive medicine.

Some described Depo-Provera as having taken an enormous toll on their emotions and personal life. Kay, for example, sought legal advice about the drug after experiencing severe side effects. She recalled that she was not given any warning about these risks and did not sign any consent forms. She experienced heavy bleeding from her 250-mg dosage and told her doctor she did not want to receive any more injections, but he suggested increasing the dosage to 400 mg instead. "Since I have received these shots," she declared in an affidavit, "I have experienced such spells of weakness that I felt like my body was encased in a huge block of cement, and I could hardly drag it around." When trying to retrieve a piece of paper that had fallen under her bed, she claimed that she could not get back up off the floor for half an hour, due to weakness. She also experienced depression, vision problems, painful intercourse, and weight gain, though she did not initially connect these effects to the drug. "Then I discovered the truth about Depo Provera, and all of my mysterious symptoms fell into place," she wrote.[62]

This notion of "discovering the truth"—or the belief that the drug's actual effects were finally coming to light as a result of the women's health movement—influenced many women who chose to join the NWHN registry. Several discussed their frustration with a physician or clinician who made them feel like it was "all in their head." One recalled, "I was so uncomfortable—even miserable—on this medication that I pleaded with the dr. to tell me if certain symptoms could be related to the drug. I would say 'does this medication cause nervousness or depression?'; he'd say—always 'do you feel nervous or depressed? Are you sure you're not just feeling overly emotional about your failure to get pregnant?' so I'd drop it. Or he'd relate any symptom to my being overweight only."[63] Another remembered, "When I began having very severe pain in my breasts and hot spots I mentioned this to the doctor and he replied 'all you women are alike. You all think you have cancer. Just keep up with the injections.'"[64] One presented her theory as to why patients encountered this phenomenon. "I'm sure you and other women in your group have run into the 'I can't find out what's wrong—so it must be in your head' syndrome so many physicians suffer from," she wrote. "It's easier and less ego-damaging than saying 'I don't know what's causing the problem.'"[65]

For some, learning what they believed to be "the truth" about Depo-Provera—in other words, that it might be responsible for their symptoms—brought them relief along with frustration. One declared, "I am sorry that I ever took this drug; however, I am finally at peace as to explain why so many medical things have happened to a 'healthy' person—I know that the headaches (vascular—severe in nature), the acute depression, the screwed up periods, the tremendous weight gain (still gives me trouble), the hair loss, and many other lesser side effects are due to the Depo Provera injections and provera pills. For years (11) I have thought, 'what is wrong with me? is it in my mind?' now, I know!!!"[66]

Most of those who chose to participate in the NWHN patient registry indicated that they were not aware that Depo-Provera had not been approved by the FDA for contraceptive use, or that it had potential side effects. For example, only 16 out of 322 women who filled out one particular version of the registry checked that they were satisfied with the drug. As a result, many presented themselves as unwitting subjects of an experiment rather than as informed patients. Many compared themselves to test animals. Janice remarked, "I feel like a lab rat," after one injection of Depo-Provera was followed by crippling leg pain, weight gain, and depression. "It pains me to think that before this happened I was a normal 30-year-old single woman working on my college degree at the University of Texas," she continued.[67] Renee wrote, "I can't believe that on top of everything else that happened to me they would give me a drug that had not been fully tested or approved. I feel like a human guinea pig."[68] Celestine, who was diabetic, had two injections of Depo-Provera at the Grady Clinic in Atlanta and experienced "overwhelming symptoms. . . . I think I was just a guinea pig."[69] She added that she had kept the drug in her refrigerator as a reminder. Though she did not specify what she wanted to be reminded of, we can assume that it was Depo-Provera's misuse. Patricia, diagnosed as having endometriosis, expressed anger that she had trusted the doctor and was not told about side effects. "The only positive result of the experience was that I began to be greatly concerned about the medical/pharmaceutical world's use of women as guinea pigs."[70]

Others portrayed themselves as unwitting human subjects. "I was a Depo Provera victim for one year in 1967–68," recalled Sarah, blaming the drug's side effects for ruining her marriage. "At the time I took the Shot I was happily married. After one year of hating it when my husband touched me, and being depressed so chronically, so much damage had been done to our bonds of trust and love that we proceeded to get a divorce." Her anger stemmed from her sense of betrayal, and she portrayed herself as an unknowing subject. "To be part of a study and to be ignored when you are the one to report side effects is an unconscionable act by the drug companies pushing their wares."[71] Another wrote that although she believed her case was not "as serious as others," she felt "violated that I was used in negligent medical practice."[72] One woman, who was fifteen when she had been given the shot as a contraceptive at the Grady Clinic, felt in retrospect that she had been too young and naïve in her willingness to be injected with Depo-Provera. "If I knew then what I knew now I would have never taken the shot," she wrote on her registry form.[73] Underscoring the coercive use of the drug on some poor women of color, another Grady patient wrote that her welfare caseworker ordered her to take the drug. "She said that if I didn't take it my check would be cut off."[74]

The stories about Depo-Provera use that emerge from the majority of the NWHN registry forms (and attached letters) are filled with emotion—anger, frustration, fear, confusion, and determination. Most complained about an unexpected side effect—or a condition that they believed to be a side effect—of the drug. Many would not have thought about the risks were it not for the "Stop Depo-Provera" campaign launched by the NWHN, or the media coverage it promoted (including special episodes on Phil Donahue's talk show and *Hour* magazine, to which many registrants referred). There is a feeling of injustice and outrage that a drug they now believed to be hazardous was used so freely on healthy women. The registrants also shared the assumption that since the FDA had not approved Depo-Provera as a contraceptive (which many claimed not to understand when they had agreed to the injections), it was unsafe.

Activist Strategies

These were precisely the images that the NWHN wanted to capture—indeed, helped to create—to draw attention to what it believed was reckless use of the drug. These were the testimonials that it wanted entered as evidence in the PBI. The network did, in fact, submit a stack of letters and registry forms into the public record. And *Our Bodies, Ourselves* coauthor Judy Norsigian carried a box of these documents to the hearing, its weightiness a reminder of the many women negatively affected by the drug.

But because of the nature of the hearing—a scientific board of inquiry—the NWHN was discouraged from presenting this type of anecdotal, emotional evidence. As soon as the FDA commissioner granted Upjohn's request, the network sought legal counsel to investigate ways in which it could remain involved in the hearing, despite its scientific format. Its attorneys stressed that the hearings would be "extremely scientific," unlike congressional or legal proceedings, "which tend to be imprecise and involve more sociological/political presentations." Instead, presentations and rebuttal would be very technical; speakers would be engaged in "complex scientific discourse." They cautioned the NWHN to restrict witnesses to real experts—in order to be taken seriously. The group must put forth "hard scientific evidence" and "refrain from including presentations on the sociological, political or economic aspects of the problem."[75]

This warning—limit their presentation to "hard scientific evidence" and expert witnesses—forced these activists to confront problems with their ideology. If they truly believed that expertise is rooted in individual bodies, and that knowledge is experience-based rather than acquired through advanced medical degrees, then this was a fruitless task. All women are thereby experts, and it would be impossible to refrain from sociological aspects of the problem.

This resistance is apparent in some of the activists' preparations for the hearing. Most notably, Gena Corea, a strong-minded feminist activist and journalist who had published *The Hidden Malpractice: How American Medicine Mistreats Women* in 1977, struck a controversial chord in the first draft of her PBI testimony:

> It is not often the voices of women are heard in such rooms as this and they may occasionally be loud for having been stifled so long. We will speak in a different voice. The words we choose may sound strange to the experts gathered here. We will not speak of "therapeutic modalities" in referring to drugs which may cause cancer in our bodies or impair our ability to resist disease, nor will we describe that devastation to our bodies, to our very beings, as "epidemiological fall-out," a phrase which moves like fog across the mind to obscure tremendous female suffering.[76]

This draft elicited concern from other NWHN supporters planning to testify—one even threatening to withdraw unless the testimony was changed—because they believed such comments would only antagonize. "Gena's written testimony is an attempt to interject her own value judgments into a scientific setting and call it a scientific paper," declared Vicki Jones, MPH, whom the network had asked to testify. She found that most of Corea's paper consisted of assumptions, not facts. "I cannot follow a testimony that is unscientific, hostile, and inappropriate," she explained. "I feel this type of testimony will create a hostile and unreceptive atmosphere and will ultimately discredit those like myself who are qualified and trained to give scientific testimony in a professional manner." Instead, she believed that "the surest approach to get scientists to listen, rather than just to hear, is to fight expertise with expertise."[77]

The difference between the two approaches—one emotional, the other rational—speaks to the fundamental dilemma faced by feminist health activists by the 1980s. On one hand, they criticized science and scientific inquiry for ignoring women's experiences and perspectives. On the other, they wanted to influence scientific regulation and policy, which required playing by the rules—fighting "expertise with expertise." But in attempting to present themselves as both outsiders and insiders, they threatened their legitimacy in both groups. They sought to "reform science by exerting pressure from the outside," in the words of sociologist Steven Epstein, "but also to perform science by locating themselves on the inside."[78] At the PBI, this tension was apparent even before the hearing began, with the controversy over whether videotaping would "encourage theatrics or emotional statements rather than . . . objective scientific testimony," as Upjohn's attorney suggested it would—an obvious attack on feminist politics.[79]

Incorporating an evidenced-based approach to the Depo-Provera debate required outside counsel. The Washington, D.C., firm of Steptoe & Johnson agreed to provide the NWHN with pro-bono legal representation in connection with the hearing by providing assistance on procedural matters. While the firm expected the NWHN to "take the lead in developing its position and contacting witnesses and formulating their testimony," it was "consulted concerning strategy and the general development of the Network's position." It also agreed to represent the group at the hearing.[80]

But most of the preparation work for the hearing was done by individual members of the NWHN—primarily Belita Cowan, Gena Corea, and Judy Norsigian. One of their intentions was to generate as much publicity on the case as possible, to educate women, especially women of color, about the side effects of Depo-Provera. They did this through network "Newsalerts" and advertisements in women's magazines and African-American newspapers. Health activist Byllye Avery, the only woman of color involved in the founding of the Gainesville Women's Health Center in 1974, also made important connections between the African-American community and women's health activists. She joined the board of the NWHN in the mid-1970s, and along with other women of color in the network began to organize the first national conference on black women's health, to be held at Spelman College in Atlanta in 1983. She moved to Atlanta in 1981, just as the Depo controversy was heating up. The city was home to Grady Memorial Hospital, the site of the controversial Depo-Provera trials.[81]

The Grady Trials

At the center of the political and scientific debate about the use of Depo-Provera as a contraceptive in the United States was a birth control clinic in downtown Atlanta. The Grady Memorial Hospital Family Planning Clinic, founded in 1964, treated over fifty thousand lower-income neighborhood women, primarily women of color, in its first few years.[82] From 1972 to 1978, lower-income women of color received injections at Grady Memorial Hospital as part of the largest U.S.-based clinical trials of Depo-Provera. Birth control advocate Dr. Robert Hatcher, known to

his friends and family as "Captain Condom," oversaw the trials as director of the clinic and remains on the faculty at Emory University, in the
Department of Gynecology & Obstetrics.[83] Approximately nine thousand African-American women were injected with Depo-Provera as part
of the study before it was terminated by the FDA in 1978. The Grady
trials quickly became controversial. Supporters and opponents, policy-
makers, researchers, and activists debated whether the Grady patients
were victims of racist policies that endangered their health, or recipients
of a "superb contraceptive," in Dr. Hatcher's words.[84] Much of the data
later debated at the PBI centered on the controversial Grady studies.

In his own analysis, Hatcher found that Grady patients were enthusiastic about the drug, stressing its convenience and reliability during
interviews he conducted in 1978. "I want the 'shot,'" stated one. "I
don't want to use the pill or anything else. I'd go crazy; I'd worry all the
time about getting pregnant. If they said no more Depo I'd cry. I used it
for five years, stopped and got pregnant one year later. I've been using
it again now for one year. It's the only thing I trust." Far from sounding
like a victim, this patient clearly felt empowered by her ability to receive
the injections. "The shot's the best for me," another Grady patient announced. "I've used it for two years; if they stopped it I'd go through the
floor. . . . It's our choice, not the Government's."[85] Note her emphasis
on choice, suggesting that she was not coerced into receiving Depo injections and believed women should have access to it.

"I'd be very upset about them taking the 'shot' away," another patient
explained. "I've had no problems. I used the pills and my periods were
very long. I also got vaginal cysts. This was an alternative. I enjoy not
having a period. I was so tired of it. . . . It's more convenient; there's no
forgetting. I need it."[86]

Stressing convenience, accessibility, and reliability, these three patients painted a very different portrait of Depo-Provera from those used
by the NWHN. Hatcher and his colleague Dr. Elizabeth Connell (who
also served on the FDA Ob-Gyn Advisory Committee) viewed these types
of comments as more representative of the patient population. "I do not
understand the motivation of people who say out of one side of their
mouth that they care about women and out of this side of their mouth,
based on no scientific data whatsoever, very effectively deny women all
over the world of a very safe and effective method of contraception,"
Connell argued. "I don't understand it."[87] In her assessment, and in
Hatcher's, the real enemy of women's reproductive choice was not Depo-
Provera or the Upjohn Company, but health feminists more interested in
censorship and regulation than freedom of choice. Yet, as the authors of

Undivided Rights point out, " 'choice' implies a marketplace of options in which women's right to determine what happens to their bodies is legally protected, ignoring the fact that for women of color, economic and institutional constraints often restrict their 'choices.' " Many of those opposed to the use of Depo-Provera believed that it was not a safe option, regardless of its reliability or effectiveness.[88]

Judy Norsigian recalls Hatcher's surprise that many feminists did not agree with his position on Depo-Provera.[89] In a letter to Norsigian just days before the PBI began, he wrote, "In spite of the fact that we will be in opposing camps at the hearings in Washington, I look forward to seeing you." Then he clarified his statement. "Actually, we are not in opposing camps at all. We both have the same hopes for sexually active couples—that they be able to use contraception safely and effectively. We just interpret the DMPA data differently." Norsigian disagreed with his position, though she noted that as a father of five daughters, he saw himself as a feminist.[90]

Despite his enthusiasm for Depo-Provera as a contraceptive, Hatcher had to tread carefully in his testimony at the PBI. When he took the stand on January 13, the fourth day of the hearing, his Grady trials had already come under attack. Some witnesses, including Dr. Robert Hoover, an epidemiologist from the National Cancer Institute, pointed out that there were major flaws with the study. There were no controls, nearly 50 percent of the patients were lost to follow-up, and most received minimal exposure to the drug (less than one year). "I think you would want a combination of both a prospective follow-up study and a series of case control studies," Hoover explained, when asked to define what an adequate study would look like.[91] "It should be designed to include a substantial number of women who received meaningful doses or a number of years of use." His final words on the subject probably made Hatcher wince. "I guess I am a little surprised at the inadequacy of the case from the human side given the fact that there is an opportunity to do it."[92] Dr. Renate Kimbrough of the Center for Disease Control agreed. "I feel that this study, number one, is too short in duration. . . . You should follow patients at least for twenty years. . . . In addition to that, the number of patients is really quite small."[93]

But Dr. Howard Ory, also of the CDC, defended the Grady studies. "When you don't know and there isn't a lot of other data available I think any addition to our collective knowledge is worth going ahead with. . . . I think it's worth studying, regardless if it is not a flawless study."[94] He was the author of a report on mortality among young African-American contraceptive users, in which he drew his data from death certificates of 218 women whose names appeared in the Grady records. Seventeen of these women died of cancer, but the majority of these patients had relied on oral contraceptives rather than Depo-Provera. He therefore concluded that the risk of death from cancer for users of the Pill was three times higher than that for Depo users. The study did not allow for patients who had used more than one method, nor did it track women who turned to other hospitals for treatment. "All I can say is that Grady is the mainstay of the medical care for black women in Atlanta," he argued.[95] Atlanta was racially stratified, and "the blacks are hemmed in a way and they go to Grady Hospital because it's right there in the middle."[96]

Hatcher, too, emphasized the racial imbalance at Grady. "Our patients were predominantly black," he explained. "In 1974 it was 91.2 [percent] and in 1978 in was 92.1." But, he stressed, the percentage of Depo-Provera users was roughly the same as for those taking oral contraceptives, suggesting, at least to himself, that there were no racist implications in the decision to offer Depo-Provera.[97] This claim further distanced him from NWHN activists, who argued that the drug was a racist tool of population controllers interested in keeping down particular patient populations.

On the defensive, Hatcher presented himself as a clinician whose time was consumed by running a large and much-needed family planning program. "I do minimal research and I am not a sophisticated epidemiologist," he explained.[98] He emphasized that Grady was a "service setting," one in which funds were consistently cut, which prevented the staff from doing "some things we might have liked."[99] After receiving some critical questions from PBI chair Judith Weisz, he noted, "To be very honest with you, we are not a research unit. I mean, it's not like a research unit. And when we have not had the funds to do something specific we haven't done it."[100]

Though Hatcher felt strongly that Depo-Provera should be approved by the FDA, he knew he needed to exercise caution in his appeal. Five years before the hearing, the FDA had audited, then terminated, the Grady Clinic Depo-Provera study. In its report, the agency's Clinical Investigations Branch noted that "the contraceptive use of Depo Provera at Grady Hospital Family Planning Clinic is routine in nature and is in no way investigational."[101] Complaints included poor record keeping ("No meaningful medical information is recorded and the form is apparently used primarily for billing purposes") and lack of follow-up.[102] Members of the Clinical Investigations Branch committee learned from patient interviews that while most had signed a consent form, they were unaware that Depo-Provera was not FDA approved as a contraceptive. Based on their findings, the committee determined that "the use of Depo Provera at Grady provides neither evidence of safety nor of effectiveness of the drug."[103] At the PBI, Weisz was well aware of these findings. "It's quite clear from the documents that you have admitted that the intent was excellent," she commented. "However, if one reads the report of the audit by the FDA in 1978 it is—it appears that there were some flaws in the translation of the intent into actual action."[104] Hatcher agreed. "I think it was a serious failure. But, however, I do not believe that it was detrimental to our patients."[105]

The NWHN members in attendance disagreed. Though deterred from providing anecdotal evidence at the PBI, they knew from the descriptions in their patient registry that Depo-Provera could be detrimental. Rather than offer individual stories of suffering to the inquiry board, they raised questions about the assumed objectivity of the human studies. Dr. Helen Holmes, science and society scholar at Spelman College, expressed concern about the inadequacy of studies on Depo-Provera; particularly those that "purport to demonstrate absence of harmful effects. . . . Many tests are so designed and conducted that they cannot yield meaningful information about Depo Provera."[106] Her first concern was with the inadequacy of follow-up. "Over the past few days we have been given some amazing figures about the numbers of women who have had Depo Provera, millions of women, and each speaker doesn't seem to agree with the next. I'm concerned about these women; if so many of them have had Depo Provera, where are they and why haven't they been followed?"[107] Such a question begs comparison with the 1970 Nelson pill hearings, during which feminists from D.C. Women's Liberation demanded to know why Pill users were not allowed to testify. But this time around, the concern was being voiced by an investigation participant, not an outsider. As a scholar, Holmes could challenge the methodology of the studies in a way that activists without advanced degrees previously could not.

But it was not just the absence of the women themselves from the data that disturbed Holmes. She also questioned the remarkable absence of reported side effects. "Depo Provera users have complained of completely unpredictable spells of bleeding, of splitting headaches, of loss of sexual desire," she reminded the board. Why was this absent from the data? Holmes provided a sociological explanation, underscoring the critical divisions of gender, class, and race. "The user may be ashamed to describe any of these to a stranger, especially to one of a different social class or race. . . . She may have heard from her friends that their complaints were doubted and/or dismissed as not relevant. Even a normally assertive American woman may be intimidated by the power of the so-called medical mystique."[108] So perhaps the absence could be attributed to the reticence of patients. But another, perhaps more critical problem, Holmes maintained, was that doctors failed to ask about side effects in the first place, or failed to take those they heard about seriously. Was heavy bleeding or depression or migraines a minor issue? These were effects that "can completely ruin the quality of a person's life."[109]

Holmes's strategy—to offer possibilities for the absence of data—indirectly brought the voices and stories from the NWHN patient registry into the hearing. She avoided anecdotal evidence, but still created a setting in which a listener could imagine an innocent woman debilitated by heavy bleeding or blinding headaches. Given that the board's task was to determine whether the benefits of the drug outweighed the risks, such testimony could be interpreted as scientific, because it suggested that quality-of-life issues played a role in determining the risk/benefit ratio. This was thus a subtle yet powerful contribution to the hearing, because it paved the way for a more critical feminist assessment of scientific methods. To dismiss a woman's complaints as being "all in her head" was no longer just sexist—it was bad science.

In the end, the Public Board of Inquiry agreed. On October 26, 1984, it submitted its final report and publicly announced its recommendation that the FDA not approve the drug. As a reporter for the journal *Science* noted, this was a "severe blow" to the Upjohn Company.[110] As Judith Weisz explained in the report, "The facts relating to the long-term consequences of the use of the drug are inadequate and insufficient to provide a basis for risk assessment. This is a serious deficiency in light of the specific questions that have been raised that the drug may have major adverse effects following its long-term use or that may become evident only after a latent period."[111]

Weisz was predominantly critical of how studies at the Grady Clinic had been conducted. "It is particularly unfortunate that the opportunity was missed to collect meaningful information at the Grady Clinic. . . . This was a setting in which, at least theoretically, resources might be expected to have been available for adequate collection of data relevant to the population in the United States."[112] In the absence of substantive data, many of the scientists pooled data to describe the number of "women-years" studied. Significantly, Weisz credited a health feminist with successfully challenging this methodology. "The fallacy of this approach has been stated most aptly by a witness for the Women's Health Network to the effect that while it takes nine months to produce a baby, nine women, each one contributing one month, cannot produce a baby."[113]

Despite Weisz's disdain for how the Depo-Provera studies had been conducted, she agonized over her final report. "I was up all night saying, you know, how am I going to summarize all this experience," she recalls. She knew the PBI's decision would have political and international ramifications. "But if science has anything to say about this, it has to be the best science possible."[114]

Though Upjohn withdrew its appeal as a result of the report, not everyone, of course, supported the PBI's decision. Dr. Elizabeth Connell, Dr. Robert Hatcher's colleague who had testified at the hearing, wrote the newly appointed FDA commissioner, Frank Young, to express her concern about the PBI's report. "Women all over the world will be deprived, either directly or indirectly, of the use of an excellent method of fertility regulation. Thousands of these women will die as the result of unwanted pregnancies and/or illegal abortions."[115]

Commissioner Young disagreed, telling Weisz that she'd "tackled a truly Herculean task in an exemplary manner." He was particularly impressed with what a thorough job she had done. "I know that you worked many nights and weekends wrestling with how to strike an appropriate balance among competing and conflicting concerns." As with Commissioner Edwards and General Counsel Hutt before him, Young supported the idea of professionalizing the FDA with the use of outside experts. Though neither he (nor any of his followers) would oversee another PBI, he found Weisz's role to be "an excellent model of how outside experts can improve public policy decision-making." Weisz had been invaluable, he concluded, "in helping to resolve a very important scientific and public health issue."[116]

Not all outsiders, however, were granted the same honor or authority as was Weisz. Health feminists had come a long way in terms of their political and professional roles in regulatory decisions. They participated in the hearing, and one was even quoted in Weisz's final report as most aptly criticizing the use of "women-years" as legitimate scientific evidence. But they were in a more complicated position than was Weisz (though she, too, calls herself a feminist).[117] They were torn between the experiential evidence provided by the bodies of individuals (the testimonials) and the scientific evidence of experts.

In the end, individual stories played only an indirect role in the hearing. Instead, NWHN activists chose to highlight women such as Adele Butterfield and Barbara Askinosie, victims in a proposed (but unsuccessful) class action lawsuit, at a separate press conference. Professionalism compromised their commitment to these stories, forcing them to develop "insider" credentials. They appropriated the language of scientists, turning to a more traditional type of expert—one whose credentials were listed after her name, not derived from any "authentic experience" as women. Activists now provided more statistics than stories, touting evidence-based medicine over antimedicalization. This compromise resulted in a mixed legacy for women's health. On one hand, it allowed for greater recognition and potential impact within organized medicine, generating more legislation and regulation of women's health research and practice. On the other, it weakened the movement's ideological basis—albeit slippery to begin with—by undermining the notion that knowledge and power are rooted in the biological body.

5 Choices in Childbirth: A Modern Midwife's Tale

When author Joan Haggerty declared her attempt at natural childbirth a failure, she was hardly alone. Her story, "Childbirth Made Difficult," published in *Ms. Magazine* in 1973, represented just one voice in an ever-increasing chorus of American women's complaints about their difficulty in controlling their birth experience. Haggerty had delivered her first child in a British clinic, where she encountered little opposition and lots of support for her desire to remain awake and aware during her baby's birth. But when she tried to recreate the experience in the United States, she met with resistance. She published her story in *Ms.* not to gain sympathy, but to encourage women to respond in kind. "Rather than simply feel martyred," Haggerty urged, "we should pool our energies and revolutionize the system so that we can go to the delivery room fully aware of what will happen there, and confident that our expectations will not be betrayed."[1] Her faith in the ability of American women to revolutionize childbirth in the 1970s is part of a larger story about a movement in transition. This chapter tracks the successes and struggles of expectant mothers and childbirth practitioners to transform the process of childbirth by reclaiming it as a natural rather than a medical event.

Haggerty's birth experience was strikingly similar to that of another author, who had published her experiences more than a decade earlier. Marjorie Karmel had delivered her first child in Europe in the 1950s and hoped to repeat her positive experience of so-called natural childbirth back home in New York City. Karmel learned about the Lamaze method of childbirth from none other than the French obstetrician Fernand Lamaze, who had delivered her first child in Paris. She is credited with introducing and popularizing the technique in the United States with her story *Thank You, Dr. Lamaze*, which was published in 1959 (and reprinted in 2005 "to inspire a new generation of parents-to-be"). In this detailed account, Karmel described the impossible task of "shopping around" for a doctor willing to use the Lamaze technique in the 1950s. Physician reactions ran the gamut from horror (at the backwardness of Europeans), to impatience, to feigned sympathy, to antagonism. Nonetheless, she was determined to give birth without anesthesia, and without pain, by utilizing the series of breathing and muscular exercises designed to manage labor pains.[2]

Like Karmel, Joan Haggerty delivered her first child in Europe without drugs. Pregnant again back in New York, she was optimistic that she would be able to recreate her initial experience with childbirth in an American setting. After all, she had read Marjorie Karmel, along with a growing literature on natural childbirth published in the ensuing decade. She had some reservations about the private clinic she chose, but she was assured that the staff was trained in Lamaze and told that she "probably" would be permitted to have her husband with her in the delivery room, keep her legs out of the stirrups, and refuse anesthesia. But when she finally went into labor (three weeks past her due date), Haggerty had a rude awakening. Five different doctors performed five internal exams. Concerned about the baby's heart rate, one inserted a monitoring device in the middle of a contraction—in her pain, Haggerty swore, only to be reprimanded by the nurse, who said, "Language!" and slapped her wrist. Two other nurses gossiped about boyfriends as she and her husband struggled through Lamaze breathing techniques.[3]

Then things got worse. Wheeled into the delivery room, Haggerty clung to her husband, who was quickly sent out. "Sorry, you make me nervous," the obstetrician told him. Haggerty recalled, "They lowered the stirrups and tied my legs in; I demanded they take them out. More assistants were called to hold me down; they tied my wrists to the table in leather thongs, and when I struggled to sit up, they laughed at me. The doctor told me to push before I was fully dilated, and he manipulated my cervix manually. . . . It was just plain hell. The staff did everything possible to undermine my control and then inferred because women can't control themselves in labor, they have to be strapped down."[4]

Months later, Haggerty remained haunted by her experience. "Everyone is telling us to forget," she reflected in the opening of her birth story. "They say, 'You have a beautiful son. The birth is over. Put it out of your mind.'" But she remained unable to do so. "Every time I nurse my baby, I re-run the scenes of his birth, trying, in fantasy, to deliver him *my* way, rather than the doctor's way." Her expectations that she could remain in control—indeed, reassured by hospital staff that she would be—contributed to her devastation at the outcome. "Despite what was promised me—and so many other women—by the doctors, nurses, and midwives, the hospital did not treat me as a person with individual needs."[5]

If anything clearly divided Haggerty's childbirth experience from Karmel's, other than a decade of social unrest, it was the level of expectations about giving birth "naturally." Karmel expected to encounter resistance about her choice; Haggerty didn't. "My mistake," Haggerty noted, "was that I relied on fantasy. I saw an image in my mind of how the birth was going to go and mistook my wishful thinking for reality."[6]

By 1973, when Haggerty's story was published in *Ms.*, her feminist-based "fantasy" struck a chord with many middle-class educated women who had read *Thank You, Dr. Lamaze* and an ever-increasing literature on childbirth. Growing up in the midst of a burgeoning feminist movement, they struggled to incorporate its principles into the ritual of giving birth. They read *Our Bodies, Ourselves*. They learned that "knowledge equaled power," and that challenging sexism included standing up to doctors and questioning their authority and power. Through "consciousness-raising," they came to believe that their personal experiences had political significance. They made choices—shopped for physicians, questioned procedures, and made new demands. They talked about "rights"—patients' rights, consumers' rights, women's rights, believing that by bringing these stories into public view, they could change the system.

Much to the surprise of these women, the sometimes revolutionary idealism they theorized about did not automatically change the realities of the birth experience. On one hand, they ran up against hospital policies, reluctant physicians, and resentful nurses. As Haggerty noted, "Unfortunately, the more demanding and assertive one is around conservative medical people, the more one is likely to be disliked and even punished." She became, in essence, "the difficult patient."[7]

On the other hand, these women encountered resistance from a divisive feminist community reluctant to embrace a philosophy that had its roots in a conservative celebration of motherhood. Feminist author

Barbara Ehrenreich found the fascination with birth "strangely nostal-gic," hearkening back to a time when "there was no Women's Move-ment to challenge us with totally new options and life-styles."[8] When sociologist Barbara Katz Rothman discovered she was pregnant in 1973, she, too, acknowledged this tension. "I did not want my consciousness raised on the delivery table," she wrote. "I was a feminist and I was pregnant. Those terms should not be mutually exclusive, but in 1973 it often felt as though they were. There had to be a way of having a baby with dignity and joy—as a feminist, not in spite of being a feminist," she declared.[9]

Even within the natural childbirth community (which included both feminists and more traditional women), there existed divisiveness over just what constituted natural childbirth, and who should provide it.[10] As Suzanne Arms wrote in her 1975 childbirth classic, *Immaculate Deception*, "Ask any ten people what the term 'natural childbirth' means and you will probably receive ten different answers. A mother who watched her second birth in a tilted overhead mirror will proudly attest to the joys of 'natural childbirth.' Questioned further, however, she may reveal that she was referring only to the fact that her eyes were open throughout the procedure, and not to the spinal anesthesia which deadened one-third of her body."[11] Doctors also disagreed about how to define natural childbirth—it could mean the absence of an episiotomy, or that the mother remained conscious.[12] Arms concluded that anything short of a C-section could constitute natural childbirth. Yet despite its trendiness by the mid-1970s, "the process itself," she argued, "[was] sel-dom achieved."[13] She noted the "high number of disappointed women who have attempted natural birth in hospitals and found that having a baby hurt like hell, that medication helped, and that the 'joy' of natural childbirth was either a lie or an impossible dream."[14]

Birth in Transition

Individual stories that emerge from *Ms.*, *Our Bodies, Ourselves*, midwife memoirs, and childbirth newsletters capture a process in transition in the 1970s and '80s. Nurses deserted delivery tables to "catch" babies in bathtubs. Hippies flocked to the Farm in Tennessee to recapture the spir-itual element of childbirth under the stars. Middle-class suburban house-wives in places like Bethesda, Maryland, and Beverly, Massachusetts, at-tempted natural deliveries in birth centers. "Lay" midwives battled not only with the law but with nurses, physicians, and nurse-midwives for the right to tend to women at birth.[15] Decades later, malpractice insurance and legal restrictions have devastated home birth practices of both lay and certified nurse-midwives. Cesarean section and infant mortality rates remain higher than most would like. Independent birth centers have been swallowed up by hospitals. Given the growing momentum of natural childbirth in the 1970s, why did it fail to capture a wider range of supporters?

Part of the problem stemmed from varying definitions and types of midwives. Lay midwives (sometimes also referred to as direct-entry midwives) practiced home births without a nursing degree, while certified nurse-midwives received professional training in nursing and met the criteria for certification by the American College of Nurse-Midwives. Many lay midwives who emerged in the 1970s had plenty of training as midwife apprentices but did not participate in a formal education program. They interpreted childbirth as a natural event that should not require medical intervention. Therefore, they felt little affiliation or identification with certified nurse-midwives, whose training and practice took place mainly in hospitals under the supervision of physicians. By the 1980s, the two groups became mired in factionalism over questions of identity and practice, with increasing hostility expressed concerning where and how to deliver (or "catch") babies.

Within these groups, one particular midwife developed a "special place in the modern midwifery movement" as someone uniquely qualified to bridge the gap between the two fields.[16] In 1975, Fran Ventre became the first licensed lay midwife in Maryland since 1924. Two years later, she attended Georgetown University to obtain a degree as a certified nurse-midwife. Georgetown, she explained, "had an outstanding program, one that nurtured rather than rejected my background in lay midwifery."[17] Despite her professional degree, she continued to practice home births and identified primarily as a lay midwife. Her credentials, however, allowed her to represent both groups of midwives. As a founding member of Midwives Alliance of North America in 1982, she attempted a reconciliation between lay and certified nurse-midwives.[18] Her position as both an insider and an outsider to organized medicine provided her with a unique perspective on alternative approaches to childbirth.

A Modern Midwife's Tale

"I shall never forget your help last Wednesday and how you gave me the confidence to last through a long labour and birth my child for myself," Helena wrote on July 18, 1990. "It was a rare gift you gave to me and my daughter, few people are able to give another being such a gift in a whole lifetime and that you can and do help women daily in this most intense experience (often several times a day too) is a remarkable marvel to me."[19] Helena's letter was just one of many thankful responses Fran Ventre received for her role as a midwife. Robin wrote that of her three births, the one with Fran was "truly the most special"; her "calming mannerism and style was exactly the type of support I had hoped for."[20] Ellen and Steve reflected that the birth of their daughter Alicia "was a great experience for both of us because you truly made us feel in control."[21] These grateful parents viewed their midwife as a supportive and affirming presence in what had become an increasingly medicalized process in the United States. What they may not have known are the serious difficulties she encountered on her journey to becoming a midwife.

Fran Ventre was a mother of three living in Montgomery County, an affluent suburb of Washington, D.C., when she began working as a childbirth educator in 1971. She taught expectant parents what was becoming increasingly popular in the 1970s—prepared, or managed, childbirth. Influenced by the work of Lamaze, she taught them breathing and relaxing techniques for pain management. She stressed the importance of being awake and aware for the baby's birth, and bonding with the baby afterward. Much to her frustration, however, hospitals quickly whisked the baby off after delivery, making much of her teaching fruitless. "The anticlimax! I gradually came to realize that what I was teaching in my classes was not natural childbirth but 'defensive childbirth.'"[22]

Up until that point, Ventre had not been an advocate of home birth, considering it "foolhardy"; but what she saw happening to her clients caused her to rethink her position. Her own three birth experiences pushed her further away from hospital births. By the third one, she came to believe that change "would not come from within the institutional establishment, but rather from outside channels of alternatives." She concluded that home birth was "the logical answer," and prophetically announced that "the beginning of the making of a midwife had begun." In 1975, she became the first licensed lay midwife in Montgomery County since 1924, but only "through a combination of contemplation, hard personal work, rigorous self-directed academic preparation, and just plain dogged determination." What kept her on course, she claimed, was her "personal commitment that the practice of midwifery, even in a medically sophisticated technological society, is desperately needed and morally right."[23] In her view, midwifery was not a career but a calling.

Like many modern midwives, Ventre recalled an epiphany in which all the complications of modern childbearing disappeared, replaced by a vision of natural simplicity. For her, it was a trip to the National Zoo. She was there to observe Jenny, a new orangutan mother, who was refusing to breast-feed her baby. Ventre was saddened to see how the zookeepers had quickly taken the baby away from Jenny to feed and raise. She saw a connection between what happened to Jenny and human mothers—medical intervention in the natural processes of birth, bonding, and breast-feeding.

When Ventre brought her children to visit Jenny a few weeks later, she noted the indifference with which Jenny treated her baby. "A frightening realization reverberated through my mind as I returned," she reflected. "Jenny had become civilized. I then knew that I was on my way toward making a decision on how I could help change things."[24] Similar to the mindset of environmentalists in the 1970s, she perceived technology and the American quest for "progress" as destructive not only to humans, but to animals as well.

Ventre was not the only midwife to encounter a primate whose anthropomorphic qualities inspired revelations about midwifery. Ina May Gaskin, who in 1971 settled on "the Farm," a self-contained agricultural collective in Summertown, Tennessee (where she still practices midwifery), recalls how a capuchin monkey taught her about the power of touch. "I learned something from her in touch language that has stayed with me, and this is part of what I have felt I must pass on to any midwife that I teach." When the monkey took hold of her finger, she recalls that she had "never been touched like that before. Her touch was incredibly alive and electric. . . . I had a flash of realization then that my hand wasn't made any different from hers—same musculature, same bony structure, same nervous system. . . . As I transmit the knowledge of spiritual midwifery to other women, I feel that compassion and true touch are of foremost importance."[25] The decision of both Gaskin and Ventre to portray their inspiration as coming from a primate is significant, because it underscores their desire to "naturalize" the birth process. They, along with a growing number of women in the 1970s, believed that most human births require no medical intervention. Birth was primal and instinctive, and required only a safe space in which the mother felt in control. Midwives would lead late twentieth-century American women, overburdened by civilization and technology, back to that safe space.

The first birth Ventre witnessed happened unexpectedly. Her best friend wanted to deliver at home with the assistance of a physician, but the birth happened while the physician was in scheduled surgery. Ventre and another childbirth educator, who happened to also be an underground midwife, delivered the baby. "What I witnessed that day transformed my entire conception of birth," Ventre recalled. "The skill, sensitivity, and caring of one woman for another in helping her at this crucial time to gently give birth to her child was a very powerful and moving experience for me." Family members crowded into the room along with Ventre to witness the "miracle of the birth process," and while Ventre shared their elation, it was tinged with a sense of personal loss. "I inwardly grieved for what I had deprived my family. I realized then that I, without questioning, had relinquished my rights as a woman and mother in the births of my own three children." This was the final turning point for Ventre. "It was then I decided: I will become a midwife."[26]

Like Ventre, Ina May Gaskin remembers the first birth she witnessed, an event that affirmed her earlier impression of the primal power shared by humans and monkeys alike. She was leaning over Anna, who was experiencing strong contractions in her camper-school bus, in a Northwestern University parking lot. It was 1971, and Anna was part of a caravan of buses—between twenty and thirty—following San Francisco State professor and theologian Stephen Gaskin across the country to spread his message of peace and hope. As Anna's contractions got stronger, she asked for Stephen's assistance at the birth (he was not a physician, but he had received first-aid training while with the Marines in Korea). But Stephen had already begun his lecture to several hundred people at Northwestern, so his wife, Ina May, came to help. "I was no midwife at the time," she recalls, "but I was able to help the mother stay relaxed during this quick labor."[27] She managed to do this despite the increasing number of faces that appeared in the windows of the bus, as Stephen announced that the group's first child was in the process of being born. "I didn't count the people, since I was mainly dealing with my contractions, but I know I was surrounded," Anna remembers. "Okay, I decided. I'm on stage. I had always loved acting since I was a young child, and I had been on stage before. Once an actress, always an actress. This was my duty. The show must go on. I knew this was what I had to do, and I knew this was going to be the best creation I had ever done. I was really looking forward to the finale, and so was everyone else. They were just standing there in awe."[28] Ina May included herself in the group of astonished onlookers. She had never before witnessed someone's birth, nor had she seen a photo of one (though she herself had given birth, she did not see her baby until the infant was almost a day old). "Even before the baby came, I knew I was witnessing something sacred."[29] She felt a calling to become a midwife—although with a master's degree in English, she also felt completely unprepared for it. Her time on the caravan would provide her with the hands-on experience she needed.

Though Ventre's journey to midwifery did not cover as much terrain, her transition was also dramatic. After she witnessed her friend's birth, she began assisting other lay midwives. But circumstances on August 13, 1974, propelled her into a leadership position. While attending a home birth that day, meconium (fecal discharge) appeared in the mother's membrane waters—a potential sign that the fetus was in distress and needed emergency care. The midwife, fearing retribution (for practicing medicine without a license), sent Ventre to accompany the laboring couple to the hospital in their van. They didn't make it; the mother's urge to push was too strong. "There was nothing to do," Ventre recalled, "but put out my hand and catch! I used everything I had read and learned in assisting in various home deliveries and the baby was born in excellent condition en route to the hospital."[30] With this move, Ventre officially joined the underground network of midwives in the Washington, D.C., metropolitan area.

As an underground, unlicensed lay midwife, and later as a certified nurse-midwife, Ventre sought to dispel popular misconceptions of her calling.[31] "Contrary to the stereotype, we are not a modern day version of the old crone of midwife folklore, unkempt and illiterate," she announced at a local American College of Nurse-Midwives conference in 1976. They were educated, politically active, and well-read. Ventre held a B.S. in education with a major in Russian from the University of Wisconsin, and suggested that such background was typical. They were drawn to midwifery not because of an interest in medicine per se, but because of their own childbirth experiences. "The lay midwife started out as a consumer of maternity services and in her enthusiasm for natural childbirth became a consumer advocate. Often she became a natural childbirth educator and because many of her prospective parents were dissatisfied with hospital confinement for maternity care, she also became increasingly aware of something called 'home birth,'" Ventre continued, clearly drawing from her own experience. Through apprenticeship, these women gained the confidence and experience necessary to provide healthy couples with an alternative model of labor and delivery. "Eventually, our names spread in an underground network and in increasing numbers women requested our services," she said. "It may not have been a sophisticated or accepted way of entering a profession, but someone needed to do the job."[32] Her explanation and defense of lay midwifery echoes the sentiments of Jane members in Chicago, who chose to provide underground abortions, not from any specific medical interest, but from a sense of compassion and duty to women interested in maintaining reproductive autonomy.

Underground networks of lay midwives began to appear across the country in the 1970s. For example, when certified nurse Peggy Vincent moved to Berkeley, California, in 1970, she discovered such an underground network. She had worked as a delivery room nurse in North Carolina's Duke University Hospital before moving across the country, where she began teaching natural childbirth courses in her home and assisting deliveries at Alta Bates Hospital. She was pregnant with her first child, and, like many converts to midwifery, would find that having a baby transformed her perception of childbirth. When her contractions kicked in, she consulted her Lamaze books. "I resembled the composed woman in the booklet about as much as a toad resembles a prince," she recalled of the smiling, peaceful woman in the photograph. "My labor quickly became a global experience. My toenails curled backwards. . . . I imploded into a black hole of efficient, uncaring pain and . . . disappeared. It wasn't even me anymore. I became Labor." Her sense of self was completely wiped out by the intensity of the pain, far from the empowering process she had imagined. "Painless childbirth? I don't think so," she concluded. "Furious at the line I'd been sold, I wondered about this conspiracy to avoid the word 'pain.' My labor had hurt like hell, and I knew I'd never teach a straight, formulaic approach to childbirth preparation again."[33]

Vincent found herself drawn to the local lay midwives, who were "a shadowy presence lurking on the fringe of organized medicine." She encountered them only when complications occurred and they came with a client to the emergency room. "Usually they ducked into the bathroom or hid behind a pillar at the approach of any doctor or nurse." Lacking any hospital privileges or a backup physician, they feared exposure. "When her patient's labor stalled or problems developed, the lay midwife had two choices: abandon the woman, or stay and risk prosecution for practicing medicine without a license. No wonder they were elusive."[34] Vincent was drawn to their "experiential and holistic" approach to childbirth, and shortly thereafter applied to a midwifery program.[35] She wanted to deliver babies at home, but with a license, so that she would have emergency medical backup and hospital privileges. Her transformation to a licensed home birth midwife involved more than just a career change, however. Vincent described her footwear shift as being from "Adidas to Birkenstocks," signaling a lifestyle change that would result in the delivery of nearly three thousand central California babies at home.[36]

Fran Ventre's entry into midwifery—catching her first baby en route to the hospital—turned her into one of the "shadow midwives" that Peggy Vincent saw lurking in emergency rooms. Both women were well aware of the lack of protection that working without a license introduced. "I traveled to attend these women in birth with pangs of fear of being arrested," Ventre recalled. "Not having sufficient medical backup and denied the right to training programs, I agonized over my ability to handle emergency situations alone."[37] This risk became even greater when she received a call in 1974 from fellow midwife Tina Long, with whom she had witnessed her first home birth. Long was under investigation for practicing medicine without a license. One of her mothers had suffered a second-degree tear when the baby's shoulder first emerged, and had to go to the hospital for stitches. A vice squad detective followed this mother's case and threatened to arrest Long if she did not sign a document promising to never practice midwifery again. Getting licensed was no easy task; Long had attempted to apply the previous year in Virginia, but legal loopholes made it impossible.

Ventre vowed not to suffer the same penalty. She contacted health officials in Montgomery County to inquire about lay licensure and was told that no one had applied since 1924. Nonetheless, she obtained an application and provided evidence of assisting at forty births, along with character statements. State and county officials responded with resistance. County Health Officer Dr. Roy Lindgren wrote her that he would prefer to see nurse-midwives assist home births. "If they are not available and the alternative is between trained lay midwives and husbands, I would opt for the lay midwives. But I would not like to see midwives in this county, no matter how well-trained, unless they are working in close association with physicians."[38] Months passed, and when pressed again, Lindgren declared that he had no intention of licensing lay midwives and that it was not his responsibility to deal with the application. Ventre then learned from another source that the State Board of Health was attempting to repeal the law sanctioning the use of lay midwives, as a result of her application. She had two days to prepare a statement if she wanted to try to prevent the repeal. She panicked as she thought of her full day of college physiology lab, her husband out of town, her three children at home, and a Lamaze class to teach in the evening. "I felt overwhelmed. There was so little time and so much at stake," she recalled. On the day of the hearing, she worked until 3 a.m. on the statement, typed it up, and went to bed at 5. Two hours later, she got up, took her children to school, and drove to Annapolis. "It was a clear spring-like day and I felt a surge of confidence," she remembered. "If I lost the battle, I would at least have tried."[39]

Ventre did not realize until she entered the state senate building that it was her midwifery application that had started the war; nor was she prepared for the presence of enemies. The sign-in sheet included a number of certified nurse-midwives working for the Public Health Service. All the officials she had been working with were also on the register. Anxious, she crept into the hearing room of the Economic Affairs Committee and sat in the corner, still the shadow midwife. Then her small group of supporters arrived—one pregnant, one nursing an infant, and another with a toddler—physical reminders of the nature of the debate.

Ventre then turned and studied the group of Public Health Service nurse-midwives, who conveyed a "stale resolve. I could see that at one time, when they started their careers perhaps, [there] was a spark of an excitement of being involved in life's miracle," she observed. "But, the reality of what the physicians allowed them to do set their determined faces."[40] Despite their training, most of what they did, according to Ventre, was paramedical services rather than delivering babies. Limited by the power of physicians, their aspirations had shriveled. (Indeed, most nurse-midwives at the time were practicing in public hospitals under the supervision of physicians.[41]) This observation—and this animosity between lay and nurse-midwives—would characterize relations for the next few decades, and inspire Ventre to attempt a reconciliation between the two groups. Relations were not helped by a comment made in 1978 by the American College of Nurse-Midwives president, Helen Burst, that reflected the feelings of many nurse-midwives of the time. "While there are some lay midwives serving the consumer well, . . . there are other lay midwives or birth attendants who quite frankly scare me and make me fearful for the unsuspecting consumer," she said, because they relied primarily on "repeat emotional experiences with little concern or knowledge pertaining to safety."[42]

Ventre's confidence was raised when the Economic Affairs Committee chairman noted that he had been born at home, delivered by a granny midwife. Although at moments Ventre emphasized that the modern lay midwife was a far cry from the "old crones," in this instance she was relieved to have that association. When the chairman called her name, she nervously approached the podium, noting the surprised reaction from the public health midwives and health officials, who had assumed she would not learn of the hearing. She explained the origins of the natural childbirth movement and the growing dissatisfaction of American women with hospital births. She compared maternal and infant mortality rates of the United States with countries that routinely utilized home births, to argue that it was in fact safer to give birth at home than in a hospital. And she stressed the inevitable trend toward home births, urging the committee to allow experienced lay midwives to ensure the safety of such a trend. During the 1970s, in fact, the number of out-of-hospital births more than doubled, from 0.6 percent in 1970 to 1.5 percent in 1977, mostly attributable to the increasing popularity of planned home births.[43] Much to Ventre's relief, the committee allowed the law sanctioning the use of lay midwives to remain on the books. The positive impression she made on the committee elicited one senator's own home birth story in the lobby after the hearing, along with assurance that the law was safe.[44]

Nonetheless, Ventre's struggle continued. Only after her lawyer threatened action against the state, which continued to delay processing her application, did she have success. She agreed to create a formal training plan, which included her assisting Dr. James Brew, a local physician who did home births (an extremely rare phenomenon). Once this was completed and she passed an examination, she became fully licensed in the State of Maryland. In the fall of 1975, she drove to Rockville to officially register, bribing her children to accompany her by bringing several of their friends along. Along with her "boisterous entourage," she arrived at the Circuit Court to sign her name. "When I opened the dusty old Registry for Lay Midwives, I was moved by the honest names of these old granny midwives before me carefully inscribed in calligraphy," Ventre recalled. Only four names were listed: the first in 1913, the last in 1924. "Here I was, some fifty years later, a continuing link with three dedicated ghosts of the past. . . . I was now one of them."[45] Clearly, despite her interest in portraying 1970s midwives as something new and different, she also identified with this earlier generation.

Ironically, Ventre found herself with little time to deliver babies after receiving her license. Together with the two women she was with at the first birth she witnessed, Esther Herman (the birth mother whose physician was in surgery) and Tina Long (the underground midwife forced to resign to avoid being arrested), she created an aptly named advocacy group, H.O.M.E., or Home Oriented Maternity Experience. Ventre served as treasurer, Herman as breast-feeding expert and correspondent, and Long as chairperson. They formed the organization in the spring of 1974, and incorporated in 1976. Within seventeen months, H.O.M.E. had received over six thousand letters, mailed over two thousand quarterly

FIGURE 10 Sandy Schildroth, Tina Long, Fran Ventre, and Esther Herman discuss their H.O.M.E. publication. Photograph © Fred Ward. Reprinted by permission of The Schlesinger Library, Radcliffe Institute, Harvard University.

newsletters, and had over one thousand members and thirty-five affiliated groups nationwide.[46] Newsletters reported on midwifery legislation, medical findings, conferences, and the history of childbirth. All work was conducted from Long's Takoma Park basement and with the help of local volunteers. As they explained in their initial mailing, H.O.M.E. "offers the information, support, and encouragement to enable parents to achieve their goals" in childbirth. "Humanizing birth is a challenge that we of H.O.M.E. are willing to meet with those who ask," they stressed, though Ventre's earlier impression of Jenny the orangutan suggests that the more appropriate word choice would be *naturalizing* birth.[47]

Ventre's other reason for not birthing more babies in Montgomery County after receiving her license was her competition. In October of 1975, two certified nurse-midwives opened the nation's first incorporated nurse-midwifery service, Maternity Center Associates, Ltd. Like Peggy Vincent, the self-acclaimed "baby catcher" mentioned earlier, Janet Epstein and Marion McCartney were registered nurses assisting obstetricians at deliveries when they decided to become midwives. Their situation was unusual, however, because they had worked for Dr. Brew, the obstetrician who did home deliveries (and under whom Fran Ventre agreed to train to obtain her Maryland license).

In their case, then, the physician was not an enemy but an advocate of home birth. Brew had delivered Epstein's own baby in 1968, and then approached her about the possibility of assisting him with home births. His clientele were women who preferred a home birth for religious reasons—primarily Christian Scientists and Sikhs. "I was shocked," Epstein revealed. "I didn't believe that he delivered women at home." But she agreed to attend a home birth, which she described as "spectacular . . . I was struck by the simplicity of it." There were no towels or instruments. He wore a white long-sleeved shirt. The birthing mother wore her own nightgown and delivered in her own bed. "I was amazed and really turned on by it. So I set myself up to do home births as a nurse."[48] Epstein began assisting Brew, but as he became inundated with requests, he suggested that she become a midwife and take on some of his clients. Epstein agreed, and attended a one-year nurse-midwifery course at Georgetown University, where Ventre would enroll a few years later. She graduated in June 1975, and contacted Marion McCartney, another nurse-midwife working for Brew, about the possibility of going into practice together. Epstein recalled that "everybody I asked looked at me like I was really out of my mind," but she was determined. The same Maryland law that had stymied Ventre presented another problem for Epstein and McCartney. It stated that nurse-midwives could not function independently or charge a fee for their services. They could only assist physicians. "To get around that," Epstein explained, "and I elected to get around it rather than fight it, was to form a corporation." She employed Brew as a backup and got the center up and running.

Though Dr. Brew had encouraged Epstein's independence, she remembered the first time she felt fully capable of delivering without him present. "The day inevitably came when we 'caught' a baby because the physician was unable to come to the home," she recalled along with McCartney. "It was an exhilarating experience for us." Like Vincent, Ventre, and Ina May Gaskin, witnessing a birth without a physician present transformed their sense of purpose, relegating them to a leadership position regardless of licensing or accreditation. Although these women were helping to bring life into the world, their revelation was undoubtedly similar to that of the Abortion Counseling Service members who learned how to perform an abortion once they realized their doctor was a fraud. These women—abortion providers and midwives alike—were the living and breathing examples promoted in Our Bodies, Ourselves. Experience, in this case, having borne their own children, made them experts.

Within a year, Maternity Center Associates was delivering twenty-five babies a month on average. Epstein and McCartney emphasized the importance of providing an alternative, empowering environment for the expectant parents. They chose to refer to them as clients rather than patients, "because they are healthy people who have just come to us for advice and assistance."[49] They encouraged women to review their own charts and express their needs. "We feel it is vital that clients be responsible for their own health care and contribute as much as they can to their own health maintenance." Like Dr. Brew, they did not shave their clients, give them enemas, or regularly perform episiotomies. They wore jeans and shirts that read "Happy Baby Home Delivery Service" to "keep things casual and optimistic."[50] A year's experience suggested that this process was successful for both clients and midwives: Epstein and McCartney had received positive feedback and found their service to be "a tremendous satisfaction and joy to us as nurse-midwives."[51] They noted a "clear demand" for home birth services in the Washington, D.C., metropolitan area, one that was unquestionably increasing. The popularity of their services, and the establishment of H.O.M.E., attested to the "growing consumer interest."[52] By 1981, the corporation employed 4 certified nurse-midwives, 25 registered nurses, 2 physicians, and 12 back-up physicians. It provided prenatal care, intrapartum and postpartum care, well-woman gynecology, and family planning. In addition, its staff oversaw 250 to 300 home births a year.[53]

But their popularity was limited to a particular clientele. Epstein explained that only 3 to 5 percent of their clients were black families, and those represented were primarily middle class. Though midwives such as Fran Ventre hearkened back to her midwifery predecessors as her forebears, they had actually served a different clientele. As childbirth moved from home to hospital around the turn of the century, midwifery came close to disappearing. Midwives attended approximately 50 percent of births in 1900, but only 12.5 percent by 1935. Most midwives (80 percent) still practicing in the 1930s were located in the rural South and referred to as "granny midwives." In Washington, D.C., and other urban centers, midwives attended only 4 percent of births by 1923.[54] Most Americans believed that childbirth was safer and more hygienic in a hospital environment. Even the National Negro Health Movement (formed in 1930) called for the elimination of granny midwives, whom many African Americans perceived as "unclean and dangerous."[55]

Race continued to be a clear factor in childbirth choice after the midwifery renaissance of the 1970s; in 1989, for example, 93 percent of those who were attended by certified nurse-midwives were white (and 96 percent of those attended by lay midwives). The average woman who chose a home birth was white, between the ages of 20 and 34, married, with a college degree.[56] Those who attempted to establish nurse-midwifery programs noted the different reactions based on both race and class. Dr. Henry Theide, chair of the Obstetrics and Gynecology Department at the University of Rochester, noted in 1976 that he was "being encouraged by the middle-class white community through the Childbirth Education Association program—and more recently, a women's health collective—to bring nurse-midwives into the community to deliver patients. At the same time," he continued, "I have been served a warning by the black community that they will have no part of the second-rate kind of care being provided by nurse-midwives."[57] The negative association with granny midwives continued to distance some who believed that the technology of the hospital represented the most advanced, and thus the best, form of care.

In her recent study of American midwives, sociologist Wendy Simonds pointed out the irony in that assumption. She found "a general sense among midwives that poor women and women of color were least likely to have their desires and needs met by conventional medicine as clients, and that they therefore had the most to gain from midwifery." Several of the midwives believed that midwifery would appeal more to these women if they encountered more midwives of color. Midwife Renie Daley noted that "the way we educate nurse-midwives is very elitist . . . and so we end up with a whole bunch of white nurse-midwives. And we really need midwives of color—more, many many many more, midwives of color. And I don't see it happening."[58] As with other aspects of women's health and reproductive issues, different perspectives and experiences limited coalition-building across race and class within the midwifery community.

By 1981, Maternity Center Associates founder Jan Epstein noted a new trend among her clients: those who did not want a home birth, but who wanted a nurse-midwife attending them at the hospital—not because it was cheaper, but because they wanted the increased individual attention. Her observation was part of a nationwide shift in the use of certified nurse-midwives. Between 1970 and 1982, the number of certified nurse-midwives grew from 629 to 2,500. During the same period, the number of educational training programs in midwifery doubled in the United States.[59] "Increasingly, choice is a factor in the utilization of nurse-midwifery services," noted Ann Slayton in 1981. "No longer is it primarily low-income women who must use the services of a nurse-midwife for childbirth or face the alternative of no medical attention at all."[60] Instead, their services were sought after by middle-class women dissatisfied with traditional obstetrical care.

As Epstein offered increased opportunities for her clients to give birth in a hospital setting, she encountered more friction from those who now viewed her as a direct competitor: obstetricians. Unlike Dr. Brew, most obstetricians delivered in hospitals, and expressed reluctance to accept competitors. "If there is anything that gets the profession's back up," observed Dr. John Maeck, professor of obstetrics and gynecology in Burlington, Vermont, "it is competition for fees." Speaking at a 1976 medical symposium on the role of nurse-midwifery, he continued, "I really think that's the key to physician resistance to nurse-midwifery.... When the nurse-midwife is put into a competing role with the obstetrician, the obstetrician just won't accept it."[61]

Fran Ventre encountered such resistance when she left her home birth practice and H.O.M.E. work to resettle in Newburyport, Massachusetts, in 1978. She was reluctant to leave Maryland, but her husband's career as an educational consultant took the family to the Boston area. "Maybe I've been sent here for a reason," she reflected in a local newspaper interview.[62]

While Ventre had encountered difficulties with legal loopholes in Maryland, they were nothing compared to the Massachusetts laws regulating midwifery. She was newly endowed with a nursing degree from Montgomery College and midwifery training from Georgetown University, which allowed her to deliver babies in hospitals—but not at home. Lay midwifery was illegal in Massachusetts at that time, and while home births were legal in the state, neither certified nurse-midwives nor any nurses at all could attend them. When nurse Janet Leigh rushed a home-birthed newborn with a prolapsed umbilical cord to an emergency room in 1982, the state filed charges against her for gross misconduct.[63] In 1987, the state supreme court upheld the law barring nurses and nurse-midwives from home births. (Only three other states prevented these types of attendants at home births: Alabama, South Dakota, and Wisconsin.) This ruling affected some 140 certified nurse-midwives practicing in Massachusetts. "The law is hysterically stupid," commented Boston University professor of health law George J. Annas, "and limits the choices for women who want home births."[64] Thus, despite Ventre's additional training, she was no longer able to deliver babies at home. Though this had been her passion, she now poured her energies into transforming the hospital birth experience, attempting to change regulations at Malden, the local health-care facility, regarding the father's role at birth, the mother's choices during labor, and the baby's right to stay with the mother in her room rather than being whisked away from the parents soon after birth.[65]

Ventre's observations and visions for Malden Hospital, reported in the local newspaper, did not go over well with its chief of obstetrics and gynecology, Dr. Peter G. Fanikos, who responded with an angry rebuttal. "The Malden Hospital has a long and proud history of providing obstetrical and gynecological facilities to meet the changing needs of the women of the communities which it serves," he wrote. "Their success in this area can be easily verified by the thousands of happy parents who have been very pleased with their birthing experience at The Malden Hospital." But to Fanikos, and to many other obstetricians who spoke out against the growing use of nurse-midwives, shunning hospital technologies and procedures was not only unnecessary—it was dangerous. Ventre's "disapproval of moving babies to the protective nursery during visiting hours," for example, "evidences callous disregard of the infant's well being." Fanikos believed the potential spread of infection was far more detrimental to an infant's well-being than separation from its mother. His true rage, however, was directed at Ventre's espousal of home births. "Local history is replete with home birth disasters of recent and distant occurrence. To advocate a return to home deliveries is evidence of a total disregard for the present and future well being of the infant and mother involved," he snapped. He referred to such practice as a kind of "barnyard obstetrics" that was "totally irresponsible." Then came the threat. That Ventre, with her "limited" nurse-midwifery training, "should believe that she is going to bring any fountain of new knowledge to the local situation may be ego satisfying," he quipped, "but delusional."[66] Clearly, Ventre would have no future at Malden.

North Shore Birth Center

Instead, she became the first director of the North Shore Birth Center at Beverly Hospital in Beverly, Massachusetts, the first freestanding, hospital-owned, midwife-run birth center in the country.[67] Located on the hospital grounds in a small gray building, the Birth Center represented a new trend in childbirth options. Facilities such as this initially carried the potential for transforming what had become a sanitized and medicalized event. In the mothers' rooms, flowers, wallpaper, rocking chairs, and beds that turned into delivery tables enabled women to feel more at home during their labor, while still having access to medical technology and obstetrical backup. Many of these birth centers were affiliated with a hospital in the vicinity, which made emergency transfer more efficient.

Peggy Vincent, the California-based "baby catcher," opted to become director of the first alternative birth center in the East Bay, housed at Alta Bates Hospital in Berkeley, where she had worked as an obstetrical nurse. She described the transformation of part of the hospital as workers gutted a postpartum room and "trucked in a queen-size bed, foldout couches, brass lamps, and enough potted plants to rival a rain forest." Soon the room resembled an "upscale southwestern motel." As the director, she initially moved through hospital protocols with little resistance from the practicing physicians. Vincent began to realize, however, that the doctors "did not understand what was about to hit them." They had estimated that perhaps six to eight women would sign up in the first month; instead, forty showed up at the first meeting. She recalled physicians being a little confused by the whole birth center concept, while the nurses "basked in our newfound power. We volunteered extra hours of work for the satisfaction of choreographing very special births for women who hoped to experience the births of their babies as potentially transforming events."[68] Vincent's optimism, though tangible at that moment, would not last long. In 1980, after three years as director, she left the center and began a practice in home births.

One major reason for the new birth center trend was the changing market. In the 1980s, health-care marketing research indicated that as the market became more consumer-driven, hospitals competed for insured obstetric patients. Consultants "advised that 'catering to the maternity market segment is critical to patient acquisition.'"[69] Thus, it is no coincidence that both Peggy Vincent and Fran Ventre directed hospital birthing centers at this time, attempting to ride the wave of consumer interest and introduce a wider clientele to their birth philosophies. Many hospitals across the nation adopted similar trends to attract paying clients who preferred the domestic touches. But for Fran Ventre and for many others, it was an experiment that ended disastrously.

Ventre began her tenure at the North Shore Birth Center in 1980. Under her direction, the staff of nurse-midwives grew from two to three, and the number of births rose from 125 babies the first year to 225 each year for the next three years. North Shore's status as the region's only birth center drew national attention, as it was touted as a model facility.[70] As with many birth centers, its cesarean rate was far lower than at neighboring hospitals, and the cost was significantly less. Perhaps Ventre began to believe that she *had* been sent to Massachusetts for a reason.

Beneath the surface, however, all was not well. Though the Birth Center ostensibly operated separately from Beverly Hospital, in reality, hospital standards increasingly encroached on Ventre's terrain. Just as Dr. Fanikos at Malden Hospital had dismissed her ideals as "barnyard obstetrics," so, too, did obstetricians at Beverly. Problems began when-

ever a midwife accompanied an emergency case from the Birth Center
to the hospital. She frequently met with resistance, and in Ventre's case,
doctors once forbade her to accompany her client into the hospital's
labor unit. In June of 1984, the hospital introduced a protocol that required midwives to consult with an obstetrician if a woman had been
pushing for more than two hours, a situation which frequently resulted
in the obstetrician demanding a transfer to the hospital.

Harvard MBA professor Regina Herzlinger characterized the tensions between North Shore and Beverly as arising from management
style. "The hospital managers were uncomfortable with the full implications of customer mastery," she explained. "On the other hand, the
nurse-midwives were uncomfortable with the traditional, hierarchical
model of hospital management, in which one person supervises others
and strict protocols guide organizational relationships."[71] Ventre desired
independence and the freedom to respond to a laboring woman's needs.
She considered the Birth Center essentially an adaptation of home birth,
while Beverly's managers and obstetricians viewed it as an extension of
the hospital. In December of 1984, Beverly's budget director complained
that the midwives "had difficulty accommodating to institutional policies," such as merit evaluations and other hospital protocols.[72] Ventre
responded that these standards were "appropriate for a hospital, not a
birth center, and that she was being judged solely on management, not
midwifery." She resigned the following morning, and was replaced by
not one but two other certified nurse-midwives: one in a full-time management role, the other in a clinical position.[73]

Ventre was shattered by the outcome. "What happened to me demonstrates the precarious place of the unorthodox practitioner within the
system," she reflected later. "They kept me as long as I was useful and
then circuitously found a way to coerce my resignation." In retrospect,
she believed it was "impossible to reach an accommodation with those
physicians, because they were bent on exerting control and reinforcing
the medical model." The North Shore Birth Center, potentially the middle
ground between two models of childbirth, could not sustain the ideals
promoted by women's health activists. "Leaving aside the personal loss
I suffered," Ventre claimed, "the greatest casualty was the professional
trust, sharing, and interdependence built up among the midwives at
Beverly. . . . It was like a Camelot for midwives and families."[74] It was
not long before a growing cynicism became apparent among health activists and natural childbirth advocates. Sociologist Wendy Simonds
notes, "You can domesticate the surroundings by hanging floral wallpaper and providing padded rocking chairs. But redecorating will not

alter conventional power dynamics, as long as the precepts of obstetrical monitoring remain in place and the operating room is right down the hall from the labor and delivery rooms 'suites.' "[75] Though the new birth centers may have been a positive experience for some laboring mothers, they did not represent the transformation of childbirth that activists such as Vincent or Ventre had hoped for.

Nevertheless, many obstetricians and hospital administrators acknowledged that the increasing numbers of certified nurse-midwives represented a force to be reckoned with. In 1981, approximately 2,200 nurse-midwives were certified by the American College of Nurse-Midwives, with an additional 220 receiving certification each year thereafter. Most worked for hospitals or physicians, but about 200 were actively employed in the hundred or so birth centers nationwide. A reporter for *Ob. Gyn. News* noted that they had "attracted a new customer: the affluent middle-class woman who wants to call more of the shots in a different birth experience." Along with Ventre and Vincent, they sought to "pioneer new arrangements in their professional ties with physicians."[76] And they were frustrated with physician resistance. In response, Congressman Albert Gore Jr. called for a special hearing before the House Subcommittee on Oversight and Investigation of the Committee on Interstate and Foreign Commerce, on "Nurse Midwifery: Consumer's Freedom of Choice." The hearing focused on the issue of possible restraint-of-trade violations against midwives who were denied hospital privileges. Certified nurse-midwife Sally Tom, representing the ACNM at the hearing, testified that opposition was coming from not only physicians, but also from hospitals, insurance companies, medical societies, and state officials. *Our Bodies, Ourselves* coauthor Judy Norsigian testified to the growing dissatisfaction with current obstetrical care among American women, particularly what she deemed as unnecessary intervention in the birth process, as exemplified in the growing rate of cesarean deliveries in U.S. hospitals.[77]

After the hearing, the ACNM established an Ad Hoc Committee to Study the Relationships Between Nurse-Midwives and Physicians. The committee called the problematic relationship between the two professions one of "definite urgency requiring immediate attention and action."[78] Comments from committee members reflect the sense of urgency felt among certified nurse-midwives. "We either believe in ourselves and our viability or we are lost," remarked Bonnie Stickles. Barbara Goddard noted, "In many ways the ACNM is still a young, immature and naïve association. We are still trying to get medicine to like and understand us." She recommended a new strategy. "We should work harder at just being ourselves, autonomous and accessible to the public." In her opinion, nurse-midwives had wasted time and energy bending over backward to accommodate and explain their philosophy to physicians. "Now is the time to end our conciliatory behavior," she declared. "Being friendly and agreeable has not substantially changed our professional ability to practice over the past twenty years."[79] Overall, committee comments portrayed the ACNM's relationship to organized medicine as similar to a rebellious teenager ready to break away from her parents, but not yet able to do so. Like women's health activists involved in the Depo-Provera campaign, these committee members recognized the importance of developing a professional status recognized and respected by organized medicine. As the authors of the childbirth chapter in the first edition of *Our Bodies, Ourselves* noted, women must work both from the "outside in" *and* from the "inside out" to demystify medicine and put the mysticism back in childbirth.[80]

Part of the problem, however, was not just nurse-midwives' relationship with physicians; it was also their relationship with other midwives. As the ACNM ad-hoc committee chair, Sandi Dietrich, commented, "The differences between a midwife and nurse-midwife continue to cloud the issue."[81] Many lay or direct-entry midwives viewed nurse-midwives as part of the problem rather than the solution; most of their training and background was in the hospital rather than the home. Nurse-midwives, meanwhile, frequently viewed direct-entry midwives as unprofessional and potentially incompetent. The ACNM, founded in 1955, has treated direct-entry midwives as "rather embarrassing lower-class relatives; as completely unrelated non-professional practitioners who give midwifery a bad public image," and occasionally as colleagues.[82] Direct-entry midwives were only allowed to join the ACNM if they had graduated from an ACNM-endorsed program.[83]

Transcending Titles: MANA

As with abortion and birth control, then, tensions among women who believed they had women's best interests in mind limited the possibilities of coalition building. And in the 1980s, these conflicting visions of how to approach organized medicine presented a major challenge to the midwifery movement. In October of 1981, the president of the ACNM, Sister Angela Murdaugh, called a small organizational meeting at the ACNM offices in Washington, D.C. She realized from her interactions with the American College of Obstetrics and Gynecology president, Dr. George Ryan, that he did not seem to understand the difference between lay midwives and nurse-midwives (sometimes applying the term "lay nurse-midwives").[84] Such confusion was indicative of a larger misconception regarding the status of midwives, one that Murdaugh felt was essential to resolve before continuing negotiations with ACOG. She called together seven prominent midwives, including Fran Ventre and Ina May Gaskin, representing both schools of midwifery. The group agreed unanimously to form a national panel "to discuss ways to open and improve communications between certified nurse-midwives and non-nurse-midwives" and to "create an identifiable body representing professional midwives."[85] Participants called it a very exciting, "historic" gathering.[86] They agreed to meet again with others at the annual ACNM convention in Lexington, Kentucky, in April 1982. There, over 150 midwives discussed the possibilities of creating an alliance.

What would an "identifiable body representing professional midwives" look like? At the Lexington meeting, each member of the original group from the ACNM meeting tried to address this challenging question. "The first issue that came up for us was the issue of membership. Who shall join?" Susan Leiber asked. "Right now we realize that there's very little uniformity among us midwives and therefore it would be impossible to have a category of membership." She believed that the group of seven "[sees itself] in the middle of a very broad spectrum of nurse-midwifery through the spectrum of lay midwifery. And we realize that there's no way that we are going to create anything that satisfies everybody but we're trying to build a structure from the center and build whatever there is as common ground." But, Leiber warned, "we are going to create vulnerabilities. We are going to bring people out of their hiding places. We're going to expose them to the dangers of being a midwife in this society."[87]

Not everyone in the room believed that such a middle-of-the-road position was feasible, just as birth centers were not an actual compromise between two different philosophies of birth. One side would always dominate—the one with more power and prestige. Diana Kraus, a lay midwife from Wisconsin, did not believe that lay midwives could "afford to homogenize ourselves with the nurse-midwife goals and principles for practice and operation."[88] Paula Murphy, also a lay midwife from Wisconsin, had previously felt at odds with nurse-midwives, but believed that the culture was changing. "I've observed real radical changes in myself," she announced. "A CNM to me was the last person that I was going to go to to ask any opinion or even have the idea that she might want to know." But now, "those kind of connections have begun to occur personally in my life."[89] Carol Leonard, a lay midwife from New Hampshire, attempted to reassure her colleagues that it was time to work together. "Our main focus is to homogenize the two schools of midwifery, to eradicate the dichotomy. I think, in philosophy, we're beginning to feel that we're all sisters and that we all need to start banding together so that we can be stronger. We need the numbers."[90] Ina May Gaskin agreed. "I think a lot of us have been thinking for several years, 'Well, what about organizing? When is the right time and how can you tell?' Like a lot of other people, I had reservations about becoming highly visible in a national sort of orientation. Is this going to turn up the heat in certain ways? Is this going to attract more oppression or repression?" She decided it was worth the struggle. "There's been a growth of understanding between certified nurse-midwives and lay midwives over the years, that we have enough friendships and bonds of trust between enough of us now, that we have started to see the ways that we can help each other."[91]

With that belief in mind, the group created the Midwives Alliance of North America, a nonprofit, incorporated, professional organization that still exists. Gaskin offered up her journal, *The Practicing Midwife*, to be a "vehicle for dialogue among all midwives about the different issues" of MANA.[92] Fran Ventre and Carol Leonard, two of the original core group (one a nurse-midwife, the other a lay midwife), wrote optimistically of MANA's founding in the *Journal of Nurse-Midwifery*:

> We appreciated each other as sister midwives with acceptance of the individual variations in approach to practice, but more important, we realized the similarities. We became more aware of the strengths and resources that each group has to offer each other. Our eyes were opened to the common bond that binds us together—a love for childbearing women and their families. Our aims could be better served by replacing misunderstanding with trust, dichotomy with coalition. We are not a threat to each other, but can sustain one another through this trust. The mutual respect we are beginning to build as midwives transcends titles.[93]

This somewhat syrupy analysis may have been an attempt to suggest a unified front in the larger battle between midwives and organized medicine. In a different context, Ventre emphasized the importance of downplaying differences between lay and nurse-midwives, claiming that they were "about as unimportant as the distinction between field slaves and house slaves"—an interesting comparison, given the overall whiteness of the midwife population.[94] Neither type of midwife had any power compared to physicians.

It was one thing to agree on the creation of a midwives' alliance. But the bigger challenges were still in front of them, including coming up with an official definition of midwifery and a system of accreditation that recognized the role of lay midwives without formal training. These challenges could not be met without the support of the larger and more powerful organization, the ACNM. In 1985, MANA members complained that at the annual ACNM convention, tension arose between the two groups over the official definition of a midwife. In an angry letter to Teddy Chavret, the president of MANA, board member Elizabeth Davis took exception to Chavret's characterization of relations between the two groups. "I do not believe that the lay-midwives were responsible for the tensions that came up over certain issues," she wrote in response to Chavret's claim that they had "trashed" the nurse-midwives. Instead, Davis blamed ACNM leadership and its "persistently communicated, anti-lay-midwife, pro-formal education challenge and attack[s] . . . made repeatedly on our membership."[95]

Chavret's response indicated that problems existed not only between different groups of midwives, but also among themselves. "If MANA is to succeed as an organization," she wrote, "its leaders must have the vision to see issues in the larger context and not take them as some kind of personal insult that incites all kinds of personal rage that then leads to inappropriate response." She was clearly angered by the alleged actions of some of her colleagues. "As midwives we are always in the middle of controversy, and always being challenged from any number of corners," she continued. "We have to have the maturity to see the *real* issue, apart from our sense of personal anger, outrage, indignation, self-righteousness, feeling victimized, etc. etc. We cannot allow ourselves to say 'fuck you' to the president of ACNM, ACOG, or whoever challenges us," she chided. "We need to have the maturity to see that sometimes our 'enemy' may be speaking some truth; and the clarity to articulate our side of the argument free from self-righteousness and closed minded-ness."[96] Chavret's condemnation of what she viewed as improperly directed rage reflected the changing cultural climate of the 1980s. It was time for the midwifery movement to come of age, these women believed; to adopt the professional strategies of enemies and competitors rather than retreating underground.

A "Human Bridge"

In 1995, Fran Ventre and two other midwives published a study entitled "The Transition from Lay Midwife to Certified Nurse-Midwife in the United States." The authors were struck by the number of women who, like themselves, began their career as lay midwives and later decided to become certified nurse-midwives. They contacted them with survey questions. What motivated the change, and what was the impact of their decision to professionalize? Sixty-five women responded to the survey—sixty-two of them white, two black, and one Hispanic—representing twenty-eight states. Most of those surveyed identified as a "midwife" rather than a "CNM," but they had obtained the additional credentials to serve a wider clientele and for job security. Like Ventre, the survey responders indicated that they chose to become lay midwives as a direct result of their own birth experiences. They wanted to "offer an alternative to the hospital birth model, and they brought a set of nature-based, feminist convictions to this experience."[97]

But their reasons for becoming certified were different from Ventre's, and signaled a larger shift within the women's health movement by the 1980s. "They said they were interested in having an impact *within* the health care system and being able to influence policy and to effect political change," Ventre noted.[98] Notably, as they became CNMs, their membership in MANA declined, while membership in the ACNM increased—another indicator of increased professionalization. Were they "copping out," compromising, becoming "too professional" in their approach, as Ventre had been accused of when she chose to become certified? Ventre did not believe so. "Becoming a 'professional' doesn't necessarily mean compromising human values and ideals," she argued. "In my heart, I will always be a lay midwife combining a profound respect for the women and their families in making birth a meaningful event with the technical skills of a nurse-midwife. . . . I hope to have the credibility needed to institute those changes from within the establishment."[99] She and her coauthors envisioned those women who had opted to become certified as a "human bridge spanning both factions: the lay midwife and the certified nurse-midwife. They have been outside of the system and inside of it."[100]

Yet with an ever-increasing cesarean rate and a steady rate of hospital births, one wonders how possible spanning such a deep divide really is, or how readily one can turn back. Ventre, for example, gave up home births for good when she became certified and moved to Massachusetts, despite her passion for the practice and her initial desire to work in "outside channels of alternatives."[101] As with the story of Depo-Provera, becoming an insider meant the inevitable loss of a following invested in fundamental rather than incremental change. As these midwives moved out of the home to deliver in birth centers and hospitals, they sacrificed ideology and independence. Professionalization, however, gave them credibility and status within organized medicine, and the possibility of gradually reforming the health-care system.

: : :

On November 18, 2008, a coalition of midwives and mothers congregated on the lawn of the North Shore Birth Center, protesting a meeting of the Northeast Hospital Corporation's Board of Trustees that was under way. At stake was the future of the Birth Center, now owned by Northeast Health System, a company that planned to close it and move all births back over to the Beverly Hospital. Hospital officials explained why the decision was financially necessary: "As with other birth centers around the nation, North Shore Birth Center is experiencing a significant rise in the cost of malpractice insurance premiums."[102] But protesters demanded that the board reconsider its decision. Carrying signs that read "Please Don't Take Away Our Choice," mothers shared "passionate" birth stories in an emotional setting. Though the number of babies born at North Shore was significantly reduced from Fran Ventre's day, some eighty to ninety babies continued to enter the world within its walls annually.

Picketers were not the only ones who decried the decision. *Our Bodies, Ourselves* coauthor Judy Norsigian helped to draft a letter to the Board of Trustees, urging it to reconsider its decision and instead "open a dialog with community members and women's health advocates who are deeply concerned about the critical importance of this reproductive choice."[103] Rebecca Hains, an assistant professor of communications at Salem State College, started a group, Save the North Shore Birth Center, on the Facebook Web site to exchange information and share personal stories about births at the center. Within two weeks, 839 people had joined the group.

Stories posted on Facebook from the mothers who gave birth at the North Shore Birth Center attest that demands for reproductive choice include choices in childbirth. "Choice" usually suggests the issue of abortion, but for a growing number of women involved in "birthing rights," choice centers on not just whether to have a child, but where and how to have the child.[104] "It's an outrage. It's unacceptable," wrote Jennifer Shea on the closing of North Shore. "And we mothers want more choices. We want safer, low-intervention births. We don't want to be pressured by hospital staff treating numbers instead of our children. We want birth centers. We shouldn't have to choose between home and hospitals. Birth Centers are safe. And it is imperative that they remain a choice for women." Mira Clarke, who delivered a son at the center on September 15, 2008, wrote, "I firmly believe that although I could have had a healthy baby in any hospital, it would not have been the life-changing experience I had at the Birth Center. Every family deserves to have the opportunity to choose this kind of birth."[105]

Three weeks later, on December 15, 2008, the Board of Trustees of the Northeast Hospital Corporation voted to keep the Birth Center open. "Victory!" posted Sarah Shamel, an organizer of the Steering Committee to Save the North Shore Birth Center, on the Facebook group page. "Our voices have been heard and all our hard work has made a difference! Thank you!" Shamel noted that the group's legal counsel assured her that its success is "remarkable and rare," attributing it to "the loud public support of the community."[106] But the trustees made the agreement contingent on instituting the use of electronic fetal monitoring at all births, an unwelcome form of technology according to the Steering Committee , which views it as "controversial" and "clinically questionable."[107] Current North Shore practice is the use of a hand-held Doppler system to monitor the fetus, recommended by the American Association of Birth Centers as the best practice. The Steering Committee is concerned that North Shore will lose its accreditation with the Commission for the Accreditation of Birth Centers, which does not allow routine use of EFM. Thus, the committee finds itself trapped: accepting the trustees' plan could result in the loss of the center's accreditation, while refusing it could result in the center's closure.

The position of the Steering Committee at the close of 2008 is a testament to the complexities of women's health activism in the twenty-first century, inherited from the previous generation. Feminist health activists put reproductive health front and center in their campaigns to empower women's lives, practicing what others sought to displace: self-definition based on reproductive function. This uncomfortable alliance of mind and body has contributed to a new climate, one in which women have very different expectations and choices than they did before 1970. But it has also resulted in problems for those who seek to radically transform women's health care.

Epilogue: Daughters of Feminism

On November 13, 2008, the *Our Bodies, Ourselves* Web site posted "Choices in Childbirth," a statement opposing current restrictions on maternity care in the United States. *Our Bodies, Ourselves* executive director Judy Norsigian explained why she had initiated this "rather unusual 'group writing' project." The Boston Women's Health Book Collective had just published *Our Bodies, Ourselves: Pregnancy and Birth*, the latest in a series of publications that include a new edition of *OBOS* and a book on menopause. On her speaking tour, Norsigian was "struck by how many people were deeply concerned about current trends in childbirth" as birth choices for American women become increasingly restricted. "Choices in Childbirth" urges that "communities preserve the option of VBACs" [vaginal birth after cesarean] and maintain options for hospital-based midwifery care, and that midwives continue to be licensed and regulated to provide home births. The statement concludes, "It is time to create a system that allows women all reasonable choices in childbirth, and to encourage practices that produce optimal outcomes for both mothers and babies."[1]

Nearly forty years after the original edition of *Our Bodies, Ourselves* encouraged readers to "act together on our collective knowledge to change the health care system," childbirth remains on contested terrain. Out-of-hospital births are by far the exception—in 2006, for example, out of more than four million births in the United States, 24,910 occurred at home and 10,781 in freestanding birth centers. These statistics represent only 0.59 percent of the birth population.[2] Choices in childbirth today are more likely to involve *when* a woman in labor will receive an epidural rather than *if* she will. As historian Jacqueline Wolf argues, epidural anesthesia and elective cesarean section have "come to represent the essence of female empowerment in relation to birth."[3] The term *choice* is parceled out by the American College of Obstetricians and Gynecologists and the American Medical Association as if to suggest that their recommended guidelines matched the rhetoric of reproductive rights.

But it is not just the fault of organized medicine; as author Judith Warner describes it, "it's us—this generation of mothers" in the first decade of the twenty-first century, a generation of "control freaks" who have embraced "the choice myth." As she sees it, "we approached the enormous upheavals of pregnancy and childbirth as though they were normal life events we could in some way control."[4] Ricki Lake's 2007 documentary, *The Business of Being Born*, also emphasizes how birth has become more medicalized than ever before. "In America today, giving birth is a billion-dollar business," the trailer begins, "but who is benefiting? Is this an improvement or are we making things worse?"[5]

This question—whether things have gotten better or worse for women—is being asked persistently by a new generation of female writers who have chosen to focus on motherhood. They are responsible for the publishing boom of the "momoir"—a shelf full of portrayals of motherhood. With their books bearing such titles such as *Bad Mother: A Chronicle of Maternal Crimes, Minor Calamities, and Occasional Moments of Grace, Dispatches from a Not-So-Perfect Life*, and *The Bitch in the House*, these writers capture the conflicts of a postfeminist era and its emphasis on "total motherhood." Many are daughters of 1970s feminists, and express the frustrations and expectations their mothers placed on them. "Before I had children," Ayelet Waldman writes, "I knew what kind of mother I would be: my mother had told me." Her mother was a product of the "consciousness-raising, pro-choice-marching, self-speculum-wielding school," whose primary goal was to ensure that her daughter would not have to suffer the same injustices that she had. "My mission as her daughter was to realize the dream of complete equality that she and her fellow bra burners had worked so hard to attain," Waldman concludes.[6] She owed it to society, to herself, and most important, to her mother.

After the birth of her first child, however, Waldman realized that success was unattainable. She began "ranting that we daughters of feminists had essentially been lied to. Our mothers and the professors of our women's studies courses had told us that it was our job to do it all, without warning us how impossible that task would be."[7] Having graduated from the judgmental *What to Expect When You're Expecting*, mothers of newborns now face an onslaught of advice books on mothering that run the gamut from safety-proofing to attachment parenting, reminding them of the 24/7 nature of their new role.

While mothering advice is nothing new—Dr. Spock had quite a following in the 1950s—the pressure to succeed at "total motherhood" as a choice is at an all-time high. As women's studies professor Joan Wolf explains, "Total motherhood obligates mothers to be experts in everything their children might encounter, to become lay pediatricians, psychologists, consumer products–safety inspectors, toxicologists, educators, and more."[8] Scholars Susan Douglas and Meredith Michaels label this phenomenon the "new momism," which they define as "a set of ideals, norms, and practices . . . that seem on the surface to celebrate motherhood, but which in reality promulgate standards of perfection that are beyond your reach."[9] No woman can be truly complete or successful without children, to which she must devote almost all her physical, psychological, and intellectual energy.

An example of the high standards, judgment, and expectations arising from the "new momism" is the "breast is best" phenomenon. Dr. Amy Tuteur, who calls herself the "skeptical OB," writes on the publishing platform opensalon.com about the disturbing quest of "lactivists"—breast-feeding activists—to condemn bottle feeders.[10] *Atlantic* contributing editor Hannah Rosin notes, "In certain overachieving circles, breast-feeding is no longer a choice—it's a no-exceptions requirement, the ultimate badge of responsible parenting." She found this out the hard way, after announcing to fellow mothers on the playground that she was considering switching her newborn to a bottle after a month. "In my playground set," she writes, "the urban moms in their tight jeans and oversize sunglasses size each other up using a whole range of signifiers: organic content of snacks, sleekness of stroller, ratio of tasteful wooden toys to plastic. But breast-feeding is the real ticket into the club."[11]

Some readers criticize these "memoirs" as upper-middle-class laments from women with too much time on their hands. "Choosing between work and home is, in the end, a problem only for those who have a choice," writes *New Yorker* book critic Elizabeth Kolbert. "In this sense, it is, like so many 'problems' of twenty-first-century life, a problem of not having enough problems."[12] Nonetheless, she acknowledges the "veritable baby boom of books on motherhood" that attest to a newfound angst about the high expectations surrounding the role.

Many writers and critics of the "mommy myth" argue that it is a direct descendant of what Betty Friedan called the "feminine mystique."[13] Friedan's 1963 national bestseller identified "the problem that has no name" as the "growing despair of women who have forfeited their own existence" in their retreat to suburban motherhood.[14] In some ways, though, the more recent "mommy mystique" is even more insidious because of its emphasis on alleged individual choice. Douglas and Michaels argue that central to the new momism "is the feminist insistence that women have choices, that they are active agents in control of their own destiny, that they have autonomy."[15] Author Judith Warner calls this the "choice myth"—in reality, she maintains, "these were choices that didn't feel like choices at all."[16]

So what has happened to the daughters of the feminist generation? For one thing, they are more likely to be in a book club than in a consciousness-raising group, seeking advice and navigation through the complexities of motherhood and selfhood rather than strategies for revolt. Self-control has replaced collective empowerment. "Most of us in the post-baby boom generation did not learn our feminism through consciousness-raising sessions or marches," Warner writes. "We learned it by going to school and through the popular media. The watered-down, power-through-control version of female selfhood we imbibed became the backbone of our identity."[17] What that has meant for many women is an intensive and critical focus on controlling one's body. Dieting, eating disorders, and fitness fanaticism have become this generation's vehicle for self-empowerment.

Though the body has never been "for feminist thinkers, *just the body*,"[18] it has become in the last few decades a cause that has accomplished just the opposite of what 1970s feminists had hoped it would. Rather than expand and enhance knowledge and power, and create a collective consciousness, it continues to restrict and contain women. Feminism's attempt to create a universal body of knowledge out of a plurality of individual bodies has not been entirely successful. "I'd been a feminist in my head since eighteen, but my body lagged behind," writes Faulkner Fox, author of *Dispatches from a Not-So-Perfect Life*. Even in childbirth, she found difficulty relying on what she called her "body knowledge." "I don't think people always, or even often, have clarity about what's going on in their bodies," she explains.[19] Such observations suggest that the dreams and goals of 1970s health feminists—to convert physicality into knowledge, and to transform that knowledge into power—have not been able to provide all the solutions their daughters are looking for.

Notes

PREFACE

1. Adrienne Rich, *Of Woman Born: Motherhood as Experience and Institution* (New York: W. W. Norton, 1986), p. 284.

INTRODUCTION

1. This self-published first edition was actually entitled *Women and Their Bodies: A Course* (1970); quotation is from p. 9.

2. See Ann Snitow, "A Gender Diary," in *Conflicts in Feminism*, ed. Marianne Hirsch and Evelyn Fox Keller (New York: Routledge, 1990), pp. 9–43.

3. See Steven Epstein, *Inclusion: The Politics of Difference in Medical Research*, Chicago Studies in Practices of Meaning (Chicago: University of Chicago Press, 2007).

4. See Regina Morantz-Sanchez, "Feminist Theory and Historical Practice: Rereading Elizabeth Blackwell," *History and Theory: Studies in the Philosophy of History* (1992): 51–69.

5. Ibid., p. 66.

6. Evelyn Fox Keller, *Reflections on Gender and Science* (New Haven, CT; Yale University Press, 1985), p. 117. Emphasis added.

7. Adrienne Cecile Rich, *Of Woman Born: Motherhood as Experience and Institution*, 10th anniversary ed. (New York: W. W. Norton, 1986), p. 285.

8. Ibid., p. 39.

9. Janet Epstein and Marion McCartney, "A Home Birth Service That Works," *News from Home* 1, no. 4 (Fall 1976): 4, Ventre papers, Schlesinger Library, Harvard University, Cambridge, MA.

10. Boston Women's Health Book Collective, *Our Bodies, Ourselves* (New York: Simon & Schuster, 1973), p. 2.

11. Linsey, response #218 to Kline survey, "Reading *Our Bodies, Ourselves*," submitted January 1, 2005. This is an online survey that I created with the financial and technical assistance of the Center for History and New Media at George Mason University. To date, 275 people have submitted responses to the survey. http://chnm.gmu.edu/tools/surveys/467/.

12. See Sonia Kruks, *Retrieving Experience: Subjectivity and Recognition in Feminist Politics* (Ithaca, NY: Cornell University Press, 2001), p. 131.

13. See Joan W. Scott, "The Evidence of Experience," *Critical Inquiry* 17 (1991), pp. 773–97.

14. For more on how the women's health movement was co-opted and institutionalized in the late 1980s and 1990s, see Sheryl Burt Ruzek and Julie Becker, "The Women's Health Movement in the United States: From Grass-Roots Activism to Professional Agendas," *JAMWA* 54, no. 1 (Winter 1999): 4–9.

15. Bethany Davis, response #154 to Kline survey, submitted December 20, 2003.

16. Morantz-Sanchez, "Feminist Theory and Historical Practice," p. 66.

17. Wendy Holt and Archie Brodsky, "Midwife Profile: Fran Ventre," *Midwife Advocate* 2, no. 3 (Autumn 1985): 1; Fran Ventre papers, carton 4 (unprocessed collection), Schlesinger Library, Harvard University, Cambridge, MA.

18. Susan Reverby, "Thinking through the Body and the Body Politic: Feminism, History, and Health-Care Policy in the United States," in *Women, Health, and Nation: Canada and the United States since 1945*, ed. Georgina Feldberg, Molly Ladd-Taylor, and Kathryn McPherson (Montreal: McGill-Queen's University Press, 2003), p. 415.

19. Rima D. Apple, *Perfect Motherhood: Science and Childrearing in America* (New Brunswick, NJ: Rutgers University Press, 2006); Feldberg, Taylor, and McPherson, *Women, Health, and Nation*; Stephanie Gilmore, *Feminist Coalitions: Historical Perspectives on Second-Wave Feminism in the United States*, Women in American History (Urbana: University of Illinois Press, 2008); Judith A. Houck, *Hot and Bothered: Women, Medicine, and Menopause in Modern America* (Cambridge, MA: Harvard University Press, 2006); Rebecca M. Kluchin, *Fit to Be Tied: Sterilization and Reproductive Rights in America, 1950–1980*, Critical Issues in Health and Medicine (New Brunswick, NJ: Rutgers University Press, 2009); Judith Walzer Leavitt, *Make Room for Daddy: The Journey from Waiting Room to Birthing Room* (Chapel Hill: University of North Carolina Press, 2009); Ellen Singer More, Elizabeth Fee, and Manon Parry, eds., *Women Physicians and the Cultures of Medicine* (Baltimore: Johns Hopkins University Press, 2009); Christabelle Sethna, "The Evolution of the Birth Control Handbook: From Student Peer-Education Manual to Feminist Self-empowerment Text, 1968–1975," *CBMH* 23 (2006): 89–118; Rickie Solinger, *Pregnancy and Power: A Short History of Reproductive Politics in America* (New York: New York University Press, 2005); Jacqueline H. Wolf, *Deliver Me from Pain: Anesthesia and Birth in America* (Baltimore: Johns Hopkins University Press, 2009).

CHAPTER ONE

1. Boston Women's Health Book Collective, *Our Bodies, Ourselves: A New Edition for a New Era* (New York: Simon & Schuster, 2005), p. xiii.

2. Joanne Williams, response #63 to Kline survey, "Reading *Our Bodies, Ourselves*," submitted January 1, 2003 (see introduction, n. 11).

3. Estelle Freedman, response #260 to "Reading *Our Bodies, Ourselves*," submitted May 20, 2006.

4. Linsey, response #218, submitted January 1, 2005.

5. Michelle Murphy, "Liberation through Control in the Body Politics of U.S. Radical Feminism," in *The Moral Authority of Nature*, ed. Lorraine Daston and Fernando Vidal (Chicago: University of Chicago Press, 2004), p. 347.

6. See Snitow, "A Gender Diary," pp. 9–43 (see introduction, n. 2).

7. For a more in-depth analysis of the changes within the BWHBC and the text over the span of its history, with an emphasis on its global circulation, see Kathy Davis, *The Making of "Our Bodies, Ourselves": How Feminism Travels across Borders* (Durham, NC: Duke University Press, 2007).

8. James T. Patterson, *Grand Expectations: The United States, 1945–1974* (New York: Oxford University Press, 1996), p. 444.

9. Paul Starr, *The Social Transformation of American Medicine* (New York: Basic Books, 1982), p. 334.

10. Ibid., p. 379.

11. David Rothman, *Strangers at the Bedside: A History of How Law and Bioethics Transformed Medical Decision Making* (New York: Basic Books, 1991), p. 5.

12. See ibid., pp. 15–29.

13. The Patient Bill of Rights was introduced by the National Welfare Rights Organization in 1970, and adopted by the American Hospital Association in 1973. Its preamble was the only document written by health-care professionals that was reprinted in *Our Bodies, Ourselves*. See D. Rothman, *Strangers at the Bedside*, p. 145.

14. Ibid., p. 128.

15. Ibid., p. 245. See also Jonathan Imber, *Trusting Doctors: The Decline of Moral Authority in American Medicine* (Princeton, NJ: Princeton University Press, 2008).

16. Starr, *The Social Transformation of American Medicine*, p. 371.

17. Jennifer Nelson, *Women of Color and the Reproductive Rights Movement* (New York: New York University Press, 2003), p. 92.

18. Sheryl Burt Ruzek, *The Women's Health Movement: Feminist Alternatives to Medical Control* (New York: Praeger Publishers, 1978), pp. 60–61. She notes that the Haight-Ashbury Free Clinic, which opened in 1967, became the model for approximately four hundred additional facilities.

19. Sara Evans, *Tidal Wave: How Women Changed America at Century's End* (New York: Free Press, 2003), p. 18.

20. Becky Thompson, "Multiracial Feminism: Recasting the Chronology of Second Wave Feminism," *Feminist Studies* 28 (2002): 337.

21. Evans, *Tidal Wave*, pp. 3–4.

22. Ibid., p. 29.

23. Ibid., p. 30.

24. Carol S. Weisman, *Women's Health Care: Activist Traditions and Institutional Change* (Baltimore: Johns Hopkins University Press, 1998), p. 72.

25. Ibid., pp. 73–74.

26. Ruzek, *The Women's Health Movement*, p. 144; see also Myra Marx Ferree and Beth B. Hess, *Controversy and Coalition: The New Feminist Movement across Four Decades of Change*, 3rd ed. (New York: Routledge, 2000), p. 108.

27. Other groups have also produced feminist health literature, although none as successfully as the BWHBC. For example, the Vancouver, B.C., Women's Health Collective published *A Woman's Place* in 1972. Newsletters included Lolly and Jeanne Hirsch's *The Monthly Extract—An Irregular Periodical* and the Women's Health Forum's *HealthRight*. In addition, feminist newspapers and journals, including *Off Our Backs* and *Ms. Magazine*, regularly covered women's health issues. By the early 1970s, traditional women's magazines such as *Vogue* and *Redbook* published articles on women's health that challenged traditional medicine. See Ruzek, *The Women's Health Movement*, pp. 147, 210, and 218, and appendix B.

28. Ruzek argues that "selective utilization" of physicians was a strategy of health movement activists, noting that lay referral systems began as informal affairs. See Ruzek, *The Women's Health Movement*, p. 162.

29. Wendy Sanford and Judy Norsigian, "Ten Years in the *Our Bodies, Ourselves* Collective—Draft"; BWHBC papers (unprocessed), 99-M147, box 5, p. 2, Schlesinger Library, Harvard University, Cambridge, MA.

30. Barbara A. Brehm, "Knowledge Is Power: *Our Bodies, Ourselves* and the Boston Women's Health Book Collective," in *Women on Power: Leadership Redefined*, ed. Sue Freeman, Susan Bourque, and Christine Shelton (Boston: Northeastern University Press, 2001), p. 156.

31. Susan Wells, "Narrative Forms in *Our Bodies, Ourselves*," in *Women Physicians and the Cultures of Medicine*, ed. Ellen Singer More, Elizabeth Fee, and Manon Parry (Baltimore: Johns Hopkins University Press, 2009), p. 189.

32. Judith Baker, response #214 response to "Reading *Our Bodies, Ourselves*," submitted November 22, 2004.

33. Boston Women's Health Book Collective, *Our Bodies, Our Selves: A Course By and For Women* (Cambridge, MA: New England Free Press, 1971), p. 1.

34. Brehm, "Knowledge Is Power," p. 157.

35. Boston Women's Health Book Collective, *Our Bodies, Our Selves* (1971 ed.), last page (not numbered).

36. K. Davis, *The Making of "Our Bodies, Ourselves,"* p. 24.

37. Lynn, letter to BWHBC, July 31, 1972; BWHBC papers (unprocessed), 99–M147, box 1.

38. In an interview with Susan Wells, Ruth Bell Alexander characterized the BWHBC as essentially a consciousness-raising group. See Wells, "Narrative Forms in *Our Bodies, Ourselves*," p. 189.

39. See Jo Freeman, "The Tyranny of Structurelessness," in *Dear Sisters: Dispatches from the Women's Liberation Movement*, by Rosalyn Fraad Baxandall and Linda Gordon (New York: Basic Books, 2000), p. 73.

40. Joan, letter to group, Fall 1974; BWHBC papers, box 1.

41. Nancy, Joan, and Ruth, letter to group, July 25, 1974; BWHBC papers, box 1.

42. Nancy, letter to group, Labor Day 1976; BWHBC papers, box 1.

43. Nancy, Joan, and Ruth, letter to group, July 25, 1974.

44. Jane, letter to group, Summer 1975; BWHBC papers, box 1.

45. J. Freeman, "The Tyranny of Structurelessness," p. 74.

46. Judy, letter to group, April 19, 1976; BWHBC papers, box 1.

47. Wendy, letter to the parenting group, August 24, 1976; BWHBC papers, box 1.

48. Ibid.

49. Norma, letter to group, September 5, 1976; BWHBC papers, box 1.

50. Ibid.

51. Ibid.

52. Joan, letter to group, September 4, 1976; BWHBC papers, box 1.

53. Nancy and Joan, memo #2, p. 2, April 3, 1979; BWHBC papers, 99-M125, box 6, Parenting folder.

54. Victoria K. Musmann, review of *Ourselves and Our Children*, *Library Journal Review*, 103, no. 17 (October 1, 1978): 1967. Negative reviews include Pat Hosking, *Broadsheet* (New Zealand), April 1979; and Molly Lovelock, "Narrow Viewpoint," *Sojourner*, February 1979, p. 13. BWHBC papers, 99-M125, box 6, Parenting folder.

55. Meeting minutes, June 2, 1980; BWHBC papers, box 1, p. 3.

56. Ibid., box 1, p. 2.

57. Wendy, letter to group, August 24, 1976; BWHBC papers, box 1.

58. Norma, letter to group, September 5, 1976; BWHBC papers, box 1.

59. Boston Women's Health Book Collective, *Our Bodies, Ourselves* (1973 ed.), p. 2.

60. Susan E. Bell, "Translating Science to the People: Updating *The New Our Bodies, Ourselves*," *Women's Studies International Forum* 17 (1994): 10.

61. Ibid.

62. Kathy Davis, "Feminist Body/Politics as World Traveller: Translating *Our Bodies, Ourselves*," *European Journal of Women's Studies* 9 (2002): 241.

63. There are approximately 215 letters filed under Reader Correspondence in the BWHBC papers. In the summer of 2001, I read through the entire collection of letters.

64. This is not the first time that women's responses to medical literature led to activism. Carol Weisman interprets recurring episodes of women's activism in the United States as waves in a women's health "megamovement" that began in the early nineteenth century. From the popular health movement to late nineteenth-century and Progressive Era movements, women have responded to health products and information and demanded that the health-care system be sensitive to their needs. See Weisman, *Women's Health Care*, p. 29.

65. Lisa Maria Hogeland, *Feminism and Its Fictions: The Consciousness-Raising Novel and the Women's Liberation Movement* (Philadelphia: University of Pennsylvania Press, 1998), p. 4.

66. Ibid., p. 10.

67. Ibid., p. 30.

68. Libby, letter to BWHBC, November 25, 1979; BWHBC papers, 99-M147, box 2, PID folder.

69. Mary Elizabeth, undated letter to "Jane and everyone in the collective," BWHBC papers, 99-M125, box 1, History: 10th Anniversary folder.

70. Helen McMillan, letter to BWHBC, July 8, 1981; BWHBC papers, 99-M147, box 2, Menstruation Brochure Requests folder.

71. Names of readers are fictional; the BWHBC had blacked out names and addresses from reader correspondence.

72. Name blacked out, letter to "Ms. Pinkas," April 14, 1980; BWHBC papers, 99-M147, box 2, Correspondence to File '79, '81–'82 folder. Susan Reverby recalls that when she gave public talks about criticizing the health industry, she would run into the "body/body politic difficulty. No matter what I said, the questions after my talk were always bipolar in their distribution. Half would be about how we should take on United States capitalism *in toto*; the other half would be about what advice I would give about a vaginal itch or the latest breast cancer treatment." See Reverby, "Thinking through the Body and the Body Politic," p. 409 (see introduction, n. 18).

73. Ibid.

74. Name blacked out, letter to Judy Norsigian, September 23, 1979; BWHBC papers, 99-M147, box 2, Correspondence to File '79, '81–'82 folder.

75. Ibid.

76. Catherine Stimpson, interview with Marcia Storch, MD, review of *Our Bodies, Ourselves*, by the Boston Women's Health Book Collective, *Ms.*, April 1973, p. 33.

77. Imber, *Trusting Doctors*, p. 114.

78. Name blacked out, undated letter to BWHBC (received February 1979), BWHBC papers, 99-M147, box 2, Correspondence to File '79, '81–'82 folder.

79. Ibid.

80. Ibid.

81. Barbara Herbert, letter to Pastor Marge Ragona, August 24, 1976; Women's Action Alliance records, box 247, folder 8, Sophia Smith Collection, Smith College Library, Northampton, MA.

82. Ruzek, *The Women's Health Movement*, p. 9. Concern over routine gynecological care fueled a much larger debate among medical schools and feminist health activists in the 1970s, the subject of the next chapter.

83. Boston Women's Health Book Collective, *Our Bodies, Ourselves* (1973 ed.), p. 268.

84. Name blacked out, letter "to those who wrote this book," February 17, 1979; BWHBC papers, 99-M147, box 2, Pap Smears folder.

85. Boston Women's Health Book Collective, *Our Bodies, Ourselves, Revised and Expanded* (New York: Simon & Schuster, 1979), p. 147.

86. Name blacked out, letter to Norma Swenson and Jane Pincus, June 28, 1979; BWHBC papers, 99-M147, box 2, Pap Smears folder.

87. Name blacked out, letter "to those who wrote this book."

88. See, for example, Sandra Morgen, *Into Our Own Hands: The Women's Health Movement in the United States, 1969–1990* (New Brunswick, NJ: Rutgers University Press, 2002), chap. 7.

89. Ibid.

90. Name blacked out, letter to Norma Swenson and Jane Pincus.

91. Amy Erdman Farrell, *Yours in Sisterhood: Ms. Magazine and the Promise of Popular Feminism* (Chapel Hill: University of North Carolina Press, 1998), p. 151.

92. Barbara Ehrenreich and Deirdre English, *Complaints and Disorders: The Sexual Politics of Sickness* (Old Westbury, NY: Feminist Press, 1973), pp. 86–87; quoted in Ruzek, *The Women's Health Movement*, p. 187.

93. In her study of *Our Bodies, Ourselves*, Davis also notes that most readers did not directly address the issue of race. She notes, "In a racialized context where whiteness is treated by many people as being without race, a condition of invisibility not available to people of color, this would indicate that many of the letters were probably written by white, Anglo-American women." K. Davis, *The Making of "Our Bodies, Ourselves,"* p. 152.

94. Ruzek, *The Women's Health Movement*, p. 192.

95. Martha Scherzer, "Byllye Avery and the National Black Women's Health Project," *Network News* (May–June 1995): 4.

96. Morgen, *Into Our Own Hands*, p. 43.

97. Wini Breines, *The Trouble between Us: An Uneasy History of White and Black Women in the Feminist Movement* (Oxford: Oxford University Press, 2006).

98. Alba Bonilla, April Taylor, Mayra Canetti, and Jennifer Yanco, "An Open Letter to the Board of Directors, Boston Women's Health Book Collective," *Sojourner: The Women's Forum*, December 1997, p. 4.

99. Greta Giving, letter to BWHBC, February 1, 1979; BWHBC papers, 99-M147, box 2, Correspondence to File '79, '81–'82 folder.

100. Nelson, *Women of Color and the Reproductive Rights Movement*, p. 74.

101. See Wendy Kline, *Building a Better Race: Gender, Sexuality, and Eugenics from the Turn of the Century to the Baby Boom* (Berkeley and Los Angeles: University of California Press, 2001).

102. Kluchin, *Fit to Be Tied*, p. 184.

103. Boston Women's Health Book Collective, *Our Bodies, Our Selves* (1971 ed.), p. 60c.

104. Greta Giving, letter to BWHBC, February 1, 1979.

105. Boston Women's Health Book Collective, *The New Our Bodies, Ourselves* (New York: Simon & Schuster, 1984), p. 256.

106. Name blacked out, letter to Wendy Sanford, August 6, 1980; BWHBC papers, 99-M147, box 2, Abortion folder.

107. Ibid.

108. Boston Women's Health Book Collective, *Our Bodies, Ourselves, Revised and Expanded*, p. 222, n. 67.

109. Name blacked out, letter to Wendy Sanford, August 6, 1980.

110. Ibid.

111. Wendy Sanford, undated response to August 6, 1980, letter; BWHBC papers, 99-M147, box 2, Abortion folder.

112. Boston Women's Health Book Collective, *The New Our Bodies, Ourselves*, pp. 305–8, 293.

113. Jane Gulko, letter to BWHBC, March 9, 1977; BWHBC papers, 99-M147, box 2, Pre-1978 folder.

114. Boston Women's Health Book Collective, *Our Bodies, Ourselves, Revised and Expanded* (New York: Simon & Schuster, 1976), p. 41.

115. Mary-Elyn O'Grady, undated letter to BWHBC, BWHBC papers, 99-M147, box 2, Pre-1978 folder.

116. Wendy Sanford, "Body Image," in *The New Our Bodies, Ourselves*, by the Boston Women's Health Book Collective (New York: Simon & Schuster, 1984), p. 6, n. 87.

117. Alice Echols, *Daring to Be Bad: Radical Feminism in America, 1967–1975* (Minneapolis: University of Minnesota Press, 1989), p. 212. See also Karla Jay, *Tales of the Lavender Menace: A Memoir of Liberation* (New York: Basic Books, 2000); Susan Brownmiller, *In Our Time: Memoir of a Revolution* (New York: Random House, 1999); and Kimberly Springer, *Living for the Revolution: Black Feminist Organizations, 1968–1980* (Durham, NC: Duke University Press, 2005).

118. Boston Women's Health Book Collective, *The New Our Bodies, Ourselves*, p. 141.

119. Barbara Smith, letter to Wendy Sanford and Lily, July 7, 1981; BWHBC papers, 99-M147, box 2, Correspondence to File '79, '81–'82 folder. See also Ruzek, *The Women's Health Movement*, p. 190.

120. Boston Women's Health Book Collective, *Our Bodies, Ourselves*, "In Amerika" chapter, p. 56, n. 1 (1973 ed.), p. 81 (1976 and 1979 eds.).

121. Wendy Sanford, letter to "the women who worked on the lesbian chapter of *Our Bodies, Ourselves*," December 15, 1974; BWHBC papers, 99-M125, box 1, History—1976 *Our Bodies, Ourselves* folder.

122. Meeting minutes, "Tuesday March 28" [1978?]; BWHBC papers, 99-M125, box 1, Minutes/Memos 1974–76 folder.

123. Name blacked out, letter to BWHBC, March 14, 1982; BWHBC papers, 99-M147, box 2, Orgasm folder.

124. Boston Women's Health Book Collective, *The New Our Bodies, Ourselves*, p. 141.

125. Stimpson, *Our Bodies, Ourselves* review, p. 35.

CHAPTER TWO

1. Martin Stone, quoted in Pamela S. Summey and Marsha Hurst, "Ob/Gyn on the Rise: The Evolution of Professional Ideology in the Twentieth Century— Part II," *Women and Health* 11, no. 2 (Summer 1985): 117. In response to this embattled environment, the American College of Obstetricians and Gynecologists moved its offices from Chicago to Washington, D.C. (see chapter 3).

2. Morgen, *Into Our Own Hands*, p. 71 (see chap. 1, n. 88).

3. See chapter 3.

4. Morgen, *Into Our Own Hands*, p. 95.

5. Women's Community Health Center, Third Annual Report, September 1977, p. 1, WCHC papers, 99-M101, Schlesinger Library, Harvard University, Cambridge, MA.

6. Ibid., p. 2.

7. Michelle Murphy, "Immodest Witnessing: The Epistemology of Vaginal Self-Examination in the U.S. Feminist Self-Help Movement," *Feminist Studies* 30, no. 1 (Spring 2004): 117.

8. Ellen Frankfort, *Vaginal Politics* (New York: Bantam Books, 1973), p. xxiii.

9. Cortney Davis, *I Knew a Woman: Four Women Patients and Their Female Caregiver* (New York: Ballantine, 2001), p. xi.

10. Although the pelvic has been a subject of study in sociology, that has not generally been the case for historians. See, for example, James M. Henslin and Mae A. Biggs, "The Sociology of the Vaginal Examination," in *Studies in the Sociology of Sex*, ed. James M. Henslin (New York: Appleton-Century-Crofts, 1971), pp. 243–72; and Susan Bell, "Political Gynecology: Gynecology Imperialism and the Politics of Self-Help," *Science for the People* 11, no. 5 (1979): 8–14. In addition, Terri Kapsalis published a fascinating study of the gynecological exam from a theatrical perspective; see Terri Kapsalis, *Public Privates: Performing Gynecology from Both Ends of the Speculum* (Durham, NC: Duke University Press, 1997). Recently, some historians have begun addressing this issue; see Murphy, "Immodest Witnessing"; Heather Prescott, " 'Guides to Womanhood': Gynaecology and Adolescent Sexuality in the Post-Second World War Era," in *Women, Health, and Nation: Canada and the United States Since 1945*, ed. Georgona Feldberg, Molly ladd-Taylor, and Kathryn McPherson (Montreal: McGill-Queen's University Press, 2003), pp. 199–222; and Carolyn Herbst Lewis, "Waking Sleeping Beauty: The Premarital Pelvic Exam and Heterosexuality during the Cold War," *Journal of Women's History* 17, no. 4 (2005): 86–110.

11. Kapsalis, *Public Privates*, p. 63.

12. Ellen Rothman, *White Coat: Becoming a Doctor at Harvard Medical School* (New York: HarperCollins, 1999), p. 73.

13. Summey and Marsha Hurst, "Ob/Gyn on the Rise," 103–22; quotation is from p. 104.

14. Lewis, "Waking Sleeping Beauty," p. 88.

15. Ibid., p. 93.

16. Ibid., p. 97.

17. Summey and Hurst, "Ob/Gyn on the Rise," p. 113.

18. Ibid., p. 114.

19. Ibid., p. 115.

20. Kenneth M. Ludmerer, *Time to Heal: American Medical Education from the Turn of the Century to the Era of Managed Care* (Oxford: Oxford University Press, 1999), p. 240.

21. Ibid., p. 241.

22. Ibid., p. 253.

23. Ibid., p. 257. By 2005, the percentage was up to 46.8 percent. See introduction to More, Fee, and Parry, eds., *Women Physicians and the Cultures of Medicine* (see introduction, n. 19).

24. Naomi Rogers, "Feminists Fight the Culture of Exclusion in Medical Education, 1970–1990," in More, Fee, and Parry, eds., *Women Physicians and the Cultures of Medicine*, p. 209.

25. Ibid.

26. Carola Eisenberg, interview with author, Cambridge, MA, August 3, 2004.

27. Janet Bickel, foreword to Eliza Lo Chin, *This Side of Doctoring: Reflections from Women in Medicine* (Oxford: Oxford University Press, 2003), p. xxi.

28. Ortho advertisement, *New Physician*, November 1971, p. 701.

29. Kapsalis, *Public Privates*, p. 66.

30. Howard S. Barrows and Stephen Abrahamson, "The Programmed Patient: A Technique for Appraising Student Performance in Clinical Neurology," *Journal of Medical Education* 39 (August 1964): 802–5.

31. Ibid., p. 805.

32. *San Francisco Chronicle* reporter, quoted in Peggy Wallace, "Following the Threads of an Innovation: The History of Standardized Patients in Medical Education," *Caduceus* 13, no. 2 (Fall 1997): 5–28.

33. Thomas R. Godkins, Daniel Duffy, MD, Judith Greenwood, and William D. Stanhope, "Utilization of Simulated Patients to Teach the 'Routine' Pelvic Examination," *Journal of Medical Education* 49 (December 1974): 1174–78; quotations are from p. 1177.

34. Robert M. Kretzschmar, "Evolution of the Gynecology Teaching Associate: An Education Specialist," *American Journal of Obstetrics and Gynecology* 131, no. 4 (June 15, 1978): 367–73; quotation is from p. 368.

35. Ibid., p. 367.

36. Ibid., p. 368.

37. Susan Guenther, "There Is No Excuse . . ." *Journal of American Medical Women's Association* 39, no. 2 (March–April 1984): 40–42; quotation is from p. 40.

38. Judith S. Jacobson, "Teaching on One's Own Body," *Journal of the American Medical Women's Association* 39, no. 2 (March–April 1984): 49.

39. Lila A. Wallis, Kenneth Tardiff, and Kathleen Deane, "Changes in Students' Attitudes Following a Pelvic Teaching Associate Program," *Journal of the American Medical Women's Association* 39, no. 2 (March–April 1984): 46–48; Jerome Herbers Jr., Lois Wessel, Jehan El-Bayoumi, Sheir Hassan, and Joan Onge, "Pelvic Examination Training for Interns: A Randomized Controlled Trial," *Academic Medicine* 78, no. 11 (November 2003): 1164–69. As Kapsalis points out, by the 1990s, over 90 percent of U.S. medical schools utilized the Kretzschmar model. See Kapsalis, *Public Privates*, p. 71.

40. Robert M. Kretzschmar, MD, and Deborah S. Guthrie, MA, "Why Not in Every School?" *Journal of the American Medical Women's Association* 39, no. 2 (March–April 1984): 43–45; quotation is from pp. 43–44.

41. Godkins, Duffy, Greenwood, and Stanhope, "Utilization of Simulated Patients to Teach the 'Routine' Pelvic Examination," p. 1175.

42. Ibid., pp. 1174, 1178, 1177.

43. Dr. James. G. Blythe, "Discussion," following Kretzschmar, "Evolution of the Gynecology Teaching Associate," p. 373.

44. Kretzschmar, "Evolution of the Gynecology Teaching Associate," p. 369.

45. Ibid.

46. Dr. Joseph C. Scott Jr., "Discussion," following Kretzschmar, "Evolution of the Gynecology Teaching Associate," p. 373.

47. Dr. William Kiekhofer, "Discussion," following Kretzschmar, "Evolution of the Gynecology Teaching Associate," p. 373.

48. The Women's Community Health Center provided educational and medical services in the Cambridge, Massachusetts, area between 1974 and 1981, when it declared bankruptcy. Members (in addition to the PTP affiliates) ranged in age from 23 to 52 and numbered from 5 to 20. The center declared that it was "the only women worker owned and controlled licensed free-standing clinic in Massachusetts," and "committed to feminism and self help" (undated flier). For more on its history, see Women's Community Health Center annual reports, 99-M101, WCHC papers; and Morgen, *Into Our Own Hands*, pp. 95–99.

49. The Pelvic Teaching Program, "Taking Our Bodies Back," *Sister Courage*, December 1976, unpaginated.

50. Bell, "Political Gynecology," p. 9.

51. Ibid., p. 10.

52. The Pelvic Teaching Program, "Taking Our Bodies Back."

53. Ibid.

54. Ibid.

55. Marsha Belford, "From Both Ends of the Exam Table: On Being a Gynecology Teaching Associate," *Womenwise* 5, no. 3 (Fall 1982), unpaginated.

56. Kapsalis also makes this observation. See Kapsalis, *Public Privates*, p. 70.

57. The Pelvic Teaching Program, "Taking Our Bodies Back."

58. Women's Community Health Center, "How to Do a Pelvic Examination," 1976, WCHC papers, 99-M101, box 8, "training notebook."

59. For example, members of "Jane," the underground abortion service in Chicago (see chapter 3), had shown their patients a view of their cervix when performing abortions.

60. Anthony Monaco, letter to WCHC, January 6, 1977; WCHC papers, 99-M101, box 4, Pelvic Teaching Program folder.

61. Charles Hatem, letter to WCHC, November 29, 1976; WCHC papers, 99-M101, box 4.

62. J. Andrew Billings and John D. Stoeckle, "Pelvic Examination Instruction and the Doctor-Patient Relationship," *Journal of Medical Education* 52 (October 1977): 834–39; quotation is from p. 834.

63. Quoted in ibid., p. 837.

64. Quoted in ibid., p. 837.

65. Belford, "From Both Ends of the Exam Table."

66. Margaret A. Campbell (pseudonym), *Why Would a Girl Go into Medicine?* (Old Westbury, NY: Feminist Press, 1973, 1977), p. 40.

67. Ibid., p. 42.

68. Frankfort, *Vaginal Politics*, p. 30.

69. Buchwald focused on six reactions presented in "almost every seminar session": fear of hurting the patient, fear of being judged inept, fear of inability to recognize pathology, fear of sexual arousal, fear of finding the examination unpleasant, and disturbance of the doctor-patient relationship.

70. Julius Buchwald, "The First Pelvic Examination: Helping Students Cope with Their Emotional Reactions," *Journal of Medical Education* 54 (September 1979): 725–28; quotation is from p. 726.

71. Kapsalis, *Public Privates*, p. 64.

72. Quoted in Billings and Stoeckle, "Pelvic Examination Instruction and the Doctor-Patient Relationship," p. 837.

73. Women's Community Health Center, Second Annual Report, WCHC papers, 2002-M92, box 1, p. 9.

74. Drs. Holzman, Singleton, Holmes, Maatsch, and Stenchever, "Letters to the Editor," *Journal of Medical Education* 53 (March 1978): 227.

75. Ibid., p. 228.

76. Pelvic Teaching Program, "Taking Our Bodies Back." Emphasis in original.

77. Susan Bell, "Author's Response to Letter of Elizabeth B. and Al C.," *Science for the People* 12, no. 1 (January–February 1980): 28.

78. Pelvic Teaching Program, "Taking Our Bodies Back."

79. Ibid.

80. Charles J. Hatem, letter to WCHC, March 14, 1977; WCHC papers, 99-M101, box 4, Pelvic Teaching Program folder.

81. Bell, "Political Gynecology," p. 13.

82. Elizabeth B. and Al C., letter to the editors, *Science for the People* 12, no. 1 (January–February 1980): 5.

83. Bell, "Author's Response," p. 29. Emphasis in original.

84. Ibid.

85. Handwritten notes [undated, but recounting the interaction that took place on 14 March 1977], no name, WCHC papers, 99-M101, box 4, Pelvic Teaching Program folder.

86. Kapsalis, *Public Privates*, p. 76.

87. Terri Kapsalis, interview with author, July 21, 2009.

88. Amyra Braha, "Not the Oldest Profession: Two Women Talk about Their Experiences as Professional Patients," *Healthsharing*, Spring 1985, pp. 11–14; quotation is from p. 14.

89. Nancy Tuana, "Coming to Understand: Orgasm and the Epistemology of Ignorance," *Hypatia* 19, no. 1 (Winter 2004): 194–232; quotation is from p. 225.

90. Jane F. Gerhard, *Desiring Revolution: Second-Wave Feminism and the Rewriting of American Sexual Thought, 1920 to 1982* (New York: Columbia University Press, 2001), p. 6.

91. See Nora Ephron, *Crazy Salad: Some Things about Women* (New York: Bantam Books, 1976), p. 13.

92. Kapsalis, *Public Privates*, pp. 115–16.

93. Susan E. Bell and Susan Reverby, "Vaginal Politics: Tensions and Possibilities in *The Vagina Monologues*," *Women's Studies International Forum* 28 (November 2005): 430–44.

94. Herbers et al., "Pelvic Examination Training for Interns," p. 1164.

95. Ubel, Jepson, and Silver-Isenstadt, "Don't Ask, Don't Tell: A Change in Medical Student Attitudes after Obstetrics/Gynecology Clerkships toward Seeking Consent for Pelvic Examinations on an Anesthetized Patient," *American Journal of Obstetrics and Gynecology*, February 2003, pp. 575–79.

96. Dena S. Davis, JD, PhD, "Pelvic Exams Performed on Anesthetized Women," *Virtual Mentor: Ethics Journal of the American Medical Association* 5, no. 5 (May 2003): op-ed.

97. http://www.atyourcervixmovie.com/about.html (accessed November 16, 2009).

98. Ibid.

99. Carola Eisenberg, "Similarities and Differences between Men and Women as Students," presented at the Elizabeth Garrett Symposium, "Women Physicians in Contemporary Society" at the Johns Hopkins University School of Medicine, Baltimore, October 9–10, 1979. Eisenberg file, Francis A. Countway Library of Medicine, Harvard University.

100. Regina Markell Morantz-Sanchez, *Sympathy and Science: Women Physicians in American Medicine* (New York: Oxford University Press, 1985), p. 359.

101. Carola Eisenberg, interview with author, August 3, 2004.

CHAPTER THREE

1. John Dittmer, *The Good Doctors: The Medical Committee for Human Rights and the Struggle for Social Justice in Health Care*, 1st U.S. ed. (New York: Bloomsbury Press, 2009); Naomi Rogers, "Caution: The AMA May Be Dangerous to Your Health": The Student Health Organizations (SHO) and American Medicine, 1965–1970," *Radical History Review* 80 (2001): 5–34.

2. Brownmiller, *In Our Time*, p. 54 (see chap. 1, n. 117).

3. Lauri Umansky, *Motherhood Reconceived: Feminism and the Legacies of the Sixties* (New York: New York University Press, 1996), p. 32; see also Murphy, "Liberation through Control in the Body Politics of U.S. Radical Feminism" (see chap. 1, n. 5).

4. Brownmiller, *In Our Time*, pp. 52–54; Echols, *Daring to Be Bad*, pp. 107–14 (see chap. 1, n. 117).

5. Heather Booth, quoted in Echols, *Daring to Be Bad*, p. 110.

6. Brownmiller, *In Our Time*, p. 18.

7. Jo Freeman, quoted in Ibid.

8. Echols, *Daring to Be Bad*, p. 136.

9. Rebecca M. Kluchin, "What Was the CWLU?" http://www.cwluherstory.org/what-was-the-chicago-womens-liberation-union.html (accessed November 17, 2009). See also p. 3 of "A View from the Loop: The Women's Health Movement in Chicago," by many Chicago women affiliated with Healthright: box 4, folder 9, Jenny Knauss Collection, Charles Deering McCormick Library of Special Collections, Northwestern University, Evanston, IL; and Echols, *Daring to Be Bad*, p. 136.

10. Suzanne Staggenborg, *The Pro-Choice Movement: Organization and Activism in the Abortion Conflict* (New York: Oxford University Press, 1991), pp. 175–77.

11. Kluchin, "What Was the CWLU?"

12. "Statement of Purpose" from *Womankind*, December 1972; http://www.cwluherstory.org/a-cwlu-statement-of-purpose-2.html (accessed November 17, 2009).

13. Staggenborg, *The Pro-Choice Movement*, pp. 175–77.

14. Leslie J. Reagan, *When Abortion Was a Crime: Women, Medicine, and Law in the United States, 1867–1973* (Berkeley and Los Angeles: University of California Press, 1997), p. 216.

15. Ibid., p. 217.

16. Laura Kaplan, *The Story of Jane: The Legendary Underground Feminist Abortion Service* (New York: Pantheon Books, 1995), p. xiii.

17. Brownmiller, *In Our Time*, p. 7.

18. See Barbara Ehrenreich, "What Is Socialist Feminism?" originally published in *WIN Magazine* in 1976, on the CWLU Web site under Classical Feminist Writings Archive: http://www.cwluherstory.com/CWLUArchive/socialfem.html (accessed November 17, 2009).

19. Kluchin, *Fit to Be Tied* (see introduction, n. 19); Jael Miriam Silliman et al., *Undivided Rights: Women of Color Organize for Reproductive Justice* (Cambridge, MA: South End Press, 2004); Breines, *The Trouble between Us* (see chap. 1, n. 97).

20. Kluchin, *Fit to Be Tied*, p. 185.

21. Of course, many cities witnessed the founding and failure of various feminist organizations. As Michelle Murphy so aptly describes, "cells split, fused, and propagated, forming a shifting multiplicity of feminist positions that gave birth to diverse strands of feminist thought." See Murphy, "Liberation through Control in the Body Politics of U.S. Radical Feminism," p. 333.

22. This somewhat surprising revelation is part of a project started by two local activists, Jenny Knauss and Laurie Crawford, who were instrumental in putting together an analytical paper on the Chicago women's health movement from 1969 to 1975 (which became "A View from the Loop"). As part of that project (through the Urban Preceptorship Program at the University of Illinois at Chicago Medical Center), in September of 1975 they circulated copies of working papers to a number of women active in the movement. These comments on the Abortion Counseling Service are from a particular draft that did not get published, and it is unclear who the actual author is. From box 4, folder 9, Knauss Collection.

23. Heather Booth, interview with Paula Kamen, September 1, 1992; folder 3, Paula Kamen Collection, Charles Deering McCormick Library of Special Collections, Northwestern University, Evanston, IL.

24. Ibid.

25. Jody Parsons, quoted in Kaplan, *The Story of Jane*, p. 6.

26. "A View from the Loop," p. 3; see also Kaplan, *The Story of Jane*, p. 27.

27. Judith Arcana, interview with Paula Kamen, September 1992; folder 2, p. 1, Kamen Collection.

28. Ibid., p. 3.

29. Kaplan, *The Story of Jane*, p. 100.

30. Ibid., p. 111.

31. Judith Arcana, interview with Paula Kamen, September 1992, p. 6.

32. Kaplan, *The Story of Jane*, p. 137.

33. Judith Arcana, interview with Paula Kamen, September 1992, p. 7.

34. Ruth Surgal, quoted in Kaplan, *The Story of Jane*, pp. 140–41.

35. Morgen, *Into Our Own Hands*, p. 22 (see chap. 1, n. 88).

36. The feminist self-help movement "insisted, however, that menstrual extraction was not a do-it-yourself abortion"—it was a way to control menstruation. For a brilliant discussion of the role of menstrual extraction in feminist

self-help organizations, see Murphy, "Liberation through Control in the Body Politics of U.S. Radical Feminism."

37. Judith Arcana, interview with Paula Kamen, September 1992, p. 8.

38. Kaplan, *The Story of Jane*, pp. 197–200.

39. Judith Arcana, interview with Paula Kamen, September 1992, p. 8.

40. Joan Scott, "The Evidence of Experience," p. 777 (see introduction, n. 13).

41. K. Davis, *The Making of "Our Bodies, Ourselves,"* p. 122 (see chap. 1, n. 7).

42. "Lorry," interview with Paula Kamen, November 26, 1992; folder 6, p. 7, Kamen Collection.

43. See Reagan, *When Abortion Was a Crime*, p. 226.

44. Chris Lombard and Ruth Surgal, "As a Feminist, This 'Jane' Was Far from Plain," *Women's E News*, March 20 2002, CWLU Web site: http://www .cwluherstory.org/as-a-feminist-this-jane-was-far-from-plain.html (accessed November 17, 2009).

45. Ibid.

46. Ibid.

47. Kaplan, *The Story of Jane*, p. 276.

48. Flier, October 15, 1970; box 4, folder 2, Knauss Collection.

49. Dittmer, *The Good Doctors*, p. 198.

50. Ibid., pp. 213–14.

51. Flier, October 15, 1970.

52. Alice Hamilton Women's Health Center memo, box 4, folder 2, p. 3, Knauss Collection.

53. Elaine Wessel, letter to Jenny Knauss, September 15, 1975; box 4, folder 2, Knauss Collection.

54. Ibid.

55. Alice Hamilton Women's Health Center memo.

56. Elaine Wessel, "Pregnancy Testing," CWLU Web site: http://www .cwluherstory.org/pregnancy-testing.html (accessed November 17, 2009).

57. "Emma Goldman Women's Health Center," undated flier; box 4, folder 14, Knauss Collection.

58. Ibid.

59. Ibid.

60. Terri Kapsalis, interview with author, July 21, 2009.

61. "Emma Goldman Lives!" undated flier; box 4, folder 14, Knauss Collection.

62. Tanya McHale, interview with author, July 28, 2009.

63. Ibid.

64. "Abortion Task Force: Who We Are," from *Womankind*, July 1973; on CWLU Web site: http://www.cwluherstory.org/abortion-task-force-who-we-are.html (accessed November 17, 2009).

65. Carole Joffe, Patricia Anderson, and Jody Steinauer, "The Crisis in Abortion Provision and Pro-Choice Medical Activism in the 1990s," in *Abortion Wars: A Half Century of Struggle, 1950–2000*, ed. Rickie Solinger (Berkeley and Los Angeles: University of California Press, 1998), pp. 320–21.

66. "Abortion Task Force: Who We Are."

67. "Hospital Fact Sheet," box 6, folder 1, Knauss Collection.

68. "If You Need an Abortion," box 6, folder 1, Knauss Collection.

69. "Hospital Fact Sheet."

70. See Staggenborg, *The Pro-Choice Movement*, p. 68. As noted earlier, this opposition to professionals and professional organizations began earlier, during the development of the Abortion Counseling Service. Local activists reflected in 1975 that this "knee-jerk reaction" limited their ability to forge networks and attract other women to the cause.

71. "Abortion Calendar–1973," box 6, folder 1, Knauss Collection.

72. Leatrice Hauptman, "Evaluation of the Abortion Task Force," December 1975; CWLU records, box 12, folder 1, Chicago History Museum (formerly the Chicago Historical Society). As noted earlier, there is an extensive literature on race and abortion.

73. Staggenborg, *The Pro-Choice Movement*, p. 20.

74. Ibid., p. 21.

75. Madeline Schwenk, quoted in ibid., p. 39.

76. Ibid.

77. Gilmore, *Feminist Coalitions* (see introduction, n. 19); Staggenborg, *The Pro-Choice Movement*, p. 62.

78. Hauptman, "Evaluation of the Abortion Task Force." Emphasis added.

79. For an example of a community study in which diverse groups were able to transcend differences to achieve abortion reform, see Ann Valk's study of abortion in Washington, D.C., in Gilmore, *Feminist Coalitions*.

80. Hauptman, "Evaluation of the Abortion Task Force."

81. "A Proposal to Fund a Portion of the General Costs of Maintaining and Updating the Health Care Information and Referral Services of the HERS Organization," 1988, HERS records, box 6, folder 53, Special Collections, University of Illinois at Chicago.

82. Ibid.

83. Amy Laiken, "HERS," *CWLU Herstory Project: The Online History of the CWLU*, p. 1; http://www.cwluherstory.org/hers-health-evaluation-and-referral-service.html (accessed November 17, 2009).

84. HERS brochure, undated; box 4, folder 21, Knauss Collection.

85. Source: Mim Desmond; appears to have been published but no citation—probably part of "View from the Loop" research. HERS records, box 4, folder 21.

86. "A Proposal to Fund a Portion of the General Costs of Maintaining and Updating the Health Care Information and Referral Services of the HERS Organization," 1988.

87. Source: Mim Desmond; appears to have been published but no citation.

88. "HERS Healthy Kit," from Pat Rush papers (private collection currently stored at Estelle Carol's house).

89. News Release: "Chicago Women Publish 'Healthy Kit,'" June 1, 1977; box 4, folder 21, Knauss Collection.

90. Laiken, "HERS."

91. HERS Healthy Kit, "How to Own Your Own body," 1977, Pat Rush papers.

92. Ibid.

93. N. E. H. Hull and Peter Charles Hoffer, *Roe v. Wade: The Abortion Rights Controversy in American History*, Landmark Law Cases and American Society (Lawrence: University Press of Kansas, 2001), p. 190.

94. Henry Hyde, quoted in Solinger, *Pregnancy and Power*, p. 201 (see introduction, n. 19).

95. Staggenborg, *The Pro-Choice Movement*, p. 92.

96. Ibid., p. 93.

97. Marilyn Katz, interviewed by and quoted in ibid., p. 110.

98. R2N2 was not the only organization that offered an alternative approach to framing the abortion debate. Another important organization was the Committee for Abortion Rights and Against Sterilization Abuse, founded in 1976 in New York City. See Nelson, *Women of Color and the Reproductive Rights Movement* (see chap. 1, n. 17).

99. In 1979, R2N2 split from the New American Movement and became an independent organization. It dissolved in 1984 due to lack of funds.

100. Staggenborg, *The Pro-Choice Movement*, p. 112.

101. *Reproductive Rights Newsletter*, no. 1 (February 1978): 5, 6; Pat Rush papers.

102. Ibid., pp. 2–3.

103. Ibid., p. 1.

104. 2/21 notes from Midwest R2N2 meeting, p. 3; Pat Rush papers.

105. 12/21 notes from Abortion Strategy (Midwest meeting), p. 2; Pat Rush papers.

106. Catherine Christeller, "Abortion Rights Action Week in Chicago," unpublished R2N2 report, Pat Rush papers.

107. Ibid.

108. *Healthright* 5, no. 3 (1979): 6; Pat Rush papers.

109. Staggenborg, *The Pro-Choice Movement*, 178. The group officially folded in 1989, though its sole contribution in its last few years of existence was a newsletter produced by Christeller. R2N2 folded in 1984.

110. Christeller, "Abortion Rights Action Week in Chicago."

111. Pat Rush, interview with Rebecca Kluchin, February 10, 2001.

112. 12/21 notes from Abortion Strategy (Midwest meeting), p. 2; Pat Rush papers.

113. Pat Rush, interview with Rebecca Kluchin, February 10, 2001.

CHAPTER FOUR

1. Judith Weisz, interview with author, March 4, 2008.

2. Jess Stribling, interview with author, April 23, 2008.

3. Judith Weisz, interview with author, March 4, 2008.

4. Quoted in Jenny Lindsay, "The Politics of Population Control in Namibia," in *Women and Health in Africa*, ed. Meredeth Turshen (Trenton, NJ: Africa World Press, 1991), p. 146.

5. Belita Cowan, April 29, 1979; NWHN records, acc. no. 99s-33, box 10, folder "Old" [unprocessed collection], Sophia Smith Collection, Smith College Library, Northampton, MA.

6. Rosalind P. Petchesky, *Abortion and Woman's Choice: The State, Sexuality, and Reproductive Freedom*, rev. ed., The Northeastern Series in Feminist Theory. (Boston: Northeastern University Press, 1990), p. 177.

7. See, for example, the early editions of *Our Bodies, Ourselves* (New England Free Press, 1971; Simon & Schuster, 1973, 1976, 1979, 1984). For more on the ideology and approaches of American health feminists, see Wendy Kline, "'Please Include This in Your Book': Readers Respond to *Our Bodies, Ourselves*," *Bulletin of the History of Medicine* (Spring 2005), pp. 81–110; and K. Davis, *The Making of "Our Bodies, Ourselves"* (see chap. 1, n. 7).

8. For an excellent overview of recent scholarship on drug regulation, see Andrea Tone and Elizabeth Watkins, eds., introduction to *Medicating Modern America: Prescription Drugs in History* (New York: New York University Press, 2007), pp. 1–14.

9. Judith Weisz, interview with author, April 22, 2008.

10. Ibid. At the age of eighty-one, she is still active in her community, protesting the development of an ethanol plant in her town, as well as continuing her research at Penn State.

11. Ibid., March 4, 2008.

12. Judith Weisz, Griff Ross, and Paul Stolley, "Report of the Public Board of Inquiry on Depo-Provera" (1984), p. 5.

13. U.S. Food and Drug Administration, *Official Transcript of Proceedings, Depo-Provera Public Board of Inquiry*, January 10, 1983, 1:5; NWHN records, 99s-33, box 6.

14. Upjohn Company, "Request for a Public Board of Inquiry," August 25, 1978; FDA docket no. 78-0124, suppl. p. 54. These records are stored on microform in the FDA Division of Dockets Management, 5630 Fishers Lane, Rockville, MD.

15. U.S. Food and Drug Administration, "Reply to Upjohn's Request for a Public Board of Inquiry," September 29, 1978; FDA docket no. 78N-0124, 1:25.

16. U.S. Food and Drug Administration, "Memorandum of Decision Granting Request for Public Board of Inquiry in the Matter of Depo-Provera Sterile Aqueous Suspension," FDA docket no. 78N-0124, 1:103.

17. Judith Weisz, interview with author, March 4, 2008.

18. NWHN press release, October 23, 1978, attachment to March 1979 form letter; NWHN records, 99s-33, box 10, folder Old. DES stands for Diethylstilbestrol, a synthetic estrogen prescribed to women in the United States between 1938 and 1971. In 1971, as a result of research linking DES to rare forms of cervical cancer in female offspring, the FDA issued a warning to physicians not to prescribe it to pregnant women. See http://www.cdc.gov/DES/consumers/about/index.html.

19. "Statement of Belita Cowan," NWHN records, 97S-5, box 15, Media folder, p. 2.

20. Ibid.

21. Kenneth M. Cyrus, letter to Jess Stribling, December 9, 1982; FDA docket no. 78-0124, 207:150–52.

22. Larry La Motte, letter to Commissioner Hayes, January 5, 1983; FDA docket no. 78N-0124, p. 163.

23. U.S. Food and Drug Administration, *Official Transcript of Proceedings*, 1:38.

24. Jess Stribling, interview with author, April 23, 2008.

25. Judith Weisz, interview with author, March 4, 2008.

26. Barbara Resnick Troetel, "Three-Part Disharmony: The Transformation of the Food and Drug Administration in the 1970s" (Ph.D. diss., City University of New York, 1996), p. 2.

27. Ibid.

28. Ibid., p. 5.

29. Ibid., p. 26.

30. Ibid., p. 63.

31. Ibid., p. 80.

32. Ibid., p 129.

33. Jess Stribling, interview with author, April 23, 2008.

34. Philip J. Hilts, *Protecting America's Health: The FDA, Business, and One Hundred Years of Regulation* (New York: Alfred A. Knopf, 2003), p. 206.

35. Ibid., p. 205.

36. Troetel, "Three-Part Disharmony," p. 98.

37. One of the most vivid examples of this conflict stems from the AIDS epidemic, when treatment activists challenged FDA procedures for how to conduct and interpret clinical drug trials for people with AIDS. Steven Epstein, *Impure Science: AIDS, Activism, and the Politics of Knowledge* (Berkeley and Los Angeles: University of California Press, 1996).

38. Solinger, *Pregnancy and Power*, p. 3 (see introduction, n. 19).

39. Loretta Ross, quoted in Silliman et al., *Undivided Rights*, p. 4 (see chap. 3, n. 19).

40. Silliman et al., *Undivided Rights*, p. 11. See also Nelson, *Women of Color and the Reproductive Rights Movement* (see chap. 1, n. 17), and Johanna Schoen, *Choice and Coercion: Birth Control, Sterilization, and Abortion in Public Health and Welfare* (Chapel Hill: University of North Carolina Press, 2005).

41. Carol Korenbrot, "Value Conflicts in Biomedical Research into Future Contraceptives," in *Birth Control and Controlling Birth: Women-Centered Perspectives*, ed. Helen B. Holmes, Betty B. Hoskins, and Michael Gross, Contemporary Issues in Biomedicine, Ethics, and Society (Clifton, NJ: Humana Press, 1980), p. 47.

42. Elizabeth Siegel Watkins, *On the Pill: A Social History of Oral Contraceptives, 1950–1970* (Baltimore: Johns Hopkins University Press, 1998), pp. 34–35.

43. Barbara Seaman, quoted in Adam Bernstein, "Barbara Seaman, 72; Pioneer in Women's Health Movement," obituary, *Washington Post*, February 29, 2008.

44. Watkins, *On the Pill*, p. 107.

45. Ibid., p. 112.

46. Ibid., p. 111.

47. Morton Mintz, *At Any Cost: Corporate Greed, Women, and the Dalkon Shield* (New York: Pantheon Books, 1985), pp. 27–28.

48. Ibid., p. 85.

49. Robert McG. Thomas Jr., "Hugh J. Davis, 69; Gynecologist Who Invented Dalkon Shield," obituary, *New York Times*, October 26, 1996.

50. Mintz, *At Any Cost*, p. 3.

51. Ibid.

52. Letter to *Ms. Magazine*, July 11, 1975; *Ms.* Letters 1972–80, manuscript collection no. 331, carton 2, folder 51, Schlesinger Library, Harvard University, Cambridge, MA.

53. Barbara Seaman and Gideon Seaman, *Women and the Crisis in Sex Hormones* (New York: Rawson Associates, 1977), p. 187.

54. Letter to *Ms. Magazine*, April 2, 1975; *Ms.* Letters 1972–80, manuscript collection no. 331, carton 2, folder 44.

55. Letter to *Ms. Magazine*, June 17, 1975; *Ms.* Letters 1972–80, manuscript collection no. 331, carton 2, folder 51.

56. http://www.nwhn.org/about/index.cfm?content_id=30&section=About (accessed November 11, 2009).

57. Staggenborg, *The Pro-Choice Movement*, pp. 167–68 (see chap. 3, n. 10).

58. Copies of these registries are in the NWHN records, 99s-33, box 7. The registries are difficult to compare and analyze, because two different types were used and the collection is unprocessed. I entered the answers into two different databases based on which form was used. In all, 167 registrants answered using the first form, and 362 answered with the second. The second form included more open-ended questions (such as "Is there anything else that you'd like the NWHN to know?") but also more specific guidelines, including a list of side effects that the registrant could circle. Many registrants included letters along with their filled-out questionnaires. Some are duplicated in different places, making quantification and organization all the more challenging. I have left all individual names out of the records, substituting numbers. "DP1" refers to those who used the first questionnaire; "DP2" refers to those who used the second.

59. Letter attached to registry #51, DP2, NWHN records, box 7.

60. Letter, January 23 1980, DP2; NWHN records, box 8.

61. Letter attached to registry #53, DP1, NWHN records, box 7.

62. Letter, July 25, 1980; NWHN records, box 8.

63. Registry #25, DP2, NWHN records, box 7.

64. Registry #27, DP2, NWHN records, box 7.

65. Letter attached to registry #114, DP2, NWHN records, box 7.

66. Registry #37, DP2, NWHN records, box 7. This frustration at the lack of answers–or even sympathy—from dismissive doctors has since generated an entire genre of memoirs, what Paula Kamen labels "sick lit." Paula Kamen, *All in My Head: An Epic Quest to Cure an Unrelenting, Totally Unreasonable, and Only Slightly Enlightening Headache* (Cambridge, MA: Da Capo Press, Da Capo Lifelong, 2005). Women have published "coming out"–style confessionals of their physical ailments and their frustrating attempts to be taken seriously by medical professionals. Suzanna Kaysen, who had previously written about her mental health struggles in *Girl, Interrupted*, later revealed her year-long

struggle to have severe vaginal pain diagnosed and treated in *The Camera My Mother Gave Me* (New York: Alfred A. Knopf, 2001). Anthropologist Susan Greenhalgh published *Under the Medical Gaze: Facts and Fictions of Chronic Pain* (Berkeley and Los Angeles: University of California Press, 2001), an auto-ethnography of her relationship with a doctor who misdiagnosed her as having fibromyalgia in 1996. All these autobiographical accounts link their painful stories to gender, sexuality, and assumptions about womanhood that conflict with medical definitions of health and sickness. Many of them credit women's health activists of the 1970s and 1980s for first drawing attention to these issues, despite the fact that they remain unresolved.

67. Registry #39, DP2, NWHN records, box 7.

68. Registry #156, DP2, NWHN records, box 7.

69. Registry #262, DP2, NWHN records, box 7.

70. Registry #58, DP1, NWHN records, box 7.

71. Letter, August 3, 1979; NWHN records, box 8.

72. Registry #34, DP2, NWHN records, box 7.

73. Registry #277, DP2, NWHN records, box 7.

74. Registry #294, DP2, NWHN records, box 7.

75. Office memo, October 28, 1980; NWHN records, 99s-33, box 10.

76. Gena Corea, "Draft of NWHN Testimony before the FDA Board of Public Inquiry Hearing on Depo Provera," NWHN records, 97s-5, box 16.

77. Vicki Jones, letter to Belita Cowan, December 18, 1982; NWHN records, 97-s, box 15.

78. S. Epstein, *Impure Science*, p. 13. Epstein labels this process "expertification." While he makes a reasonable claim for the role of AIDS activists in transforming the production of scientific knowledge, it is important not to downplay the earlier contributions of women's health activists to this process.

79. Kenneth M. Cyrus, letter to Jess Stribling, December 9, 1982.

80. Susan G. Esserman and Roger E. Warin of Steptoe & Johnson, letter to Sybil Shainwald, December 3, 1981; NWHN records, 99s-33, box 10.

81. Silliman et al., *Undivided Rights*, p. 65; Morgen, *Into Our Own Hands*, p. 45 (see chap. 1, n. 88).

82. Malcolm Potts, "Statement of Position," FDA docket no. 78N-0124; Boston Women's Health Book Collective records, Francis A. Countway Library of Medicine, Harvard University, Rare Books Depository H MS c 261, box 34.

83. www.webmd.com/robert-anthony-hatcher (accessed November 11, 2009).

84. Statement of Robert A. Hatcher, "The Depo-Provera Debate," in U.S. House of Representatives, *Hearings before the Select Committee on Population*, 95th Cong., 2nd sess., August 8–10, 1978 (Washington, DC: U.S. Government Printing Office, 1978), p. 213.

85. Robert Hatcher and Aliza Greenspan, "A Descriptive Analysis of Women Using Depo-Provera at Grady Memorial Hospital Family Planning Clinic, 1974 and 1978," p. 27, appendix 3, NWHN records, 99s-3, box 6.

86. Ibid.

87. Elizabeth Connell, quoted in "The Ultimate Test Animal" transcript, p. 4; Boston Women's Health Book Collective records, Francis A. Countway

Library of Medicine, Harvard University, Rare Books Depository HMS c 261, box 35.

88. Silliman et al., *Undivided Rights*, p. 5.

89. Judy Norsigian, interview with author, December 16, 2004.

90. Ibid.

91. U.S. Food and Drug Administration, *Official Transcript of Proceedings, FDA Depo-Provera Board of Inquiry*, January 11, 1983, 2:198.

92. Ibid., 2:200.

93. Ibid., 2:230.

94. U.S. Food and Drug Administration, *Official Transcript of Proceedings*, January 12, 1983, 3:72.

95. Ibid., 3:75.

96. Ibid., 3:72.

97. U.S. Food and Drug Administration, *Official Transcript of Proceedings*, January 13, 1983, 4:14.

98. Ibid., 4:5.

99. Ibid., 4:28.

100. Ibid., 4:35.

101. U.S. Food and Drug Administration, memorandum from Clinical Investigations Branch, February 23, 1979; FDA files, 248:168–72, FDA docket no. 78-0124, p. 5.

102. Ibid., p. 2.

103. Ibid., p. 5.

104. U.S. Food and Drug Administration *Official Transcript of Proceedings*, 4:26.

105. Ibid., 4:27.

106. Ibid., 4:185.

107. Ibid., 4:187.

108. Ibid., 4:189.

109. Ibid., 4:190.

110. Marjorie Sun, "Panel Says Depo-Provera Not Proved Safe," *Science* 226, November 23, 1984, p. 950.

111. Weisz, Ross, and Stolley, "Report of the Public Board of Inquiry," p. 172.

112. Ibid., p. 87.

113. Ibid., p. 88.

114. Judith Weisz, interview with author, March 4, 2008.

115. Elizabeth Connell, letter to FDA Commissioner Frank Young, November 16, 1984, FDA docket no. 78N-0124, vol. 358, CH 91.

116. Frank Young, letter to Judith Weisz, January 28, 1987; FDA administration files, Upjohn Company, AF12-868, vol. 106, January 28, 1987.

117. Judith Weisz, interview with author, March 4, 2008.

CHAPTER FIVE

1. Joan Haggerty, "Childbirth Made Difficult," *Ms. Magazine*, January 1973, p. 17.

2. Marjorie Karmel, *Thank You, Dr. Lamaze*, new ed. (London: Pinter & Martin, 2005).

3. Haggerty, "Childbirth Made Difficult." p. 17.

4. Ibid.

5. Ibid., pp. 16–17.

6. Ibid.

7. Ibid.

8. Barbarah Ehrenreich, "Childbirth: Do We Need It Anymore?" In *Proceedings of the First International Childbirth Conference*, June 2, 1973; Midwifery Subject Collection, MS 454, box 2, folder 15, p. 23, Sophia Smith Collection, Smith College, Northampton, MA.

9. Barbara Katz Rothman, *In Labor: Women and Power in the Birthplace* (New York: Norton, 1982), p. 13.

10. See Paula Treichler, "Feminism, Medicine, and the Meaning of Childbirth," in *Body/Politics: Women and the Discourses of Science*, ed. Mary Jacobus, Evelyn Fox Keller, and Sally Shuttleworth (New York: Routledge, 1990), pp. 113–38.

11. Suzanne Arms, *Immaculate Deception: A New Look at Women and Childbirth in America* (Boston: Houghton Mifflin, 1975), p. 138.

12. Richard W. Wertz and Dorothy C. Wertz, *Lying-in: A History of Childbirth in America* (New York: Free Press, 1977), p. 195.

13. Arms, *Immaculate Deception*, p. 139.

14. Ibid., p. 140.

15. While the terms *lay midwife* and *direct-entry midwife* are frequently used interchangeably, their meanings are somewhat different; as Judith Rooks explains, lay midwifery refers to home birth practice and "informal training that is founded in experience; direct-entry indicates that the attendant "went into midwifery without first being trained as a nurse." See Judith Rooks, *Midwifery and Childbirth in America* (Philadelphia: Temple University Press, 1997), p. 8.

16. Wendy Holt and Archie Brodsky, "Midwife Profile: Fran Ventre," *Midwife Advocate* 2, no. 3 (Autumn 1985): 1; Fran Ventre papers, carton 4 (unprocessed collection), Schlesinger Library, Harvard University, Cambridge, MA.

17. Fran Ventre, quoted in ibid., p. 1.

18. Ibid.

19. Helena Hughes, letter to Fran Ventre, July 18, 1990; Ventre papers, carton 1.

20. Robin and Peter Mostgrove, letter to Fran Ventre, April 5, 1991; Ventre papers, carton 1.

21. Ellen, Steve, and Alicia Anziand, letter to Fran Ventre, April 1, 1996; Ventre papers, carton 1.

22. Fran Ventre, "The Making of a Legalized Lay Midwife," *News from Home* 1, no. 2 (April 1976): 3; Ventre papers, carton 1.

23. Ibid.

24. Ibid., p. 4.

25. Ina May Gaskin, *Spiritual Midwifery*, 4th ed. (Summertown, TN; Book Publishing Company, 2002), pp. 10–11.

26. Ventre, "The Making of a Legalized Lay Midwife," p. 4.

27. Gaskin, *Spiritual Midwifery*, p. 16.

28. Ibid., p. 34.

29. Ibid.

30. Ventre, "The Making of a Legalized Lay Midwife," p. 4.

31. There have been many different types of midwives in the United States, and the word itself, as Judith Rooks points out, has had many "overlapping but different" definitions. "Granny midwives" referred to black and white women in the Southeast who attended home births until about the mid-twentieth century, and they were trained through apprenticeship. *Lay midwifery* and *direct-entry midwifery* are also terms used to describe women who practice in a home birth setting with apprenticeship-type training. Many since the 1970s refer to themselves as "traditional midwives" or "independent midwives," disliking the term *lay* with its suggestion of untrained or unprofessional. Certified nurse-midwives are registered nurses who have also completed training in an accredited nurse-midwifery program and passed a national certification examination. For more information, see Rooks, *Midwifery and Childbirth in America*, pp 1–10.

32. Fran Ventre, "The Lay Midwife," originally presented at a workshop entitled "Partners for Health," sponsored by Chapter 6 of the ACNM on October 2, 1976. Reprinted in the *Journal of Nurse-Midwifery* 22, no. 4 (Winter 1978): 33.

33. Peggy Vincent, *Baby Catcher: Chronicles of a Modern Midwife* (New York: Scribner, 2002), pp. 49–52.

34. Ibid., p. 55.

35. Ibid., p. 68.

36. Ibid., p. 74.

37. Ventre, "The Making of a Legalized Lay Midwife," p. 4.

38. Ibid., p. 5.

39. Ibid.

40. Ibid., p. 6.

41. Rooks, *Midwifery and Childbirth in America*, p. 66.

42. Helen Burst, quoted in ibid., p. 67.

43. Ibid., p. 60.

44. Ventre, "The Making of a Legalized Lay Midwife," p. 6.

45. Ibid., p. 7.

46. *News from Home* 2, no. 2 (Spring 1977): 2; Ventre papers, carton 1.

47. "Home Oriented Maternity Experience," undated, Ventre papers, carton 1.

48. Anne Kaspar, "Independent Practice as a Nurse Midwife in Bethesda, Maryland: An Interview with Jan Epstein, CNM," *Women and Health* vol. 6, no. 3/4 (Fall–Winter 1981): 177.

49. Epstein et al., "A Safe Home Birth Program that Works," in *Safe Alternatives in Childbirth: Based on the First American NAPSAC Conference, May 15, 1976, Arlington, Va.*, 2nd. ed., ed. David Stewart and Lee Stewart (Chapel Hill, NC: National Association of Parents & Professionals for Safe Alternatives in Childbirth, 1977), p. 159.

50. Ibid.

51. J. Epstein and McCartney, "A Home Birth Service That Works," p. 4 (see introduction, n. 9).

52. Ibid.

53. Kaspar, "Independent Practice as a Nurse Midwife in Bethesda, Maryland," p. 180.

54. Rooks, *Midwifery and Childbirth in America*, p. 30.

55. Ibid.

56. Ibid., p. 155. They were still a minority, however, representing only 1.2 percent of the U.S. birthing population; see p. 149.

57. Henry Theide, "Defining the Role of the Nurse-Midwife: Symposium," moderated by Sharon Schindler Rising, *Contemporary Ob/Gyn Quarterly* 8 (July 1976): 168, 173.

58. Wendy Simonds, Barbara Katz Rothman, and Bari Meltzer Norman, *Laboring On: Birth in Transition in the United States* (New York: Routledge, 2007), p. 137.

59. Sally Tom, "Nurse-Midwifery: A Developing Profession," *Law, Medicine & Health Care* 10, no. 6 (December 1982): 262.

60. Ann Slayton, "Thoroughly Modern Midwives Offer Choice of Care and Cost," *HCFA Forum* 5, no. 3 (August 1981): 17.

61. John Maeck, "Defining the Role of the Nurse-Midwife: Symposium," pp. 174, 176.

62. Fran Ventre, quoted in Donna Schnicker, "The Midwife: An Ancient Profession May Offer a New Alternative to Parents Here," *Malden (MA) Evening News*, December 12, 1978; Ventre papers, carton 3.

63. Archie Brodsky, "Court Hears Janet Leigh's Case; Decision Awaited," *Midwife Advocate* 2, no. 3 (Autumn 1985): 1; Ventre papers, carton 1.

64. "Massachusetts Midwife Curb Upheld," *New York Times*, May 24, 1987.

65. For a fascinating analysis of the expectant father's role in childbirth, see Leavitt, *Make Room for Daddy* (see introduction, n. 19).

66. "Midwifery: The Other Side of the Story," *Malden (MA) Evening News*, January 10, 1979; Ventre papers, carton 3.

67. Fran Ventre, telephone conversation with author, August 23, 2005.

68. Vincent, *Baby Catcher*, p. 57.

69. Rooks, *Midwifery and Childbirth in America*, p. 92.

70. Holt and Brodsky, "Midwife Profile," p. 4.

71. Regina E. Herzlinger, *Market-Driven Health Care: Who Wins, Who Loses in the Transformation of America's Largest Service Industry* (Reading, MA: Addison-Wesley, 1997), p. 78.

72. Ibid.

73. Holt and Brodsky, "Midwife Profile," p. 5.

74. Ibid., p. 6.

75. Simonds, Rothman, and Norman, *Laboring On*, p. 192.

76. Ann P. Wood, "Obs., Nurse-Midwives Labor to Define New Working Relationship," *Ob. Gyn. News* 16, no. 14 (July 15, 1981): pp. 1, 23.

77. Gail Sinquefield, "Hospital Practice for Certified Nurse-Midwives—Privilege or Right?" *Journal of Nurse-Midwifery* 27, no. 1 (January–February 1982): 1–3.

78. Sandi Dietrich, Ad Hoc Committee Chairperson, "Individual Committee Comments Specifically Addressed to the Board of Directors," memo to

ACNM Board of Directors, January 16, 1981, p. 1; ACNM records, MSC 330a 11.6, National Library of Medicine, Washington, DC.

79. Ibid., p. 4.

80. Emphasis added. The authors explain, "We must assume more control over what happens to us in and out of hospitals during our time of childbearing. We must work from the inside to make hospitals more humane in which to have our babies. . . . And we must work from the outside in for the development and legalization of midwife services, neighborhood clinics and efficient mobile medical units. . . . We must also work on and along with doctors and nurses to demystify, to deprofessionalize medicine, so that we become more at one with what happens to us." Ruth Bell and Jane Pincus, in *Our Bodies, Ourselves,* 1973 ed., p. 159 (see introduction, n. 10).

81. Dietrich, "Individual Committee Comments," p. 2.

82. Simonds, Rothman, and Norman, *Laboring On,* p. 148.

83. In 2006, there were ten direct-entry programs in the United States and forty-two nurse-midwifery programs accredited by the ACNM. See ibid., p. 139.

84. "Midwives Alliance of North America Original Open Meeting," April 25, 1982, transcript, p. 2; Ventre papers, carton 3.

85. "Meeting of Midwives in Washington, D.C.," press release, November 5, 1981; Ventre papers, carton 3.

86. "Dear Midwife," undated letter signed by Huzeler, Ventry, Jolly, Charvet, Leibel, Gaskin, and Withrow attached to press release, Ventre papers, carton 3.

87. "Midwives Alliance of North America Original Open Meeting, April 25, 1982," p. 7.

88. "MANA Meeting Continues," transcript of April 1982 meeting, p. 6; Ventre papers, carton 3.

89. Ibid., p. 8.

90. Ibid., p. 9.

91. "MANA Formed: Nurse-Midwives and Lay Midwives Unite," *Practicing Midwife* 1, no. 16 (Summer 1982): 4.

92. *Practicing Midwife* 1, no. 16 (Summer 1982): 1.

93. Fran Ventre and Carol Leonard, "The Future of Midwifery—an Alliance," *Journal of Nurse-Midwifery* 27, no. 5 (September–October 1982): 24.

94. Holt and Brodsky, "Midwife Profile," p. 6.

95. Elizabeth Davis, letter to to Teddy Chavret, May 30, 1985; Ventre papers, carton 3.

96. Teddy Chavret, letter to Elizabeth Davis and other MANA Board Members, June 13, 1985, p. 2; Ventre papers, carton 3.

97. Fran Ventre, Peggy Spindel, and Kate Bowland, "The Transition from Lay Midwife to Certified Nurse-Midwife in the United States," *Journal of Nurse-Midwifery* 40, no. 5 (September–October 1995): 436.

98. Ibid. Emphasis added.

99. Ventre, "The Lay Midwife," p. 35.

100. Ventre, Spindel, and Bowland, "The Transition from Lay Midwife to Certified Nurse-Midwife in the United States," p. 437.

101. Ventre, "The Making of a Legalized Lay Midwife," p. 3.

102. http://www.ourbodiesourblog.org/blog/2008/11/plans-to-close-north-shore-birth-center-temporarily-postponed (accessed November 20, 2009).

103. Ibid.

104. Jennifer Block, *Pushed: The Painful Truth about Childbirth and Modern Maternity Care* (Cambridge, MA: Da Capo Press, Da Capo Lifelong, 2007), p. 268.

105. http://www.facebook.com/topic.php?uid=33650813774&topic=5940 (accessed November 20, 2009).

106. Sarah Shamel, "Birth Center to remain OPEN!" to members of the Save the North Shore Birth Center, Facebook, December 15, 2008; www.facebook.com/inbox/?folder=[fb]messages&page=5&tid=1076394746044 (accessed November 20, 2009).

107. Mira Clark, Rebecca Hains, Amy Kreydin, Sarah Shamel, Christa Terry, and Nicole Altieri, "An Open Letter to Dr. Henry Ramini, the Administration, and the Board of Trustees of Beverly Hospital," December 18, 2008; http://savethenorthshorebirthcenter.wordpress.com/an-open-letter/ (accessed November 20, 2009).

EPILOGUE

1. http://www.ourbodiesourblog.org/blog/2008/11/choices-in-childbirth-statement-encourages-options-and-evidence-in-maternity-care (accessed November 21, 2009).

2. Births: Final data (annual report, 2006). National vital statistics reports. Hyattsville, MD: National Center for Health Statistics. www.cdc.gov/nchs/births.htm (accessed February 8, 2009).

3. Jacqueline H. Wolf, *Deliver Me from Pain*, p. 195 (see introduction, n. 17).

4. Judith Warner, *Perfect Madness: Motherhood in the Age of Anxiety* (New York: Riverhead Books, 2005), pp. 8, 44–48.

5. http://www.thebusinessofbeingborn.com/ (accessed November 21, 2009).

6. Ayelet Waldman, *Bad Mother: A Chronicle of Maternal Crimes, Minor Calamities, and Occasional Moments of Grace* (New York: Doubleday, 2009), p. 21.

7. Ibid., pp. 39–40.

8. Joan Wolf, "Is Breast Really Best? Risk and Total Motherhood in the National Breastfeeding Awareness Campaign," *Journal of Health Politics, Policy and Law* 32, no. 4 (August 2007): 615.

9. Susan J. Douglas and Meredith W. Michaels, *The Mommy Myth: The Idealization of Motherhood and How It Has Undermined Women* (New York: Free Press, 2004). pp. 4–5.

10. http://open.salon.com/blog/amytuteurmd/2008/09/17/breastfeeding_and_the_cult_of_total_motherhood (accessed November 21, 2009).

11. http://www.theatlantic.com/doc/200904/case-against-breastfeeding (accessed November 21, 2009).

12. http://www.newyorker.com/archives/2004/03/08/040308crbo_books (accessed November 21, 2009).

13. Hannah Rosin notes that Cathi Hanauer and Ellen Gilchrist's *The Bitch in the House: 26 Women Tell the Truth about Sex, Solitude, Work, Motherhood, and Marriage* (New York: William Morrow, 2002) "reframed the Feminine Mystique for my generation of mothers."

14. Betty Friedan, *The Feminine Mystique* (New York: Norton, 2001), p. 311.

15. Douglas and Michaels, *The Mommy Myth*, p. 5.

16. Warner, *Perfect Madness*, p. 52.

17. Ibid., p. 46.

18. Ibid., p. 184.

19. Faulkner Fox, *Dispatches from a Not-So-Perfect Life: How I Learned to Love the House, the Man, the Child* (New York: Three Rivers Press, 2003), p. 105.

Index

Note: Italicized page numbers indicate photographs.